MAN IN GOD'S WORLD

MAN IN GOD'S WORLD

BY HELMUT THIELICKE

TRANSLATED AND EDITED BY
JOHN W. DOBERSTEIN

HARPER & ROW, PUBLISHERS
NEW YORK, EVANSTON, AND LONDON

This book is a revision and translation of chapters 18 to 32 of DER GLAUBE DER CHRISTENHEIT, copyright by Vandenhoeck & Ruprecht, Göttingen, Fourth Edition, 1958. Chapter 12 is from FRAGEN DES CHRISTENTUMS AN DIE MODERNE WELT, copyright by J. C. B. Mohr (Paul Siebeck), Tübingen, 1948.

FIRST EDITION   F-N

LIBRARY OF CONGRESS CATALOG CARD NUMBER: 63-14971

CONTENTS

19565

5

FOREWORD

THIS BOOK HAS A VERY EVENTFUL HISTORY. PERHAPS,
therefore, the best way to salute my American readers is to tell
them something about it.

In 1941, in the midst of World War II, I was forbidden by the
Nazis to speak or to travel. I was interned in a small city. This
was their revenge for my having on several occasions rebelled
against the tyranny by word and act. Previous to this time they
had already dismissed me from my position as a university pro-
fessor. I was also forbidden to publish books and articles; this is
the way the Nazi authorities saved paper. Finally, however, permission was obtained for me to deliver one evening lecture a
week in the Stuttgart Cathedral Church (*Stiftskirche*).

At that time the bombing raids had not yet begun. I suspected,
however, that dreadful visitations were still in store for us, and
it was this that made me feel that people should be prepared for
eternity. I considered how this might best be done and came to
this conclusion: the Nazi tyranny has not only pitched us into a
ghastly war which every day is destroying our men, our brothers
and sons, on the battlefields; it is not only exercising the most
monstrous reign of terror within the country, but it has also
attacked and desecrated everything that is holy to us. It has introduced pagan gods and is bent upon using them to drive out
Jesus Christ. It interprets all of life, it interprets birth, death,
history, and eternity in a way that is different from what we
learned as Christians and also found to be true and reliable. This
has brought bewilderment and confusion to many people, and

besides, this godless interpretation of life has made an impression upon not a few. And how can young people, especially, help being susceptible to all this, particularly when they are scrupulously and consistently shut off from all contact with Jesus Christ—exactly as they are in Bolshevist countries today.

This diagnosis brought me to the conviction that I must prepare people for the terrible things that lay before them by giving them instruction—quite simply, just instruction—in the mysteries of our faith. I wanted to help them to see their life and the course of history from the standpoint of Christ. I wanted to show them that faith not only has something to do with our state after death or with our inner religious life, but that it also opens our eyes to a wholly new way of looking at life here and now, that when we meet Christ we see nature, history, our fellow man, our community life, the problem of law and justice, war, and even our death with new eyes. I wanted to try to show them that as his disciples we lead a rich and full life, that for those who have found him there is nothing that is alien, that through him joy is sanctified (and thus really made full), and that in terror and death we shall nevermore be left desolate and alone. And so I lectured to them on the fundamental truths of our faith—simply following the course of Luther's *Small Catechism*—and endeavored to show them that this also sharpens our view of real life, of politics, international relations, and everything that environs us, making it more realistic, perceptive, and penetrating. The lectures continued, with brief interruptions, for almost three years.

In this book a number of excerpts from these lectures have been assembled. My friend and translator, John Doberstein (how wonderful that I should meet with this interpreter and liaison with the United States!) gave me counsel with regard to what parts of the large body of material in the lectures might be of special interest to my American readers. Only one chapter (on the reality of the demonic) has been taken from another book, but it too originated in this same period. I shall say something further about this presently, but first I must tell a bit more about how the lectures fared.

From the beginning they drew large crowds. Evening after evening some three thousand persons gathered together: workers and businessmen, students and professors, soldiers and generals, Nazi functionaries (naturally in civilian clothes!) and Jews, Dutch compulsory laborers (they had been deported to Germany and I gathered them together secretly) and sometimes whole classes from the schools. It was an overwhelming time for me. Never since have I experienced such intense listening.

Then came the air raids. One church after another collapsed or burned, thousands of homes sank into rubble and ashes, and the original congregation of hearers was scattered; but new ones kept coming. And when the streetcars stopped running they came on foot, often from many miles away through the fields of ruins and rubble which were dark, spectral, and frightening on those winter evenings.

Finally the cathedral church, too, was destroyed by fire. I can still see the towering torch of this venerable house of God. Not even when at almost the same time my own house burned down, and I stood there holding in my hand a key to a door that no longer existed, was my heart so wrung . . .

We sought out two other auditoriums which were still standing on the outskirts of the city. Since they were smaller, I intended to speak in both on succeeding evenings. When I arrived, on a bicycle and having had often to walk and scramble my way through the fields of rubble, they too had been destroyed; not even the streets on which they were located were there any more.

But still we did not give up. I then announced that the lectures would be continued in a more distant suburb, Bad Cannstadt. Because of their fear of the Nazis, the newspapers would not allow me to insert a large advertisement but only the following notice in small print, not even mentioning my name, but only the initial: "Thursday, 8 P.M. T." But this was sufficient to mobilize the scattered congregation, and again they were there. The hall was so overcrowded that I was apprehensive of what might happen if an air-raid alarm occurred. And this actually did come during the second or third meeting. I asked everybody to leave quietly in order to go to the bomb shelters and then gave the benediction. The organist played an evening hymn as the crowd left the hall quietly and without any panic. When I went out, the last to leave, the flak was already roaring, since the fliers were beginning their attack upon us. By the light of the flashing guns I finally found a shelter. But it was already closed and because of the danger they refused to open the door. However, the faithful student who had stuck with me and I beat on the door so mightily that finally it was opened and we were quickly pulled inside. Then came the most dreadful attack I ever experienced. Two of my hearers, one of them the organist who had just been playing, were killed.

A few weeks before this I had already had a similarly moving experience. After an air attack I was helping with the clean-up operations and was standing at the edge of a huge crater opened up by an aerial bomb. It had killed an officer and fifty women auxiliary air force aides. A woman came up to me—she was the wife of the officer who had been killed—and asked whether I was Helmut Thielicke; for I was covered with dust and grime and she did not recognize me at first. She then showed me her husband's cap and said, "This is all that was left of him. Only last Thursday I was with him, attending your lecture. And now I want to thank you for preparing him for his death." Then she quietly shook my hand.

What we were doing there was teaching theology in the face of death. There the only thing that was of any help at all was the gospel itself. Everything else simply dissolved into thin air. We were living only upon the substance of our faith. And these desperate hours also helped us to find that substance.

The miracles of God which we experienced in all this time were incomprehensible. After each lecture some two hundred stenographers remained and I dictated to them a brief résumé. Stationery stores donated mountains of paper to me for this purpose. Each one made ten or more copies and those who received them through the mail did the same. They were all sent to our soldiers at the front. After the war some of my books went through a not inconsiderable number of printings, but I shall probably never again have such tremendous editions as I had with these pages written by hand. And people trusted what came to them in this written form, whereas they had the greatest distrust of everything that was printed, for all of it was censored by the tyranny. How many of those who remained on the battlefields

wrote to tell me they had received these pastoral letters and that
the eternal Word had been a comfort and a stay to them in the
cold steppes of Russia or the desert sands of Egypt!

The chapter on the reality of the demonic is taken from my
book entitled *Fragen des Christentums an die moderne Welt*
("Questions Christianity Addresses to the Modern World").[1] I
wrote this book secretly in this same period. The manuscript was
smuggled into Geneva by diplomatic pouch and was published
there by the Ecumenical Council anonymously. It was sent
primarily to prisoner-of-war camps, where it was used as a text-
book in the camp universities, especially for student courses. I
myself did not see my own book until long after the war. I could
tell a long story of the adventures of that book, too.

As I write this I am suddenly struck by the thought of how
strange it is that an author should be telling such stories about
his book in a foreword. Isn't there something dubious about
that? Ought not a book speak for itself? If one has to show that the
contents performed a service back in the past, during the war,
this still does not prove that it has anything to say to the present
generation.

Well, I believe that all the questions discussed in it are still
relevant today. Otherwise I certainly would not recommend it
to readers in the United States. Even in Germany the original
book is still being reprinted. Those times illuminated many questions about faith, human nature, history, and life with an in-
tensity and a depth that is hardly ever seen in more peaceful
times. In such tensile tests of fate one could not attract people
with the topics and clichés of the day. Only pure, hard metal was
accepted. God had sent us into a hard school in order to make
us find this metal. And that is why I have let everything stand
as it was said at that time. And this, too, is why I have felt I
might tell something of the background and the times when the
lectures originated. Terrible as those times were, times when we
were surrounded by bizarre ruins and daily expected our own

[1] *Fragen des Christentums an die moderne Welt, Untersuchungen zur
geistigen und religiösen Krise des Abendlands* (Tübingen: J. C. B. Mohr [Paul
Siebeck], 1948), pp. 170-217. (Trans.)

death, we often think of those days of terror with a certain nostalgia. We are glad, of course, that we can look forward to Sunday without wondering whether the church in which we may hear the Word of God is still standing. And yet, in this time of peace the voices of eternity have grown fainter. And never since have we perceived as clearly as we did then that God is stronger than fire and destruction and that even in the valleys of deepest darkness, rod and staff are put into our hands and bridges are thrown across the abyss. What more could I wish, than that even a little of this should dawn upon the reader today?

It is a wonderful providence that so many of my books of sermons and addresses should be the first to appear in English dress; but now it will not be long before the more scholarly works, especially the *Theological Ethics,* are presented to readers in the United States.

HELMUT THIELICKE

Hamburg
First Week in Advent, 1962

MAN IN GOD'S WORLD

MAN IN THE COSMOS | I

MARTIN LUTHER, IN THIS SMALL CATECHISM, *BEGINS HIS* explanation of the first article of the Creed: "I believe that God has created *me*." And we may well ask: Isn't this an odd way to begin to talk about the whole creation? Considering the vastness of the creation of all things, why shouldn't something more sensible have occurred to the Reformer than to talk about man, this very late though highly developed and already decadent "mammal"? Isn't this another evidence of man's incurable vanity, which is constantly betraying him into imagining that he is the center of the universe and taking himself so utterly seriously, even in the midst of and despite protestations of Christian humility? Nietzsche once said of this arrogance of man: "What is the vanity of the vainest of men compared with the vanity possessed by the most modest in 'feeling that he is a human being' in nature and the world"; in other words, in claiming that he has a special role in the rest of the cosmos?

In order, then, to get behind what Luther intended in beginning his teaching about creation with this very strange and striking phrase: "I believe that God created me," let us ask ourselves quite simply how *we,* we so-called "modern" people, would begin to explain to a friend or to our children what is meant and what is implied when we say that "God created the world," and that therefore the world is a *creation.*

If we had this task, we would probably see two possibilities of making belief in creation somewhat plausible to our children, or our pupils, or our friends.

15

1. *THE INFINITY OF THE WORLD IN TIME*

We could start out by saying that somewhere at the very beginning, where the endless succession of creatures is lost in the dark
reaches of primordial beginnings, there is *God*. We are normally
quite willing to accept some such initial beginning. It is the kind
of construction we need for our thinking, a kind of scientific
hypothesis, which we are simply *obliged* to set up. True, we do
not have to call this first beginning "God," but can, if we want
to be somewhat more matter-of-fact and less emotional, simply
call it the "first cause." Adalbert Stifter once said that to believe
in God means to be convinced that the endless chain of causality
ends finally in the hands of God.

This view is usually called "deism" and what it affirms is that
God is like a watchmaker who has constructed a clock, set it going, and then lets it go on running without concerning himself
about it any further. This view constitutes one type of belief in
evolution, a belief that, roughly and briefly stated, says something
like this:

In accord with the law of cause and effect, every phenomenon
is caused by an antecedent phenomenon. For example, man is the
effect of prehuman animal forms (whether these were apes is of
no importance at this point). These animal forms in turn are
the result of more primitive forms until we finally get back to the
one-celled animals. Then on the farthest horizon of development
in the past, we may assume an original gaseous state which had
to condense and form the most primitive phenomena of nature.

It is of the very nature of such an evolutionary series that it
should be endless both forward and backward. But even the original gaseous state prompts us to ask: Who or what was its cause?
The very thought of this unending series is painful to the human
mind and is borne only with difficulty. Therefore the mind puts
a stop, as it were, to this ever-continuing line of development by
setting an ultimate starting point, which it then may or may not
call "God." This God would then be the first beginning, or as
Aristotle called him, the "prime mover." In so far as one con-

ceives of this prime mover as having some kind of "personal" power, one can call him the Creator.

Undoubtedly this is an impressive view. We see the "infinity of the world in time" spread out before us. And yet this infinity flows from and is finally caught up in the hands of God—hands which we see in our mind's eye mysteriously shining at the beginning of all things, as our thoughts, stretched to their farthest limits, grope ceaselessly backward to the primordial dawn; hands which, because they brought everything into being, are still creatively and sovereignly at work in all that is happening now.

But here, despite the impressiveness of this grand view of the world, we are compelled to ask some fundamental questions. What significance does man have in this view? And growing out of this, what meaning does this view have for our own life in concrete terms? What can it give us in the way of purpose and a meaningful goal?

Asking these questions, we find out two things. First, in this infinite realm man is a very late point, which is separated from those hands of God by a stupendous series of preceding phenomena. And second, he is really *nothing more* than a point, a fleeting minute in cosmic time, a minute which will vanish without a sound when it is past as eternal silence falls upon its forgotten grave. Nietzsche, whose thinking was dominated by this idea of evolution, saw this futility and nothingness of man with unusual clarity. Therefore he felt that man's assuming to himself any unique position in the cosmos was simply absurd and grotesque vanity.

Nietzsche, acting in thorough consistency with this belief in development, never wearied of stressing this *momentary* character of human existence. He speaks of inorganic, *dead* nature as being the real nature and says that it is a "boundless process of becoming, without any delusions," and within this eternal succession organic points emerge or rather flash up for a moment. "The drops of life in the world are of no significance for the total character of the vast ocean of becoming and passing away." "Life on earth is a moment, an incident, an exception without a consequence." Before and after it there broods only the silence of primeval time and the silence of the time of the End. And even within these brief moments the time of *human* life itself is only a tiny atom of time. "Man is a small eccentric species of animal that has its time."

So there is nothing specifically "human." Man is almost nothing, an atom floating completely lost in infinity along with the whole long line of his generations, from the days of his original ancestors. (Within this tiny space of time how much tinier is the life of an *individual* man!)

And now a cold chill comes over us, whereas at first we were inclined to find this view of the world so impressive. In the light of this world view our life looks like this: Our love for one another, the sufferings of the great war, Goethe's *Faust,* Michelangelo's sculptures, Beethoven's *Ninth Symphony,* Bach's *St. Matthew Passion,* the joy of a man standing on some alpine peak, the high courage to die for an idea, the love of a mother for her child, the creative devotion of a great scientist—all of them nothing more than an unsubstantial drop in a ghastly, gigantic ocean, nothing but a feckless, puling peep between two icy zones of silence. Hardly born, and already forgotten and engulfed in nothingness: *is this the meaning of our life?*

But that is what it *must* be, if this view of the world is correct. And Nietzsche then proceeds to draw the consequences of this view with all the heroic coldness and despairing courage that characterize his thinking.

Starting from this point of view, he says, I fulfill my life when I accept and affirm its transience, its swift and fleeting evanescence and reabsorption into inorganic nature; when I make up my mind to abandon any hope or claim upon eternity in my life and embrace its nothingness. Then ultimately the meaning and fulfillment of my life consist in affirming its meaninglessness and accepting the nothingness of Mephistopheles' "eternal emptiness." "To be released from life and become dead again can be a happy thing." "We become utterly truthful . . . death must be reinterpreted! In this way we reconcile ourselves with what is real, that is, with the dead world." This, then, would be the meaning of life—to affirm and accept the nothingness in which our tiny bit of human life with its little leaping flame of idealism is set. So the last word of the world view based upon this idea of development, this belief in the infinity of time, is this: *first,* the ultimate futility of human life; *second,* its transitional character, with no significance of its own; and *finally,* one's personal acceptance of nothingness. And at the same time we see how absolutely unimportant it is whether we give this belief in development a religious foundation, as deism does, by calling the ultimate cause "God," or whether we follow Nietzsche and allow the development to end in the unknowable silence of primordial time.

So we are confronted with a completely negative end result, an absolute, unconditional devaluation of life, the utter bleakness of which can hardly be covered by the contrived phantom of the "superman." Anybody who really knows Nietzsche knows what that means. There is a tendency today whenever Nietzsche is quoted to put forward only one side of his thought, the seemingly bright side about propagating the human race upward and the shining goal of attaining the superman. It is important therefore to show the other and less well-known side, the bleak backdrop of his thought, in front of which these shining phantoms and dreams appear in order to brighten and glorify its deadly darkness.

Recall once more the starting point of our train of thought. We began by asking how we might explain to modern man our faith in creation, and we attempted to do this by thinking of God the Creator as the original beginning of the evolution of creatures. We have seen that this belief in development ends in nihilism, the absolute futility of human existence, and we cannot avoid recognizing that here the road that leads to any real faith in the Creator and the knowledge of our human creatureliness is blocked.

2. *THE INFINITY OF THE WORLD IN SPACE*

There is, however, another possibility which seems to present itself to us as a way of communicating this faith in creation to modern man. It, too, should be examined. We have been speaking about the infinity of the world in *time*; perhaps the infinity of the world in *space* may be more impressive.

And the fact is that many books on religion and even more

teachers of religion prefer to begin with the infinity of the world of the stars in order to illustrate the unfathomable glory and infinity of the Creator God.

Think for a moment of just one example, which may illustrate the infinity of space. Several years ago, by means of the most powerful astronomic telescope there was discovered a faint half-moon-like nebula which indicated the existence of a whole new universe.

It was formerly thought that the Milky Way, to which our solar system and our small planets belong, was the only existent universe. But now we know that there are not only thousands of individual stars but also thousands of complete universes in the universe. This universe is 500 million light years away and—what is equally prodigious—it is moving away from us at a speed of 80,000 kilometers per second—as are the other universes, too. One therefore has the impression that the total universe is expanding every second in an utterly appalling way. Naturally, we can have no adequate conception of this speed; it is so rapid that one could round the earth one and a half times between two pulse beats. In its tremendous flight away from our range of vision this may have been our last opportunity to catch sight of this new universe; otherwise we might never have known about it at all. And how many other universes there may still be behind it in the infinity of cosmic distance, universes which humanity in the brief seconds of its existence will never see or even suspect!

Such thoughts—far as they may seem to take us away from the subject of our question—should give us a vivid impression of this infinity of space and at the same time help us to understand why the human spirit, and especially the *religious* spirit, has always looked up into the cosmic distances of the firmament in order to find an illustration of the eternity and infinity of God. The Holy Scriptures do this too, of course; but they do so in a way that carries a completely new undertone. In any case, they are referring to this upward look into the firmament when they reverently speak of him who "gives songs in the night" (Job 35:10).

The sight of the stars has always, as long as men have existed and long before the modern concept of infinity was formed, led to religious veneration. For in this upward look humanity gained a sense of something greater than man; because we lifted our eyes to the stars, many a care, many a quarrel, which might have swelled all out of proportion because they were so close to our feelings or our daily life, have been reduced to their proper significance and have suddenly become very small and petty things.

And here again we put the question: What does this infinity mean for *man,* what does it mean, quite simply, for us *personally* and for our *life?*

Let me answer that question by simply asking another question: If we ask what this means "for us personally," isn't the answer exactly the same as in the case of the infinity of time? There the life of man is only a microscopic particle of time. Here the life of man is a mere atom, subject to the same futility in the face of the infinity of space as it is over against the infinity of time.

If, just for a moment, we really take this infinity in utter seriousness, do we not lose all conception of our own life, of all that is great and heroic and noble, and also of all that is small and nasty and base? In view of these cosmic dimensions does this distinction have any significance at all? Or, to use another simile, when we think of World War II and the mass misery in scores of ruined cities, does it make any difference at all whether yesterday two bees on the island of Capri fought over one of the millions of flowers there, and one of them sprained its sixth leg in the fray, or whether the two of them remembered that bees must stick together and harmoniously share the flowers? It is completely unimportant, isn't it?

But if that is so, isn't it equally unimportant, or even much less important, whether we human beings are great and noble in our life or whether we behave meanly and basely? So, does not the infinity of space pitch us even more radically into utter futility? Does not this utter nothingness extinguish, not only the little things, but also the greatness in our life?

This we must get clear in our minds, if we are not only to be thrilled but also appalled by the grandeur of space and the light years—if it is true that the immensity of light years really constitutes the ultimate background of this world, cutting off our vision of anything beyond it.

If we can quote Nietzsche for the infinity of time and its terrors, we can quote Kant for the infinity of space. At the end of his *Critique of Practical Reason* he breaks out in these famous words: "Two things fill the mind with ever new and increasing admiration and awe, the oftener and the more steadily we reflect on them: the starry heavens above and the moral law within."

What this statement means is this: The sight of the starry heavens teaches me my own littleness and that which is greater than I. But this sense of the tremendous magnitude of the cosmos would be so overwhelming that I would be utterly shattered if there were not one thing that I could oppose to this infinity, namely, the moral law within me. This moral law tells me that I am a free, moral being. And this, despite my utter smallness, distinguishes me fundamentally from the starry heavens, be they never so gigantic. For these constellations must run their courses in accord with eternal, immutable laws and therefore are not free, but rather imprisoned in the unalterable cosmic curves of their orbits. And therefore I can contemplate them as a free being, infinitely superior to them all.

We shall see later that this self-assertion over against the infinity of the universe has its source in a Christian and Western heritage. What interests us at this point is just the fact that for Kant the infinity of cosmic space is tolerable only because the starry heavens are balanced by the moral law. The starry heavens alone would be dreadful.

At any rate, this much we now understand: It would be simply terrifying, we would be helplessly exposed to the awful loneliness of a chilling infinity, if we had to draw our faith in God the Creator from this concept and experience of space: "I believe that God has created the world; I believe that his arms embrace the far reaches of the light years and therefore last of all—for I am the least and smallest of all—they include *me*."

If that were so, would we not have to go on and say something like this? "I believe, O God, that you must first govern and direct the Milky Way, so that there shall be no cosmic collisions and catastrophes; and if you have a lot of time on your hands, Creator God, you may perhaps give some attention to our planet. And there at best you may be concerned about a few microscopically small so-called 'great nations' among the antlike children of men, perhaps even the handful of earth that is called the West—but what about me? No, it would be grotesque even to think of such a thing, to assume that you could have any interest in me. This could be imagined only by an old book like the Bible, which suffers from a confusion of proportions and has no conception of the ridiculous rank man holds in the whole of the universe."

In concluding this train of thought concerning the infinity of time and space, we ask ourselves two questions:

1. Would not such a Creator God be cold and forbidding? Would he have any relationship whatsoever to him whom I may call my *Father*, because Jesus told us so? No, this God would certainly have nothing in common with a father; he would have become instead an impersonal cosmic formula, and in that formula my life with its sorrow and joy, its guilt and its high endeavors, its love of life and its fear of death, would only be an X or even that appalling cipher "infinite minus."

2. Is the Bible really so naïve that it puts man at the center and thus gives him an infinite importance, thus showing that it has no conception of the microscopical minuteness of his existence?

Three times in the Bible (Ps. 8:4; Heb. 2:6-9; and Ps. 144:3) we hear this cry: "What is man that thou art mindful of him?" And that, after all, means quite simply: No man of himself can claim—indeed, no man could ever arrive in a natural way at the idea—that he, that all of us together, were anything upon which the Creator could reasonably bestow his interest. In any case, in this repeated cry the Bible undoubtedly shows that it has more sense of the proportion of greatness between God and man than many people in our time, who say on the one hand that we Christians take ourselves too seriously when we bother God with our personal affairs and even our daily bread, and then turn around and say that one should not grovel and bow before God, but rather stand up before him—almost like an equal partner.

When the Bible poses the question "What is man that thou art mindful of him?" it knows very well that there is a decisive proportion of greatness between God and man. But it sets it forth not with the undertone of despair (as does modern man despite his assurances to the contrary), but rather with the tone of utter amazement—that God should *nevertheless* be mindful of man! *Why* the Bible does this—well, the content of the gospel is meant to tell us why. Here we simply note the fact as such.

This same mystery, the "Christian" mystery, to which the Psalmist is pointing, is also expressed in that touching children's hymn,

> Do you know how many stars
> There are shining in the sky?

This song of the many, many stars in the sky is not intended to make the child conscious of how small and stupid he is within this great world. No, it tells him in simple, moving terms that even though and just because God holds all the millions of stars in his hand, he also knows him and loves him.

Do we understand, then, why it is such a liberation to hear Luther begin his explanation, *not* with light years and dizzying thought of space, but rather with the simple statement, "I believe that God has created *me*"?

Now we can sum up briefly everything that is expressed in that simple, succinct statement:

1. It says that the eternal God in all his unfathomable majesty, enthroned beyond all space and time, *knows* me and has called me by my name. Now the accent of infinity lies upon my life. Now I can say: I am his *child* and therefore I stand infinitely closer to him than all the "great possessions" of the universe and all its Milky Ways.

2. I, man, can say "Thou" to God; I can address him as "my Father, our Father." I am therefore not one of the infinite effects produced by the cause called God, but rather he is my Father. More precisely stated, I am related to God not as effect to cause, but rather as person to person. So when I say "Abba! Father!" something far more and quite other is happening than what Kant calls the moral law. Because I can say this word of prayer, I can not only face the whole cosmos in all its grandeur—I, the child of God, whom all the cosmic spaces and the mighty planets cannot harm, the child of God whom the "sun shall not smite by day nor the moon by night"; I can also reach out my hand to him through all infinite space, and he sees it and grasps it. In the

midst of "brother spheres in rival song" and the sun's resounding "thunder,"[1] I can lift up my tiny childish voice, I can bring to him my joy, my sorrow, everything, and he hears that voice through all the cosmic music of the spheres.

3. And this already suggests our third point: In the midst of this tremendous cosmic empire which is subject to the Creator God, I can have a relationship to him that makes me "directly subject to the King." Before God, I, man, am not merely a citizen of my country, not merely a child of my parents, not merely the bearer of certain more or less valuable attributes and capacities, but rather, without the interposition of any higher courts of appeal whatsoever, I am directly and solely responsible to him. Without any intermediation I can approach him; for him I am his child. And I am his child even when, and precisely when, every other court spurns me, when for every earthly court I no longer represent a value, even if I am only a feeble-minded waif whom human pride regards as a burden and treats as such or relegates to an institution. Even then I am still his child and despite what men may say I can call upon him and know that his hand is there.

This immediacy to the King was given to me by Jesus Christ, for it was he who gave me back my Father; it was he who brought me to the Father. And that's how faith in the Creator brings us to the very heart of the gospel.

To sum up, God is our Father and we are his children. We have immediate access to him, in spite of all the light-year spaces and all man's courts of appeal. All this is what Luther meant when he framed that audacious opening sentence of his explanation of creation:

"I believe that God has created me."

---

[1] Goethe, *Faust*, Prologue in Heaven. (Trans.)

II | CREATION AND COSMOLOGY

WE HAVE SEEN THAT THE BIBLICAL TEACHING CONCERN-
ing creation is not primarily interested in the question of "how
the world came into being." Its purpose is not to present a theory
of how the universe began; its sole interest lies rather in the question of what kind of a *personal relationship between the Creator
and the creature is intended in God's plan.*

In the first chapter of Romans Paul speaks quite to this effect
concerning faith in God the Creator (vv. 18 ff.). He points out
that nature is a *parable,* which is, so to speak, a transparency of
the Creator. But this transparency of the natural world was of no
help at all to men for the simple reason that "though they knew
God they did not honor him as God, or give thanks to him"; in
other words, man did not do the one thing that makes all the difference: he did not draw from it the conclusion that he must take
this belief in a Creator and make it a part of his life. This taking
one's faith in a Creator into one's own life means some very practical things, like accepting one's daily work as well as the strength
to do it every morning anew as from his hands; leaving the morrow confidently to the leadings of this Lord instead of anxiously
worrying about it; looking without fear at the bloody strife of
this world, and really acting upon one's faith that there is a knowing and purposeful power that governs above all the madness and
all the dreadful judgments in this world.

So, says Paul to us modern men, we get not one millimeter
closer to the Creator by learning to know the precise operations
of natural law and searching back to the primeval beginnings—if
at the same time we close ourselves off from his fellowship and his

26

rule over our personal life. Luther emphasizes this same implication of faith in a Creator, which is so exceedingly practical and also determinative of our knowledge, in the conclusion of his explanation of the first article of the Creed, which culminates in these words: "for all which I am in duty bound to thank praise, serve, and obey him."

From this vantage point, then, we gain an insight that is of tremendous importance. If we read Luther's *Small Catechism,* we shall find that he structured his explanation of the Ten Commandments *and* his explanation of the meaning of creation according to a strict parallelism: in both sections the one thing that governs the whole point of view is that we must enter into an I-Thou relationship with God.

The Ten Commandments, therefore, are not pursuing the purpose of setting up some kind of moral program for the improvement of the world. Their message to the world is not: If you keep all these commandments (that is, if you do not lie, steal, commit adultery, etc.), then your life and the whole world will be harmoniously balanced, then there will be no more prisons, no more wars, nor any such things. What possible good could such an assurance do us when every step we take in actual experience shows us that we cannot keep these commandments anyhow, that we live in a world which rules and allows itself to be governed by rules that are totally different from the commandments of God? What real place do they have in politics, in business, in the shaping of culture? We live in a world that grovels in the dust before some gods which are totally different from the Lord . . .

No, the real message of the commandments is this: All your unhappiness, all your troubles, crimes, and wars, all your distrust of one another and your lack of inner peace, stem from this *one* fact, that you have lost the center of your life. Only on *one* condition—namely, that you allow yourself to be called to order and brought to order through Jesus Christ at this innermost point in your life where fellowship and peace with God are at stake: in other words, that you learn to "fear and love God"—can the healing process also begin in your moral life and in the public areas of politics, business, and culture.

So there is profound meaning in the unmistakable monotony

with which Luther begins his explanation of each one of the commandments with the same words: "We should so fear and love God . . ."

To use a medical metaphor, he is not interested in symptom therapy. That is to say, he is not concerned that we should patch up and correct the manifestations of moral degeneration and the sores on the skin of human society (by trying, for example, through legal measures to reduce the amount of adultery, fraud, murder, etc.) , but rather that we go back to the center of the person. To be a Christian means nothing short of seeing the real trouble of our life at its innermost center (which is, that we have so little fellowship with God) , and then submitting this innermost center of our lives to the divine Physician in order that he may heal us from the inside out.

Now, we find exactly the same approach—and this is the parallelism of structure I mentioned above—in Luther's explanation of creation. Here again his explanation puts the decisive emphasis not upon how the universe came into being, but rather upon a man's personal relationship to the Creator, who created "me," and whom I am in duty bound to thank, praise, and obey. And that takes belief in a Creator out of the realm of theoretical contemplation and scientific reflection about the origin of our cosmos and brings it right down into the sober, matter-of-fact practice of our life in this moment. Let us consider three examples of this bringing of theory down into life, each of which will give us a different angle of it.

It is dreadfully easy, perhaps in a religious discussion, to say *in theory,* "It is my firm conviction that a creative will governs this world, that there is a God who created the nations and designed the structure and order of the cosmos"—and *at the same time* lead a life which is in no way oriented toward the holy "Thou" of this Creator. This is the egregious inconsistency of the so-called "religious man" who is loath to admit that there is any total sovereignty of God which also includes his own life, his job, his marriage, his relation to his neighbor, and so on. Instead, he wants God's rule to be operative only "outside" in the cosmos or in the world of nations. His secret interest here probably lies in the thought that God is so occupied with the stars, the phosphorescence of the sea, and the wonders of biology that he will not come too close to his personal and private life with his high-powered demands.

A second example: It is very easy to stand on a mountain peak and be thrilled and moved by the crimson marvel of a sunrise and the creative power of God, and then four hours later, back at the hotel, when you receive the news that your own house no longer exists, cast the whole mess at the feet of this same Creator and say, "How can God allow such things to happen?"

And then a third example, which is the logical completion of the other two: It is very easy to stand in some alpine meadow on a spring morning and feel a religious shiver going down your back at the thought that there is a "power" who "points the clouds their course, whom winds and seas obey," and then that same evening, tormented by worries about the coming weeks and months, the oppressive images of the future, refuse to trust that this same Lord, who so marvellously directs the clouds and winds and seas, is able to find ways where "wandering feet" may go.

These very elementary, everyday examples make it clear that genuine faith in the Creator comes into being only when we get beyond this conventional, pious-sounding theoretical recognition of a Creator and allow ourselves to be called into a personal relationship with him. In the light of these three examples we would therefore understand "personal relationship" to mean that in the structuring of our whole life we begin by reckoning with the fact that this Creator has a demanding will and therefore has some demands to make upon us. In the second place, this personal relationship means that we also accept as coming from his hands the hard—and hard to understand—lot that may come to our personal life or to our country, and not only the pleasant things such as the magic of an alpine sunrise or sunset. And finally, personal relationship means that we allow the cares for tomorrow to be dissolved and extinguished in praise of him who is and who was and who is to come, and in whose sure governance the morrow, too, is safe.

So we see how the circle of the Bible's faith in creation and all its radii point to the center of the gospel, namely, to the heart of God that is open to us and on which we should reckon.

This is also what Paul is driving at in those enigmatic phrases in which he speaks of the world as being created "through" Jesus Christ.[1] What he means is that God is never an impersonal first cause in the process of cosmogony, but that from the first moment of his creative action he was creating toward the "thou" to whom he willed to be related as a father and whom he desired to walk before him as his child. "Jesus Christ in the creation" points mysteriously to this original relationship of Father and child, to this will to fellowship in God, which determined his actions from the very first moment and which is still the goal of salvation and will be the end of history.

With the help of this basic, determinative motif in creation, namely, that its purpose is a personal relationship between the Creator and the creature, it is not difficult to draw the most important lines that mark off the Christian doctrine of creation from its apparent competitors, meaning those intellectual competitors which are found in the cosmologies and various world views.

The problem here is this: Even though it is true that this personal relationship to God is the center of the Christian faith in creation, nevertheless this faith *also* affirms that God actually created the world in a very *real* way, not merely in some "spiritual" sense. How does this square with our present scientific knowledge; for example, with our biological or astronomical view of the world? We must deal with these questions, because they cause great trouble for many people and because they are the kind of question that must concern every wide-awake person who is open to the questions of the times. We shall deal with this problem by discussing first the question of cosmology (or world picture, *Weltbild*) in the next chapter, and then the question of world view (*Weltanschauung*) in its relation to Christian faith.

What do we mean by a cosmology or world picture? By cosmology we mean the attempt to pull together all our scientific experience that tells us something about the structure of our world and to construct from it a total picture of the origin, structure, and nature of our world. This is the only way in which we can see all the individual facts and phenomena and properly arrange them in a larger context. Even a physician cannot properly judge a particu-

---

[1] Cf. Eph. 3:9, A.V. (Trans.)

lar pathological phenomenon—an abscess, for example, or a tuberculous symptom—unless he knows the total constitution of his patient and thus sees the framework in which the individual pathological symptom is to be incorporated.

ᒓ It is the same way with the world as a whole. If we want to understand properly a particular historical phenomenon, say the emergence of capitalism and the social crises and upheavals which it entailed, we must know what role industry and business play in the whole of a nation. But more, we must know how the various national economies are related to each other, and thus the place these economies have in the total organism of humanity.

But even that is not sufficient. Since economy is concerned with the production of goods and the meeting of needs, and therefore with the world of things and goods and with the production of the material and biological conditions of man's existence, we are inevitably compelled to ask what is man's *whole* relationship to the cosmos. What, for example, are the needs that pertain to his biological character (such as adequate nourishment); but at the same time, what is there in him that is more than biological, what are his peculiar needs as a "human being" (such as his so-called "human rights")? What are the characteristic traits he exhibits, for example, in determining what his needs are and how they should be met? (I am thinking, for example, of economic competition, the psychological law of supply and demand, and all those factors which specifically differentiate the economic exchange of goods among human beings from what happens in a colony of ants or bees, and which can only be understood as manifestations of man's peculiar and special position in the cosmos.) We see, therefore, how even this one area of life, that of economics—and the same applies to all the other areas of life—keeps pushing us beyond the limited sector of one area and forces us to see that there are overlapping points of view, which we must have if we are to gain a picture of man as a whole. Further, we must see what this individual area looks like in the total world and the whole of life. If we are heading a business we must have an overview of *all* the functions of life; we must have something like a cosmology, a world picture, into which we can properly incorporate our special area.

And yet this world picture keeps expanding far beyond the outlook we have already mentioned toward increasingly comprehensive and more total views. That is to say, a cosmology includes not only our planets, for our universe is itself included in larger astronomical systems. Consequently, cosmology requires a judgment concerning how our earth arose in the whole cosmos and how man came into being in it. Then we must also have a judgment concerning the structure of the earth, whether it is a flat plane swimming in a great ocean or whether it is a sphere. And finally, to complete our world picture, it is necessary that we know what place our planet has in the total universe; whether, for example, the sun revolves around the earth or the earth around the sun. The totality of all these judgments results in a total view of the world—in other words, in what we call a cosmology or "world picture."

And here arises the important and tremendously popular question: How does the Christian faith in creation relate to this cosmology? Or more precisely, is not this faith rooted in our obsolete cosmology? Does this not mean, then, that the whole framework in which the Bible views all individual events and the whole history of salvation, is simply false and long since exploded? After all, we cannot get away from the fact that the creation story regards the earth as being the center of the whole process of creation. Quite "naïvely" we are told that the stars were created after the most important part of creation was completed. And similarly in the cosmology of the Book of Revelation we are told very simply that in the final judgments and terrors at the end of history the great red dragon will appear in heaven and with his tail will sweep down "a third of the stars of heaven and cast them to the earth." After all, we know that this simply could not happen in any literal sense, for every one of these stars except the moon is incomparably larger than our earth; it is simply a quantitative impossibility that a number of stars could fall upon our earth, just as it is impossible for ten parachute mines to hit a single ant.

And that leaves us with the perilous question: Does not faith in creation fall to the ground along with this obsolete cosmology? Is not this faith bound up, for good or evil, with the cosmological framework in which it is incorporated?

And the first thing we must say in answer to that question is that it is simply true that cosmology of the Bible is antiquated and obsolete. After all, it would be a sad thing if in all these thousands of years our knowledge of the world had never budged an inch.

At the same time, however, we see how very little stress the Bible puts upon this cosmology, the completely secondary position it has. As we have already seen, it was by no means the purpose of the biblical narrators to furnish us with an account of the origin of the world in the first chapter of the Bible. Their purpose was something altogether different, namely, to bear witness *within the framework of the cosmology of their time* to three things:

First, that at the beginning of the world, above the silence of the primeval flux or the steamy cloud of primordial mist (whichever it may have been)—in any case, long before the creatures were called into being—the Spirit of God was at work.

Second, that in every moment still elapsing God is still *upholding* this world which he created (no matter whether one imagines the stars to be points of light on the inner side of a globular universe or whether one regards them as planets and fixed stars that run their courses in accord with immutable laws).

Third, that man has been called into being by God, set down before his face, and given the dignity of being his child (regardless of whether one believes that he was made of a lump of clay or that God called him forth from a line of prehuman animal forms and bestowed upon him the miracle of being the image and child of God in the context of biological evolution). When children are born do we not speak of their being given to us by God—even though, of course, they do not simply fall from heaven, but rather come into being through procreation and birth according to the natural laws of biology? Nevertheless we think of them as being given and created by God within this natural form of generation.

So we ask: Does the development of cosmology and the progress of scientific knowledge change any of these affirmations of faith in the slightest degree? On the contrary, we see that our knowledge of the cosmic dimensions of space and time only brings out more clearly the twofold wonder of God's creative power—twofold in that God encompasses these boundless spaces and yet *at the same time* knows man, that grain of dust and merest atom, and calls him by name.

Historically, the struggle between faith in creation and cosmology was brought to a head by the development of astronomy. We know what an earthquake went through the intellectual and religious world when Copernicus and Galileo broke away from the Ptolemaic cosmology, the world picture in which the sun revolved around the earth, and demonstrated that it is just the opposite. This meant a revolution, because it meant at the same time a break with the biblical view of the world. For in the biblical cosmology our earth stands at the center of cosmic events—if only because the crib of the Christ-child and the Cross of Golgotha were set down upon this earth. It was thought that if it were true that this new Copernican cosmology was correct and our earth was only one among millions of stars, then the uniqueness and the centrality of Christ's redemptive work would fall to the ground too.

For us today this objection is hardly conceivable, for we have learned that the forgiveness of sins, our homesickness for the heart of God, and the world dominion of Jesus Christ have nothing to do with the position of our planet in the totality of the universe. Through this very crisis in astronomical cosmology we have learned that God remains independent of all changes in our view of the cosmos and that he can be praised in *any* cosmic system, whether it be an earth which is supposed to be a fixed star in the center of the universe, or a planet which moves like a tiny atom in the midst of unimaginably tremendous galaxies, or the kind of earth set forth by the adherents of the "empty universe" theory.

At the same time we see that Luther, with an infallible instinct for the biblical essence of the gospel of creation, took a position in his explanation of the first article of the Creed which really does lie beyond the level of cosmology when he said, "I believe that God created me." There he laid his finger upon that personal character of faith in the Creator which can be experienced in every past, present, or future picture of the world.

Christian faith in the Creator is therefore independent of any cosmology that happens to be current; or to put it another way, it is given to us within the cosmology that we have worked out in good conscience with the knowledge we have. But the Christian faith itself never dictates what this cosmology should be.

WORLD PICTURE AND WORLD VIEW | III

THERE ARE A NUMBER OF POINTS THAT DISTINGUISH A "world picture." The chief difference can be described in this way. We said that a "world picture" or cosmology is the sum of all the scientific knowledge which combines to give us a concept of the total structure of the world.

A world view, on the other hand, has a totally different interest: its purpose is to tell us something about the ultimate meaning of life and the world. For example, the idealistic world view of Hegel puts forward the thesis that the world spirit manifests and reveals itself in everything that happens, in nature as well as history, and that just because such a rational spirit is behind everything that happens, the world too is rationally, meaningfully, and logically constructed.

The materialistic world view, on the other hand, takes the position that there is no spirit at all and that everything that happens is merely a movement of matter. Neither of these world views (to mention only the idealistic and the materialistic views as examples) can claim that they have *proved* their correctness. Nobody can prove that a rational spirit is behind all things or that everything is a movement of matter. This is something that must be *believed*. Thus Fichte says in the introduction to his principles of science: The philosophy (one can also say, the world view) one has determines what kind of a man one is. What Fichte is saying is that the kind of a man a person is, is not determined by exact scientific knowledge, but rather is rooted in an unprovable level of personal life and therefore lies in a pretheoretical stage of knowledge.

Consequently, world views, every one of them, are based upon *faith,* that is, in this case upon a presupposition which can no longer be proved. We may therefore sum up by saying that world views attempt to provide an ultimate interpretation of the meaning of the world, but an interpretation which as such is not demonstrable.

A world view, however, differs from a cosmology in still another respect:

A cosmology has a *theoretical* interest; it seeks to round out our knowledge of things by putting together all the individual data in a mosaic whole.

A world view, on the other hand, has a definitely *practical* interest. It attempts to give man ultimate motivations for his actions; indeed, it seeks to give him *strength* for these actions. The implication of this is that man can act with complete devotion of his life and his strength only if he knows that what he is doing has meaning in a larger context.

Wherever world views arise in the modern world their purpose is to communicate to man this kind of meaning for his life in the total framework of the world and thus to stimulate him to devote his full energies to what he is doing and arouse his capacity for enthusiasm. World views are a kind of combustible which is poured upon the flames of the passions and enthusiasms. Again, then, world views have an interest that is primarily practical and contributory to action.

Consequently, to advocate a world view always means that one is seeking to give a *theme* to the world, which is to say that one is setting up some entity (the spirit or life or the individual or economics, etc.) as the ultimate and controlling reality and then asserting that all other entities are derived from this *one* entity. A world view means a kind of world formula. If you know the formula, all the secrets of the world open up as if with a magic word. In other words, world view means that one sees the whole world subsumed under a definite *theme* by which all the phenomena of life are determined.

This brings us to a point where all these questions become essentially and *theologically* interesting. Here we must remember that in all the world views this theme under which the world is subsumed always consists of a *creaturely* entity. We have only to think of world views in which the supreme entity is the spirit or life or economics or the glands. All of these entities are a part of the created world. So what is actually happening here is that *creaturely* entities are being elevated to the highest possible rank and set up as the theme of the world.

This statement, which at first appears to be so simple and self-evident, is nevertheless of tremendous importance. This statement means quite simply that world views see the world as being ordered, not by the Creator, but rather by that which is created. Or to put it in another way, world views see the meaning of life, the world, history, not in God, but rather in the creature or in a creaturely entity.

This does not mean that world views need always be consciously atheistic. The word "god" may continue to be used. But the terrible thing is that the concept of God is always exclusively determined by this alleged, absolutized creaturely entity.

In the world view of *rationalism*, for example, reason was made the theme of the world, and thus every statement made about God had to be in accord with the standard of reason. So one arrived at the pale religion of reason called "deism," in which God is placed at the beginning of things as the first cause, only to make way for the logical process of natural laws and never again to appear on the scene.

In the *biological* world view God is only another term for generative life and the eternal laws that govern the world.

In the *racial* world view God is the God of a particular breed, that is, he must take on the features of a particular racial species, and thus we have such fanatical ideas as a "German" God, an "American" God, a "white" God, or a "black" God. These examples illustrate in a shocking way how God can be made dependent upon creaturely entities, in this case, a racially defined entity.

In all these cases, therefore, the Creator is constantly being defined in terms of something that was created.

In Paul's great argument with the religious world views (in the first chapter of Romans) he therefore speaks of men finally ending up in the worship of "images resembling mortal man or birds or animals or reptiles," in other words, in the open and scarcely dis-

guised worship of creatures. This process reached its culmination
in Nietzsche's idea of the "superman," in which the last bit of disguise fell away. But we know from the First Commandment that
this is the manifestation of man's primeval, original sin.

That is to say, original sin consists in worshiping the creature
instead of the Creator, the creature finally becoming an idol (for
an idol is nothing else but a deified creature).

It is against this attempt and only this attempt that the negative
part of this first and chief commandment is directed: "I am the
Lord your God . . . *you shall have no other gods before me."*

In any case, here is one deep and alarming danger in all world
views, against which the church of Jesus Christ is called to do battle in every age. But this is not merely a matter of *denying* the
world views. That cannot be the business of the church of Jesus
Christ. For the world views very often have the important and indispensable function of ordering life and combining all its diverse
manifestations under one unified point of view. Especially in
times of internal and external disintegration it is natural that
people should wish for a world view which orders and reduces
everything to a unified common denominator.

I say that here the task of the church of Jesus Christ is not simply to make gestures of denial and rejection. In its office as shepherd and guardian of the world its duty is to call attention, in the
name of faith in the Creator and the First Commandment, to this
tremendous danger of having a world view without God, the danger of any world view that honors the creature instead of the
Creator. Further, it is its duty to call attention to the simple, elementary fact that God is not mocked and that as soon as God is no
longer the Lord, but merely a phantom of our own desires or a
feeble reflection and imitation of our humankind, then darkness
and gloom descend upon the earth and the nations.

A few points may show what happens when a world view acts as
if it were autonomous and abandons God.

The world views are in danger at all times of elevating a creaturely entity to the status of God, whether that entity be the spirit
or mind, life (*bios*) or economics.

The consequence of this confusion of the Creator with the creature is always a profound disorder, disorganization—indeed, de-

cay in the world. *For the creaturely entity which is thus elevated to the position of being the theme of the world is never equal to this task, and is simply incapable of embracing and controlling all the phenomena of life.*

Assume, for example, that the creaturely entity "mind" were absolutized and exalted to the position of being the theme of the whole world. The inevitable result of this absolutizing of the mind would be a certain intellectualism which is incapable of binding the deep substrata and irrational forces in human life. It is therefore no wonder that the forces of blood and instinct rebel against an intellectualistic world view, that the vital gods demand their hearth fire and Dionysus cries out for his myth and his cult. The whole realm of instinct and elemental feeling seeks release and expression and feels that it is not understood and bound by the domination of the intellect. It feels that it has been left out of account and therefore tends to rebel. This is the only thing that can explain Friedrich Nietzsche's revolution against the intellect. His thought is one long outcry against the domination of the intellectual and abstract mind. What we hear in him is the tortured cry of man's deep, instinctual, biological nature, which had been subjugated and ignored by an alien master. And Friedrich Nietzsche was a kind of vent that sought to release the pressures of passion and instinct which had never been subdued by pure intellect.

But already in our generation we have seen that this attempt—in this case to make life (*bios*) the ultimate theme of the world—is not capable of comprehending the whole, either. For a purely biological world view leaves the mind and the spirit unsatisfied. The spirit is something more and also *demands* to be something more than a mere emanation or reflection of man's biological structure. Goethe's *Faust* and Bach's *St. Matthew Passion* demand to be taken as a struggle for an ultimate truth, not merely as products of a mind which is a mere exudation of our biological nature. Besides, the purely biological view of life does not take account of the fact that man is more than a mere organism, that he is an ethical person, an image of God, and that he has an eternal worth and dignity that remain even when in the biological sense he may be called old and useless, sick, and not worth being allowed to go on living, because he does not satisfy the ideal of perfect natural health.

So it is inevitable that these forces of the spirit and the ethical should resist the violence done to them by the purely biological view.

The same process can be illustrated in all attempts to produce a world view. Where the individual is deified, for example, and the world view proclaims only the right to personality, the right to develop according to one's own nature, to develop what Goethe calls "the minted form which develops as it lives," there the sense of *community* is likely to be ignored and the result is a protest against individualism.

On the other hand, where the *community* is deified and you have a collectivistic world view, the individual personality feels slighted or tyrannized, and in turn rebels in favor of a new individualism. If all the signs are not deceiving, we are in a new phase of a development of the latter kind. Young people who for years have lived in barracks or were regimented in parties or leagues are pressing for a more individual, private life subject only to their own control.

We have considered these facts for only one reason, and that is because these terrible crises in the history of succeeding world views can only be understood if they are seen from the biblical point of view, that is, on the basis of faith in the Creator and the First Commandment.

And what we have clearly seen is this: When men with the help of world views elevate a creaturely entity to the place where it becomes the ultimate meaning of the world and thus put it in the place of the Creator, they deliver the world over to decay and disintegration. For we see how these creaturely entities always leave whole areas of life unaccounted for and thus encourage them to rebellion. The creaturely entity, "community," drives the individual to rebellion; the creaturely entity, "individual," entails the revolt of the forces of "community." This has been so in all the world views we can think of.

Has not therefore the history of the West with its increasing secularization become one long chain of revolutions?

A survey of the inner history of our hemisphere in the last centuries makes our heads spin, so rapid has been the succession of philosophies, world views, and ideologies; so quickly has one enthroned idol been toppled and replaced by another. It is a veritable parade of idols, and how comical these gods look from behind! What we took with such deadly seriousness a few decades ago now strikes us as vapid and ridiculous. How these world views, these idols, have followed upon each other's heels! You recognize them by the suffix "-ism" attached to their names. It would be too confusing to mention them all as they succeeded each other: rationalism, sensualism, idealism, materialism, monism, biologism, and so on and so on.

And as we look at this passing parade of idols we are reminded of three basic biblical laws which are here verified in a way that is almost staggering.

1. Wherever God the Creator is dethroned as the absolute and sovereign Lord of the world and our life, there the gods replace him.

2. Wherever false gods are enthroned, there is always a struggle of the gods among themselves; the result is a battle of world views and the threat of chaos. What that means in concrete terms we have learned all too clearly in an age of nationalistic world views. We saw this kind of world view take a grip upon the whole world of nations, leading to a new form of polytheism of individual nations. The nations had their own gods and each made itself the highest one, which was to be the standard for the world. Seen from this point of view, the last world war takes on an apocalyptic character; the nations fought each other, as it were, in the airy realms of the nationalistic gods. A truly Trojan situation! Mutual understanding vanished from the world because the connecting link "God" was gone and the nations with their own gods—that is, their own absolutized spirits—are thrown into bickering and brawling. Therefore no human arm can stop this battle of the gods.

3. Finally, wherever God is dethroned and false gods are worshiped there is always a "twilight of the gods," too; the creaturely entity which has been made an absolute immediately shows its lack of ability to bind together broad areas of life, and there is able to maintain its position for only a short time. Hence the ever-

increasing and more rapid attrition of the world views.

And there is one last thing that is clear. There is no human power that can stop this development and call a halt to the parade and conflict of the gods. It is a characteristic of the gods that, though you can help them to get onto the throne, as soon as they are enthroned they begin to rule you, and then they can no longer be toppled by human strength. Only new gods can overthrow the old ones, to be immediately threatened in turn by other usurpers. So from the first day on, even the outlook of the gods is darkened by twilight and by the operation of eternal, immutable laws whose creeping shadows advance upon them. A touch of sadness lies upon the face of all the gods, and the melancholy realization that the days of their life are fleeting goads them to make haste, forcing them to overstrain their power. They know that their "time is short" (Rev. 12:12).

This is the terrible Archimedean screw, endlessly turning in the unholy history of the world views.

There are certain concepts—and this can be seen in the foregoing illustration—which we cannot present in straightforward scientific style, but for which we must employ mythological categories in order to express them adequately. We are dealing here with something in the hidden background of the world which cannot be dealt with directly, but rather requires the indirectness of a symbolic reflection in the form of a myth. Here all of us are sitting in the "Platonic cave" and cannot see directly. Nor can we make direct statements. Mythical insights are always indirect and veiled even in the style in which they are presented. They are indirect simply because they cannot be acquired by means of simple, scientific objectivity (which anyone can acquire), but one must put oneself in a definite position in order to receive them.

Here we come close to the mysteries of the world, close to those levels in which the gods rise and fall and exert their uncanny power—the kind of power they are acknowledged to have by the message of the Bible, which is the only view that penetrates into these levels, because it knows the "Light of the World," the Light that reveals and unmasks these opposing powers.

The solution to this fundamental problem of the West, which lies at the root of our intellectual and spiritual confusion, cannot be found on the strategic, military, political, or cultural level; for in the last analysis it is a question that is bound up with our attitude toward the living God. Here there are no patent solutions that can tell us how to act; there is only a call to repentance and the willingness to turn around and go back home to God.

The second thing that becomes apparent here is this: Only the First Commandment, "I am the Lord your God," and the first article of the Creed, "I believe in God the Father Almighty, Maker of heaven and earth" can give us valid directions as to how one can live in history. For God alone is the lord of *all* the areas of life, not merely of a part of it as the gods of the world views claim. God claims the obedience of our mind and spirit, but he also wants our bodies, our vitality, our urges and instincts, for his possession. The body is the temple of the Holy Spirit. God rules body, mind, and spirit.

And then further, God points us to *fellowship* with our neighbor. When Jesus summed up all the commandments in the commandment to love one's neighbor this meant quite simply that we men do not exist for ourselves, but rather belong to our neighbor. But in doing this God is not simply turning us into units in a community or collective; he is actually addressing us as *individuals.* We stand before him completely alone. We receive from his hands the *suffering* in our lives, which we can share with no other person and which is an integral part of the uniquely personal plan of our life. We stand before him completely alone with our *guilt;* no fellowship or community can relieve us of it. And we must die our own death alone; nobody can do it for us or accompany us. There we are utterly alone with God.

So God claims us as individuals, not merely as collective beings. He knows and addresses us personally, and only on the basis of our solitariness before God do we receive the power to give ourselves to our neighbor. For only in this solitariness and only as we are addressed by this divine Thou do we become a self at all, so that we are capable of giving ourselves. This is precisely the reason why the Christian fellowship is never an impersonal collective. The collective arises only when the individual personality is suppressed and consumed in the impersonal mass. In his fine book, *Justice and the Social Order,* Emil Brunner points out that collectivism takes the organic structure of social order and grinds it into atoms in order subsequently to fuse the individual particles into the artificial unity of the collective.[1]

But where *God* is the Lord, and life in *all* its aspects is enclosed in one all-inclusive totality, the individual and the community are related to each other in a strict order and each retains its own validity and dignity. Where the world views prevail, the result is either individualism or collectivism, a kind of spiritualized intellectualism or subservience to matter.

On the other hand, God wants no personality cult (the age of the individualistic world view). Nor does he desire anybody selfishly to pursue his own salvation; he wants us to live for our neighbor.

These examples show that God is a total Lord. Before him there can be no individualistic or collectivistic views, no individualistic world view of the spirit and no worship of the body and vitality.

God takes us as a whole. He is a total Lord. He alone rules the totality of our life and all the areas of life.

Two comments in conclusion:

1. I think I have sufficiently guarded myself against the misunderstanding that my purpose here has been to present a more or less clever interpretation of history. I have already said that this cannot be my task.

My concern has been only to point out one single fact, and that is that the spiritual and intellectual experience of the last centuries, or more precisely, the history of world views, the terrible consequences of which we are all suffering today, can be understood only in terms of biblical categories. We can understand it only if we see it as an "apostasy from God" and therefore as the rule of false and mutually hostile gods. Here we find ourselves very close to the message of the last book of the Bible, which sets forth the background of world history from the point of view that this is a battle of God with the false gods who are in permanent rebellion against each other and against the Lord of lords—and in so doing says something qualitatively different from what Goethe meant by history as the "struggle between faith and unbelief."

[1] Emil Brunner, *Justice and the Social Order*, Mary Hottinger, trans. (New York: Harper & Row, 1945) , p. 82.

A person who does not possess the "category of the apocalyptic" sees only the foreground of history; he sees only the intellectual battles, the struggles for political and military power, philosophical movement, economic crises, and all this in ever closer succession and more brutal proportions.

2. In everything I have been obliged to say about this struggle of gods and world views, and this profound disorder in our modern world, the intention has not been in any sense to be merely negative and pessimistic. True, I have been talking about "apostasy from God." (And this is really the key to the inner history of the Western world.) But we can make this statement only in the name of one enormous fact, namely, that this Creator, this Lord of heaven and earth actually *exists* and that Christ stands at the beginning and the end of history. And that means that we are not wandering about in a hopeless maze with no way out, surrounded by the dark, mysterious forces of fate. No, we are rather running away from a Lord who is waiting for us to come to him.

When the law of history is conceived in terms of "development" (such as the unfolding of an entelechy,[2] a "minted form which develops as it lives"), then we have no alternative but the fate of incessant advance to its end, and the best we can do in the face of this development is to stand "at attention" like the soldier of Pompeii, powerless to defend ourselves against it.

But the gospel tells us about the *kairos,* the "acceptable time," the time of opportunity, the "today," when we can hear the Lord's voice. To hear the gospel means to be granted a new beginning. To be assured of forgiveness means to be given a new future. The gospel speaks of the "new creation," because it knows him who creates. History is not left to its own autonomy or to the law of the rise and fall of the gods. It rests in hands that are reaching out for man. The ultimate impulses of history come from a heart. The threat of the end of all things is only *one* of its possibilities. The *other* possibility is for us to go back home to God.

[2] Entelechy: the inner nature of anything, which determines its development. The reference here is to Goethe's definition of the term in *Urworte, Orphisch: "Geprägte Form, die lebend sich entwickelt"* ("minted form which develops as it lives"). Cf. pp. 59, 68, 160 below and also Helmut Thielicke, *The Freedom of the Christian Man,* John W. Doberstein, trans. (New York: Harper & Row, 1963), pp. 14, 17, 26, 32. (Trans.)

IV | THE WORLD VIEW OF BIOLOGY

WE OUGHT NOT TO CLOSE OUR DISCUSSION OF COSMOLO-
gies and world views without discussing in more detail two further
implications of this basic subject. Here I have in mind especially
our young people who are constantly meeting this problem in
their thinking and schooling and are entitled to know what the
church has to say about it.[1] The two basic themes I shall deal with
in these next three chapters are the world view of biology and the
controversy over the origin of man.

I begin with the first, the world view of biology.

The term "biology" comes from the Greek word *bios,* which
means "life." The term "biological world view" means therefore
that here is a view in which *bios* or "life" is made the paramount
theme of the world and all the other phenomena of the world are
derived from it. In this view are two important assertions which
decisively affect the meaning of our life.

1. In the first place, the biological world view quite specifically
rejects the idea that the term "life" is applicable only in the physical realm. The biological world view asserts quite correctly that
formerly we were constantly making the great mistake of dividing
the world into two parts: we were applying the term "life" only to
the physical part and therefore only to a limited sector of the
whole of life, to animals, plants, and the human body. Thus the

[1] In the following chapters we are by no means dealing with a complex of
questions which can be regarded as settled, once we have disposed of biological
materialism and its philosophical propaganda, for biologism as a way of looking at the world is a much more extensive movement. It is a particular expression of materialism which we shall have to reckon with increasingly in
the future.

mental side of man was consciously split off. That is, we were saying that everything man thinks (for example, in his philosophical systems), everything he produces in the way of cultural values in the realms of art, science, and religion, is completely independent of his fundamental biological character. Indeed, we went even further and declared that the mind and spirit are actually hostile to the body, which is determined "only" by biological factors, and that human life is realized in a definite struggle between flesh and spirit, between will and instinct.

This view is now being very emphatically and vehemently denied by those who are interested in the biological world view. This whole way of thinking, which separates mind and spirit from the body, is wrong even in its approach. The mind dare not be separated from physical life and exiled to a sphere of its own, to a metaphysical ghetto as it were. For the mind rises up out of the physical sap of a man's life. For example, it is quite obvious that a healthy person thinks differently from a sick one, and therefore that the mind *does* have something to do with the physical constitution. And it is equally obvious that all man's intellectual and cultural creations are related to the species: a Chinese philosophy, for example, is something quite different from the world view of a European thinker.

So here again it seems evident that all intellectual and cultural creations clearly reflect the fundamental biological basis from which they have sprung, and that consequently they are in no way autonomous and independent of this biological foundation.

I mention this point of view, not merely to reject it, but in order to point out that it also has a positive side. It can only be understood as being a justified reaction against the bloodless kind of thinking which makes the mind independent and estranges it from its natural ties. There can be no doubt that this represents a genuine concern, and therefore we must guard ourselves against assuming a merely negative attitude toward it. The task of the church of Christ is not merely to guard the purity of divine truth, but also to understand and deal seriously and pastorally with man's philosophical search and struggle.

So there is expressed here a genuine demand that we take account of the fact that the mind, whether it expresses itself in art or philosophy or in great conceptions that give structure to life (education, economics, etc.), is bound up with "life." It is simply true that in the great creations of the human spirit, say in the Gothic cathedrals, along with the Christian confession that is inherent in these creations a very definite mentality, and actually a *bios-conditioned* mentality, is expressing itself. Therefore it is a complete impossibility (though, of course, it has been done) to imagine erecting a neo-Gothic church for a Negro tribe on the mission field. There is too great a difference between the "life-relatedness" of the Gothic spirit and that of the Negro tribe, even though this Gothic church (one must hope, despite its neo-Gothicism!) is for Western man a genuine confession of the *same* Christ to whom this Negro tribe also prays. It is well, and also spiritually significant, to point out that in the Gothic cathedrals we have a very definite kind of people, with their own particular *bios*-related structure, hewing out in stone their confession of Christ in their own peculiar way.

So when the Gothic cathedrals proclaim and confess, "Praise be to Jesus Christ," and their multitudes of vertical lines appear to be pointing upward to the right hand of God, where sits the risen, exalted Christ, then this is certainly not a bloodless, abstract truth (of the kind a cold, disinterested dogmatician might formulate). What we have here is rather the whole soul of a people living and moving in these creations; they put themselves and their whole existence into this confession. Thus there is real and permanent value in the emphasis of the biological world view upon the fact that truth is bound up with man's physical, biological structure. And the church of Christ must not overlook this either. But, of course, this is not the only thing to be said here. When we start with the Scriptures we immediately become aware of the limitations of this point of view and the deadly danger of the *merely* biological approach.

2. The second thing about the biological view is that it starts very definitely with the basic concept of the *organism*. It views the individual units of life (cells, organs, individual persons) in the light of their being bound together in a superordinate structure, that is, an organism. The individual member of the organism has significance only because of the whole.

This idea seemed perfectly self-evident with respect to the cell—

which, of course, is actually significant and capable of life only in conjunction with the whole organism. But sometimes the idea has not appeared so self-evident when applied to *the individual human being*. There undoubtedly have been times and philosophies which have taken the individual with undue seriousness, promoting a regular cult of individual personality, its development, and its emotions. I must admit, for example, that today, when we find ourselves living under the tremendous burden of the fate of the whole Western world, which goes far beyond the individual, I find it rather heavy going to read Goethe's *The Sorrows of Werther*. It is a little hard for us these days to understand how anybody can be so utterly serious about the lovesick emotions and sentiments of one individual person and make them the creative center of a man's whole life, regardless of all community obligations and objective vocational responsibilities; and to comprehend how a man could allow himself to make being a "lover" his lifework and chief calling. This is why the biological world view regards it as its chief task, so far as the individual is concerned, to see the meaning of his life only in the superordinated community (the family group or nations, for example) and to prove that the individual as such, taken by himself, is completely meaningless and impossible.

Here again we shall first have to acknowledge the positive value of this concern; for, after all, we have come out of an age which has talked much and perhaps too much about the development of individual personality. All this overemphasis upon the development of the individual personality had its bitter consequences; for in the economic area it led to the disastrous phenomenon of capitalism, i.e., to the uninhibited expansion of the individual enterpriser-personality or of individual economic interest groups, which in turn resulted in the proletarianizing, the pauperizing, and the exploitation of broad masses of people at the cost of the individuals in those masses. So there can be no doubt that it is necessary to remind ourselves first of the positive intent of this kind of thinking in terms of the organic whole.

Now I take it that we have seen that every attempt to make a creaturely entity (in this case, *bios*) the paramount theme of the world is doomed to failure by two facts:

First, the fact that one can never explain the *whole* of life in this way, and that consequently many areas of life, for example the intellectual and religious, cannot be derived from this one entity called *"bios."* And, second, this philosophical attempt breaks down on the fact that the creature (in this case, again, the *bios*) can never with impunity be put in the place of the Creator.

It is therefore easy to see why biologism is inevitably drawn into violent opposition to the Christian faith; for the Christian faith proclaims the exclusive lordship of God: *"I* am the Lord your God . . . you shall have no other gods before me." In simple, practical terms that means that the God of the Bible absolutely refuses to be in any way a reflection of a particular biologically conditioned species or race of men and therefore a product of the religious imagination of the Jewish race (named Jahweh). He is the unconditioned, sovereign *Lord* of life, but not an *"expression"* of life—as the biological world view asserts, for example, when it assures us that not only culture but also religion is dependent upon our biologically conditioned breeding.

It is therefore understandable that biologism should take the strongest kind of offense at the God of the Bible. It resists the "God of life" because it believes in "deified life." This is the deepest point of its opposition.

Then there happens what always happens when a person or a school of thought refuses to recognize the absolute lordship of God. They look for "reasons." Nobody is content merely to say, "I will have nothing to do with this God"; nobody merely shakes his fist at him. Nobody who refuses to accept God is satisfied merely to clench his fists; he always invents reasons to oppose him. He does this for the very simple reason that he needs to obtain a good conscience and justify his protest against God to himself.

In exactly the same way the biological world view seeks to obtain a good conscience by persuading itself that the God of Christianity is offensive to the fundamental insights of biology; that he constitutes an intolerable contradiction to modern scientific knowledge and the world view determined by that knowledge. It is extraordinarily important right at the outset that we see this most secret motive in its polemic against the Christian faith. This motive is far more important for our encounter with it than the individual scientific or pseudoscientific assertions it makes in the course of its polemics. Much more than in the "biological world view," we are interested in the human being who is hiding behind it and entrenching himself against God.

Let me mention briefly what people say about the church's way of thinking about these things.

1. They say that Christian systems of thought, those of the church, are characterized by the fact that they separate man from the natural, organic structures of life such as clan, race, people, homeland, language, and history, and in a mechanistic way incorporate him into international administrative and power units. In other words, Christianity severs man from all his natural ties, makes all men alike (turns them into bloodless "souls"), and breaks down all natural, organic communities into a purely mechanical sum of individuals. Whether these are Herero or Jewish or Nordic individuals makes no difference whatsoever. For according to Christian dogmatism, before God all men are a mushy mixture of molecules, or, more politely expressed, "before God all men are equal." True, their bodies are different, this simply cannot be denied, but their souls are alike. But this they say is unbiological, even antibiological, thinking—and this is the way the "anti" attitude arises, indeed, *must* arise, despite whatever piety may still be present.

2. The second objection to the faith of Christianity consists in the following. Biology, as we have seen, had derived both body and mind, or body and spirit, from the concept "life." For it everything depended upon the wholeness of life, which expresses itself in the physical as well as the mental and spiritual. For biology both body and mind are merely different aspects of the same thing. Over against this (the biological world view cries out, with all the fervor of a reformer sweeping old trash from men's minds), Christianity divides life. In the first place it divides life into "this world" and the "world to come." But not satisfied with this, it denies psychophysical unity and puts in its place a sinful body and an otherworldly soul. Says one critic, "Negation of life, contempt for life, and the demonization of nature have darkened European thought and life for centuries. Therefore both confessions [Roman Catholic and Protestant] are the chief antagonists of a world view that is based on life."

I think it fair to say that even the strongest man will not be able to assert that this is not a caricature of Christianity. We have already laid the groundwork well enough in our study of the biblical statements concerning the world and man, so that I need only recall a few important points.

First we ask what is *wrong* in this description of Christianity, and then ask the deeper and more relevant question of why it is that a person hides behind the biological world view and there takes up a defensive attitude toward Christ.

Allow me first to put the following question:

Is it really true that church dogmatism, that is, biblically grounded faith in Christ, makes men all the same in this mechanical way, reducing them all to bloodless souls? Well, just let the Bible speak for itself on this question.

Anybody who reads the first pages of the Bible will be struck by the fact that in the creation story there are five words that recur in almost monotonous fashion: "each according to its kind." Again and again it emphasizes this uniqueness of the individual kinds of animals as well as plants. The creation account in almost every verse makes it clear that the life and viability of creation consists precisely in this fruitful tension between dissimilar kinds, which complement one another and by the very diversity of their tone-values produce the full and complete chord of creation.

This consciousness of the diversity of kinds, characters, and gifts continues on various lines in the New Testament also. But I shall mention only one of them.

The Christian concept of *community,* in the Apostle Paul's view particularly, is defined in terms that are thoroughly organic and integral. If you want to check this statement, just read the twelfth chapter of I Corinthians. There it says that community in Christ is like a body of which the head is "the Lord." The individual members of the body, the feet, eyes, ears, etc., are dependent upon each other and therefore find their meaning and purpose only in the whole. It is self-evident (and therefore not spelled out further) that the body does not consist only of feet and hence of members completely alike; Paul too would have called such a being not a man, but at most a centipede. And it would be equally absurd, and here we quote Paul himself, if "the eye said to the hand, 'I have no need of you,' or again the head to the feet, 'I have no need of you.' "

The Christian community therefore does not consist of a mechanical, soulless juxtaposition of identically constructed co-ordinated individuals (as the anti-Christian propaganda of biologism would have us believe), but rather of a "unity-in-tension" of members who are naturally different in kind and function, designed to complement and harmonize with one another, and thus attuned to each other, as it were, according to the rules of counterpoint.

This is true today when we think, for example, of the world fellowship of the Christian churches, the ecumenical church. Those who attend these world conferences tell us of the wonderful way in which the diversity of peoples and races, of East and West, work together and complement one another in the totality of the church, and how through this very uniting of diverse gifts and kinds the world concert of Christendom, the many-membered richness of the *one* body, was realized.

Nor did the fundamental thesis that "there is neither Jew nor Greek . . . neither slave nor free" prevent Paul from leaving untouched the class structure of the society of his day with its freemen and slaves, and actually forbidding the abolition of social and national inequality when this kind of revolutionary abolition dared to appeal to equality before God. Here the answer was unequivocal: "Every one should remain in the state in which he was called" (I Cor. 7:20; cf. the letter to Philemon). The fact is that on every page of the Bible God is not a God of a system or of egalitarianism, but rather a God of living, tension-filled creativity, the forms of which are designed so that the unequal may complement and harmonize with one another. This is also the point in the distinction between the sexes, the confusion of which Paul rejects in many passages of his letters. He is concerned to preserve the womanliness of woman and the manhood of man.

Because God is not a God of a system, but rather the God of living, unique individuals, we may also catch this note of singularity in his creativity in that passage which declares: "I have called you by name, you are mine." God deals with every man and every kind individually, recognizing the singularity which

they share with no other man or other kind. Thus Jesus treats
the Pharisee differently from the woman who was a sinner, the
rich young ruler differently from the man who was born blind,
the malefactor on his left differently from the malefactor on his
right. He treats "each according to its kind"! The great mass of
people who crowded about him to hear his sermons, all gazing
at him with the same expectancy and their faces all turned in the
same direction, immediately resolves itself in Jesus' eyes into a
multitude of specific persons, every one different from the other
because of his special needs and hopes, his character and his social
status. In the crowd are the self-satisfied and self-assured and also
the broken in spirit and heart, the healthy and robust and also
those with unseen wounds, the rich and the hungry—all of them
gathered around him; and what to foolish human eyes may be
nothing but a formless mass of individuals is in the discerning
eyes of Jesus a tremendous, expectant profusion of widely differing individuals, each one of whom must be dealt with "according
to his kind." Only so can we understand why Jesus always sought
a personal relationship with the individual man and why he repeatedly avoided, ignored, or abandoned the crowds in order to
deal with the individual man "according to his kind."

To sum up, the Bible is fully aware that every individual man,
animal, and plant is different; it knows that every one needs complementation, physically, sexually, and in character. Nowhere in
the Bible is there the slightest trace of a tendency to reduce things
and persons to mechanized stereotypes.

But true as it is that in biblical thought the creation consists
of a multitude of kinds and species and the community is governed by the concept of an organism, it is equally true that there
is a definite level in men where they are all alike, Jews and
Greeks, Arians and Semites, Zulus and Japanese, Europeans and
Americans. Of every one of them it is true that they are called
by God and are responsible to him, that they are all "persons."
Of every one of them it is true that they have sabotaged the plan
which God had for their life and therefore must confess: "We
are all sinners"—Jews and Greeks, Paul himself, they are *all* "under the power of sin" (Rom. 3:9). Of every one of them it is true
that Jesus Christ died for them.

And here is where it becomes really true that there are neither Jews nor Greeks, but only the fellowship of the "greatly blessed." In sin, suffering, and death *all* men are equal, Bolshevists and National Socialists, plutocrats and paupers, dogmaticians and biology enthusiasts. And all of them alike are children of the Father in heaven, who "makes his sun rise on the evil and the good, and sends rain on the just and on the unjust." In an ultimate sense *the whole of mankind is a community of destiny before God, in evil and in good, in doom as well as in hope.*

Thus the Bible views man from two points of view, or one might say it looks at him with two sets of eyes, and therefore it sees him really in clear perspective. It sees him in all the profusion of types and kinds, in all the diversity of characters that supplement and complement each other. But its eye also penetrates to a depth in man at which all men stand before the Father with no difference at all between them as sinners and as children of God, and where Jesus Christ is their brother.

This particular example makes it clear that only this double view, this perspective of the Bible, makes human community life possible and that without God—that is, without this divine "binocular" view—it must inevitably fall apart. So here as we come to grips with the biological view of the world we receive an unhoped-for and welcome confirmation of our conviction that it is the commandments of God that sustain and preserve the world.

That is to say, whenever this double character of likeness and difference which men have in the eyes of God is split apart and made one-sided, immediately this results in great crises and chaotic disintegration.

When one emphasizes the difference between men, their racial peculiarities and the autonomy of individual national and other organisms—as the biological world view tends to do—then immediately the individual kinds of structures break away from each other; they seek to be inwardly and outwardly independent, demanding an autarchy which refuses to be hampered by any bonds whatsoever. Then with all the certainty of a logical process there ensues a disastrous misunderstanding, or complete lack of understanding, of other kinds, other races, other nations. Then there is no longer any understanding of that ultimate bond that binds all human beings together. Then one no longer recognizes, indeed, *cannot* recognize, the ultimate norms that apply to and bind all men, and then one also loses all sense of the sanctity and inviolability of international treaties (to name a concrete example). Then one no longer knows, and *can* no longer know, the dignity and obligation that come with the fact that we are all children of *one* Father and are all traveling together to the Last Judgment. Where this ultimate commitment under God is missing, there the gods rule. Then we have the polytheism of nationalisms which we referred to in the preceding chapter. Then above the embattled nations the national gods are still fighting each other in the upper air, and no human hand can ever unravel the tangled skein of gods and men. But the fact that this is so and that it must always come to this pass is the consequence of this mad insistence of the biological world view that men are different in kind, while ignoring the *other* point of view of the Bible, namely, that all men are equal before God.

But the opposite must also be said. When men are no longer seen from the point of view of their dissimilarity and their organic need for complementation—in other words, when the holy monotony of the creation story's "each according to its kind" is no longer taken seriously—then immediately a purely mechanistic, bloodless coexistence of co-ordinated individuals begins to gain ground. We see all around us the consequence of this one-sidedness in many of the products of modern leveling, egalitarian collectivism.

Here we pause for a moment.

These insights ought to be a forceful indication that here again it is the Bible that has the deepest thoughts about man, that only before *God* does human character emerge as it really is, in both its similarity and its dissimilarity. We now see that the world views (especially the two last mentioned) deny these deepest thoughts of the Bible, that therefore they see man only from one side, and hence, as soon as they gain control, lead to the breakdown of his existence and the order of his life.

Let me close by pointing to the Figure in whom the ultimate meaning of our life and thus also the particular ideas we have discussed in this chapter become clear, namely, the prototype of man himself, Jesus of Nazareth.

In him two things become plain:

First, that man appears only as a unique, definite person. Jesus himself was born in a very definite country, at a definite period of time, and among a definite people. The time he entered into history was a definite, though to human eyes very arbitrary, point in the time scale on which the year One falls. He is really a very particular person, he is the carpenter's son from Nazareth; he is so confined to his circle of life and so stamped by his whole environment that people could ask him, "Can anything good come out of Nazareth?" They cannot imagine that anybody so limited by geography and status could have anything to offer which would concern *all* men.

Second, despite the fact that he had this definite stamp of time and place and race, he nevertheless did not become a Jew or a Greek or a Roman, but rather—"the Man," "being born in the likeness of men."

And this means that beyond all the limitations of space and time and race we all recognize ourselves in him. When we look at him we know what God really has in mind for us, namely, that we should live in fellowship with him as *he* did, that we should become his children and his sons as *he* was.

And at the same time in everything he becomes one of us: in his temptation he entered with us as a brother into battle against doubt and guilt, and in solidarity with us he also took our death upon himself. There is no loneliness, no silence and hiddenness of God that can daunt us, which he has not suffered more deeply and more cruelly in his own body and in his own soul.

"Here is the man!" says Pontius Pilate, unaware of what he was really saying. Every one of us, wherever we live and whatever our race or kind, must confess: This is the only man who ever lived! And God be thanked that we can call him not only "Lord," but also "Brother"!

V | THIS-WORLD AND OTHER-WORLD

THE FIRST POINT OF STRESS IN OUR ENCOUNTER WITH the biological world view was the question whether Christian dogma removes man from his organic relationship to clan, people, history, race, etc., and turns him into a bloodless soul; in other words, whether it makes all men equal and alike and reduces them to one big, undifferentiated, unarticulated mass of human beings.

We turn now to another point of stress in this argument, namely, the thesis put forward by the biological world view that Christian dogma splits the wholeness of the world and puts in its place a binary structure made up of this world and the world beyond; and that in addition to and in connection with this, it also splits man into two parts, body and soul. It goes on to assert that a further characteristic of this cleavage of life is that now God is assigned only to the soul, or the world beyond, while this world and the body are left without any god or even demonized. Over against this it makes the assertion that it is precisely *in* the structures of this world that God reveals himself; God lives and has his being in the laws of nature, in growth and decay, in death and renewal; he lives in the total harmony of all the structures of the world working together.

It was Goethe, incidentally, who gave classic expression to this idea in his "Proemium" of 1816, though it is an expression which addresses us at a far deeper level than does the modern biological world view. But this is precisely the reason why I prefer to cite the classic form of this belief. With a definite side glance at the God of the Bible, Goethe says in that poem:

58

> What were a God, who, outward force applying,
> But kept the All around his finger flying!
> He from within lives through all Nature rather,
> Nature and Spirit fostering each other;
> So that what in Him lives, and moves, and is,
> Still feels his power, and owns itself still His.[1]

In other words, God is not to be found "outside" in a world beyond; he is not split off from this world, but rather moves it from "within." He moves this world in the same way that the hidden, incomprehensible life force moves and constitutes an organism from within, like the hidden life force which Goethe repeatedly calls entelechy. As against this view, the God of the Bible stands "outside" of this world and has forsaken it.

Allow me to dilate a bit upon the notions concerning this Christian concept of the world beyond that rattle about in people's heads.

Christianity, some people think, banishes God from the world and packs him off to the ghetto of the world beyond, where, as Goethe says, he keeps "the All around his finger flying." Now, after all, one could go on and say (and why don't they do so?) that this view of God and the world beyond is a private and personal fancy of the Christians and one may as well let them be happy with this idea.

But it appears that this concept of the beyond entails some fatal consequences which go beyond the sacrosanct sphere of the private and personal.

In the first place this concept of the beyond would seem to remove God from this world. Then it would appear that Christianity simply leaves nature without any god, or as we said in the last chapter, "demonizes" it. The Christian cannot find God and does not want to find God in nature simply because he isn't there. Nature, the argument goes, lives only in the mechanical operation of the law of causality; indeed, according to the Christian view nature is actually the realm of evil. Does not the Christian live in a constant battle against nature, against his urges, desires, and instincts? Does he not live in a painful dualism of flesh and

---

[1] Translation by John S. Dwight. (Trans.)

spirit? In the Christian view, is not nature (and therefore the body) the ground where all the demons and forces of evil are deployed? Is not this the place where tigers lie ready to spring, the place where the wolves howl? Is it not a fact that Christians must regard nature as one great masquerade of the devil?

But there is more to come. Three further inferences would appear to follow from this disastrous split brought about by the concept of a world beyond.

1. It would seem to follow (and how monstrous it sounds when we put it into so many words; what polemical ire it arouses!) that Christianity does not seek God in the wonders of creation, in that great series of wonders that range all the way from a blossom to the surging elemental power of the oceans; but rather finds him in a *book,* a book bound in black. And hence that it expects us to swallow the grotesque notion that God has given us "something of himself in writing." For after all, this inference would seem to be quite obvious: if one no longer finds God in the wonders of life, but rather in a book—and, what is more, in a very old book that looks as if it belonged in a museum—then inevitably you will have the kind of human being whom one can only call a "scribe" or a fanatical literalist. How different from this ugly picture is the ideal of our times, the ideal of a vital, instinctively sure man who is open and receptive to life!

2. A further inference would appear to be that the man who is dominated by this Christian concept of another world beyond this one can never give himself fully and joyously to this world; can never really be completely and unreservedly enthusiastic about anything, but rather inclines to flee from this world. With a certain malicious relish the grotesque examples are cited: the flagellants, the ascetics, the pillar saints and contemplators of the navel; the withdrawal of the priests from family and children into celibacy, and sometimes even voluntary castration (cf. the church father Origen) as a horrible sign that the natural world of generation and the man-wife relationship are evil and must therefore be renounced.

If God is really banished into the ghetto of the beyond—and this is apparently what Christianity teaches—then these occurrences in the history of the church are not to be interpreted as degenerate phenomena and departures from the norm, but rather are necessarily connected with the very nature of Christianity and are therefore "normal" in the Christian sense. How can it be otherwise? Does not this splitting apart of life drain all the divinity out of life, so that the beyond absorbs it all? And then what is left? Nothing but burnt-out cinders and slag, leached of all divinity—and this slagheap provides the raw material for this so-called "vale of tears."

3. Still a third inference seems to follow from the Christian concept of a beyond. It manifests itself in the idea of "miracles." After all, "miracle" always means that God certifies and attests himself in a sign. When Jesus, for example, heals a sick person, his purpose is to say, or show by means of a sign, two things: first, that God is the foe of diseased, degenerate, disordered creations and that they hurt him and wring his heart. And second, that God also has the power to restore and heal his creation. (Cf. the later chapters on "Miracle.")

As against this, the biological world view sees miracle in life as it is, in the wonderful harmony of its laws and in the fact that behind it we can see the creative divine nature at work.

But this "natural" view of the miracle of life, the argument runs, is completely impossible for the Christian, since for him life belongs to the realm of this Godforsaken world. Therefore the God of the Christian cannot attest himself in the miracle of the laws of life, either; on the contrary, he can attest himself only as he *breaks through* these laws. Just look at the miracles in the Bible! There you find dead persons brought to life—isn't that "unnatural"? A virgin bears a son or an aged woman like Elizabeth, the mother of John, bears a child in old age. Nothing but infractions of the laws of nature! Here one sees all too plainly the kind of God who is "outside" the world, the God who allows the world to revolve around his finger, and therefore the God whom one no longer sees in the world from which he has been banished. And just because we no longer see him, just because the world has been deprived of God, he is compelled every once in a while to call attention to himself by means of a miracle.

We shall deal with miracle in more detail later. Here our purpose is only to assemble the questions and put them in a larger context.

Allow me to summarize what Christianity looks like from the point of view of biologism. The biological world view says that Christianity splits the totality of the world into two parts, this world and the other world. And the implications of that are:

1. The world is deprived of God, and therefore God is no longer found in nature, but rather in a book; instead of a vital relationship to life the result is a dead literalism.

2. In a world deprived of God there is nothing left but to flee from the world and concentrate upon and live for the other world. Then this world takes on the character of a vale of tears and misery.

3. Because God is no longer discerned in the miracle of life and its natural laws, he must call attention to himself by means of the reverse of nature, namely, by breaking through the laws of nature in the form of miracles.

And then we are asked this question: When Christians thus split apart—*appear* to split apart—this world and the other world, is not this perhaps to be regarded as a private religious preference, a mere individual notion?

Now surely we see that this is obviously not the case. For after all, it would seem that this understanding of the world exerts a profound influence upon the type of man it produces. This type of human being seems necessarily to be the kind of person who flees the world and denies and negates life, who is incapable of throwing in his lot with the world and is numbed and stiffened by dogmatism. Can a generation which is faced with tremendous tasks, a generation whose ideal is the kind of man who is "down to earth" and open and receptive to life, tolerate, even afford, such a type of man?

But when I enumerate all these negative characteristics which are alleged to be the consequences of the Christian concept of the beyond, it probably strikes you as it does me that something is wrong here. For we all know plenty of Christians, and historical situations too, which simply do not coincide with this caricature. You have only to think of the parables of Jesus, of the lilies of the field, the birds of the air, the imagery of sowing and reaping, or even the story of creation in the Old Testament. Here wherever one turns the world is transparent, allowing us to see the Creator who is behind it, working in and through it all. It certainly does not look much like a demonizing of nature.

But perhaps all these indications of a positive attitude toward nature and life on the part of Christianity are merely exceptions and therefore fortunate but nevertheless misleading inconsistencies. In any case the problem lies too deep to permit us merely to marshal examples of Christian imagery to prove the impossibility of this caricature of Christianity. We must really pursue and examine carefully this question of what this allegedly terrible concept of the world beyond is all about.

Allow me to begin with the following very simple question: Is it really true that the Bible turns our eyes away from vital life to the world to come? Says the aged Faust:

> What's beyond is barred from human ken;
> Fool, fool is he who blinks at clouds on high,
> Inventing his own image in the sky.[2]

No, we do not want to keep gazing at the beyond, but rather keep our eyes on the divine power that moves "within" the world. But does not the Bible and its idea of a world beyond turn us into "fools"?

Well, I suggest that we turn to the Bible itself, and I remind you of a parable in the New Testament in which Jesus very significantly poses and deals with this problem. It is the parable of the Rich Man and Lazarus (Luke 16). It is so familiar that we need not repeat it except for a few allusions.

In this parable the veil that hides the beyond seems to be drawn aside for a moment. In these carefully drawn vignettes we seem to get a glimpse behind the scenes of the world to come. The rich man is in hell, which is hot and full of torment; but Lazarus the poor man dwells in the communion of saints. Between these two worlds there is no connection. When the rich man begs Abraham to send someone to cool his tongue with a drop of water, Abraham

[2] Goethe, *Faust*, Philip Wayne, trans. (Baltimore: Penguin Classics, 1959), Part II, Act V, Midnight, p. 265. (Trans.)

says No, it can't be done. Suddenly the door clicks and is locked
shut. In this painful predicament the rich man then remembers
his five brothers who are still living on earth, and driven by extreme concern he begs Abraham to *warn* these five brothers for
whom the door has not yet closed, who are still living in the time
of decision. Abraham points out that after all these brothers have
Moses and the prophets; in other words, that they have the Word
of God. The wise man, however, thinks this is not enough; the
Word of God is too quiet, too faint, too easily overlooked, and
too easily doubted. But if he would send one of the dead to tell
them what things were like in eternity and show them that the
decisions were being made there and that one would have to remain in the sphere toward which one lived his life on earth, then
surely this would make an impression on them. Abraham, however, rejects the proposal and says, "If they do not hear Moses
and the prophets, neither will they be convinced if someone
should rise from the dead." So much for the story.[3]

Now, what is really the purpose of this parable which gives us
the most detailed picture of things "beyond" to be found anywhere in the New Testament? Is this intended to be a blueprint
of the beyond, given us in order to provide us a geography of
the other world which will be so precise and vivid that it will
compel us to keep our thought fixed there instead of here on
earth?

We need only to put the question in this way and we all realize
that this is not its purpose. On the contrary, what the Lord, who
tells this story, is concerned with is not the world beyond, but
the here and now. The hidden theme is the five brothers who are
still living in the time when the final decision has not yet been
made. And these five brothers—they are you and me! *We* still
have the decision to make, *we* are still living in the here and now
when we should be hearing his voice and not hardening our
hearts. So the theme of this parable which says so much about the
beyond is my life and your life. It is as if every spotlight in the
house were focused on that spot on the stage where you and I live
out our lives—are *still* living out our lives—the place where we

---

[3] For a fuller treatment of this parable see Helmut Thielicke, *The Waiting
Father* (New York: Harper & Row, 1959), pp. 41-51. (Trans.)

must decide about eternity. And everything that is said here about heaven and hell and the beyond is only the stage setting around this spot on the stage. True, it is what gives character and meaning to this spot; but *we* are the ones who are on the stage!

Actually, it is remarkable how little emphasis the Bible puts upon the beyond or the future. We are not even to think about the "morrow," but rather leave it to God's care. We are to live *today,* in the here and now! And even when the Second Coming of the Lord is described, as for example in the Book of Revelation, the stress, amazingly, is not upon details of the life to come. On the contrary, its whole intent is to convey to the church in the *present* moment of her struggle this message: He who is the final victor will be king. And this king is Jesus Christ. You are not a poor little cult, cherishing a memory; you are a community of people who can lift up your heads because your Redeemer is drawing near from the other side. All of these pictures of the future are words of comfort and encouragement to battle for the church militant here and now, for its present hour of decision.

All one has to do is to compare the literature of that time with the New Testament and one will immediately see the difference between them. Outside the biblical literature a fantastic imagination produced great descriptions of the world to come, replete with detail. Comparing them, one is immediately struck by the holy restraint and temperateness of the Scriptures and their almost monotonous insistence that what matters is the *today* in which we hear his voice, and the *now* which is still the acceptable time. Even the account of the Ascension gives us no description of what things are like in the heaven to which Christ ascended, but is content with the terse statement that Christ is now sitting at the "right hand of God."

But what this actually says is that Christ has *not* withdrawn to "base headquarters" in the beyond, but rather that now he has been raised above the limitations of his life between Bethlehem and Calvary and is exercising his unrestricted world-dominion, so that *from* him and *through* him and *to* him are all things, all subject to his rule.

If I were permitted to make a very pointed statement, I would venture this one: The festival of the Ascension is the festival of "this world," the feast of Jesus' sovereign power over all the world!

So this is the first point we must make here: the Bible does not picture the world beyond in detail. On the contrary, it covers it with a curtain, and when it does point to it, does so, as it were, by means of dotted lines, and all these dotted lines are characterized by the fact that they point to me and to the present moment of my life—the moment in which I must "now" decide for eternity or in which I "now" need encouragement and consolation.

But even though the Bible does not expatiate in detail upon the other world, it is nevertheless there, and the Bible attaches the utmost importance to it. I mention only a few indications that point in this direction.

God "dwells in unapproachable light" (I Tim. 6:16). Though this passing world is really only a parable and only points to him, though it is transparent, allowing him to be seen behind it; nevertheless it is also true that to the man whom God does not grant his Spirit all this says nothing; the mysteries remain and the great signs are opaque.

He actually is the "wholly Other," who cannot be measured by human standards. If we try to do this nevertheless, we get nothing but an enlarged, idealized man, a reflection of our own self or the "soul of our race," but never God himself. We have already spoken a number of times of the racial God, or better, the God made in the image of man, who is constructed in this way.

The real character of God as the "wholly Other" is movingly expressed in an Old Testament story (Exod. 33:12 ff.) in which Moses pleads with God, "I pray thee, show me thy glory." What he is saying is this: Lord, I see you only in a mirror, in reflections, images, and parables. (We understand this lament very well, do we not? How often God is vague, unclear, unintelligible to *us* in the way he shapes our lives or guides the course of history! No doubt about it, we understand Moses very well when he prays: Let me see thy glory! Give me a glimpse behind the mysteries and mere reflections of thee!) And there is still another facet in this prayer of Moses: Lord, I hear thee only in mysterious words and commands which often I cannot understand; for once let me see thee face to face!

There we hear the ancient cry of man for God that echoes through all the religions of the world: "Let us see, let us see! Give us one glimpse behind the great mystery of life! How tormenting it is always to have to stand outside the 'Christmas door,' sensing a faint shimmer of light and catching the almost imperceptible breath of blessed song above the world and never being allowed to open the door! Let me see thy glory!"

God then put Moses in a cleft of the rock. "While my glory passes by I will put you in a cleft of the rock, and I will cover you with my hand until I have passed by; then I will take away my hand, and you shall see my back; but my face shall not be seen."

So he can see God only from behind, he can only see the afterglow which God's history leaves behind it on earth: the leading of his people, the cloud of witnesses, all the paths that lead to Jesus Christ, the great goal of all God's leadings, all the roads that will have reached their end only when he shall come again to judge the quick and the dead.

These are footprints of God which the yearning servant can see, but his face he cannot see, for he who sees God face to face *dies*. No man can endure it.

But why is it that no man can endure direct contact with God? Why would direct sight of his glory kill us, and why dare we not do what so many people today want to do, or at least say they would like to do—stand right up and face the Lord God? We would simply perish, that's why.

It is a noteworthy fact that in all the encounters of men with God in the Bible they are utterly terrified, filled with fear and trembling. The Goethean man and also the man with the biological world view cannot understand this. On the contrary, they would be *delighted* to have such a direct vision of God. After all, their highest goal is to discover the motivating power, the ultimate creative principle of things. The very thing Faust was waiting for, after all, was that he might see "the inmost force which binds the world and guides its course,"[4] in other words, that God would become apparent to him in the ground of things.

[4] Goethe, *Faust*, Bayard Taylor, trans., (New York: Modern Library, 1950), Part I, Scene 1, p. 16. (Trans.)

And his supreme goal was undoubtedly not merely to perceive
the divine force theoretically, but also to "see" it. Goethe quite
specifically made it his purpose to "see" the ultimate divine origi-
nals: the "original plant" from which all real plants are constructed, the "original phenomenon" which is behind all tangible
phenomena and in which they blend together visibly; or the "entelechy," i.e., the ultimate organic generative and formative power
which causes life to burgeon forth in all the abundance of its
forms. How these expectant seekers after sight have striven, and
still continue to strive, for the sight of God, whom they seek in
the ground of things and whom they describe with so many
names! What happiness and fulfillment they have expected of
that moment when the parable of life would become transparent
and the mystery of the divine would begin to gleam in the ground
of life. At the same time they have expected that they would find
in this moment their own deepest union with the cosmos, for they
have thought of themselves as tiny sparks of the fire that burns
in the ground of the world; and the spark is akin to the flame and
strives to return to that innermost fire. "I, image of the Godhead!"
says Faust therefore,[5] and this is why he waits so fervently for
the unveiling of the Godhead.

But now comes the biblical view, which stands in strange and,
at first sight, almost painful contrast with this natural view,
which is so much easier for all of us to understand: no man can
see the face of God, and even when the angels appear, when the
glory of God breaks in upon men at the Nativity, they are filled
with great fear and terror. When Peter witnessed the miraculous
draught of fish in which Jesus showed forth his marvellous power,
he did not turn to him with bright and shining face and say,
"Verily, God is in you, Jesus of Nazareth, and look, now I am an
image of the Godhead, too; now my small strength gravitates
toward your cosmic strength in order to unite with it." No, he says
nothing of the kind. He says quite simply, "Depart from me, for
I am a sinful man, O Lord." And again there is in these words a
deep sense of fear and terror.

In all these stories the same basic experience is present. In such
moments of nearness to God the men of the Bible realize that a

[5] *Ibid.*, p. 23.

great gulf separates them from him. Great fear comes over them simply *because* they know they are being called by name, and suddenly they realize what they really are—men cut off from God, men who cannot possibly appear before him as they are. God's holiness has something consuming about it, for none of us can stand before him. Luther goes so far as to say that the manifestation of God in the Law drives one either to "despair" or to "hatred of God." At any rate, there is one thing the men of the Bible cannot say in these moments of meeting with God, and that is what Faust so emphatically exclaims. "I, image of the Godhead!" They know, of course, that they are mirrors of God, but even more they know that they are dull and tarnished mirrors! They know that they are glass, through which God would shine, but most of all they know they are broken glass.

This is made staggeringly clear in the Cross of Jesus Christ, where men are suddenly confronted with the *real* image of God and not merely their own idea of God, spun out of their own heads and hearts. When they meet the *real* image of God they do not recognize him: "The light shineth in darkness; and the darkness comprehended it not" (John 1:5, A.V.). And when they did *comprehend* it, they interpreted it as a threat, for the darkness realizes that it is suddenly confronted with the light. The Cross is the most dreadful sign of all signs that show us how far man is from being the image of God; otherwise he would not have so miserably failed to recognize the whole and unbroken image of God in Jesus Christ.

Why have I mentioned all these biblical instances? Because they really show that there is such a thing as the "beyondness" of God. For every one of the instances mentioned is saying the same thing, namely, that God is not *identical* with his creatures, not identical with the world, and that even though they all came from his hand, even though he clothes the lilies of the field and feeds the birds of the air, even though we can say "Our Father" to him, God nevertheless stands at a *distance* from all these things and from all of us. We must say to him: We are sinners, but thou art the Holy One; we are the accused, but thou art the Judge; we are under the dominion of guilt and tears and death, but thy kingdom is not of this world! And when one day that kingdom comes, there will be no more suffering nor crying nor death any more, and every tear will be wiped away from our eyes—so "different," so "otherworldly" is thy kingdom!

That is the Bible's conception of the world beyond. God is not simply identical with the world, he is not merely "the inmost force which binds the world together." He is not merely another word for generative life and the harmony of its laws. God is the "wholly Other," the Creator who is at the same time strictly separate from his creatures and will not suffer them to intrude upon his sphere, as man does when he makes himself God. He is the "totally Other," the Holy One who is strictly divorced from sin. "Depart from me, for I am a sinful man, O Lord." This is what the Bible means by a God who is outside and beyond the world.

And once again: it does not dwell in detail upon this world beyond. It does not draw men's interest and concern away from life in order to shift their minds to that other world. It has only one purpose: to proclaim the difference, the awful distance between the Creator and the creature, between the Holy One and the sinner.

We see what happens when God is identified with the world and made to live only "in" the laws of nature: then we no longer face the Holy One, the "wholly Other," the dreadful Judge.

Perhaps something of this is expressed in those famous words of Goethe at the beginning of the second part of the tragedy of *Faust,* which describe Faust's situation as he finds himself in "a pleasant landscape." Behind him lies the wrong he perpetrated upon Margaret, and he is still in the toils of his labyrinthine qualms of conscience. But now he finds himself in the presence of nature, and nature begins to heal the smart of it. Thus a modern commentator says of this scene (and undoubtedly lays his finger on Goethe's intention), "Nature is able to restore even to the guilty one his happy, childlike peace of mind." "Faust's qualms of conscience are taken as an illness from which he must recover, and the *place* where he finds recovery is in nature. For in Goethe's conviction, *remorse,* like *care,* is a hindrance to that which most becomes him: unflagging activity and affirmation of God's world."[6]

---

[6] R. Buchwald, *Führer durch Goethes Faustdichtung* (Stuttgart, 1942), pp. 161, 158. Italics mine.

In other words, remorse and guilt are definite hindrances to life. Only nature is capable of ridding us of these hindrances to life, because it knows neither *care*—now we can really think of the birds of the air whom the heavenly Father feeds!—nor *guilt*.

So, what does man, what does Faust seek in nature? He seeks in it the realm beyond good and evil. He seeks in it the place where God will not meet him in person, where he feels embosomed in a sequence of events which knows no guilt and no moral values, and in which everything that burdens his life and his conscience seems to be nothing more than a great, tension-filled process which somehow possesses the necessity of a law of nature.

In contrast with this view of guilt and of nature, Psalm 104 brings us into a totally different world. I quote a few verses:

> Thou makest springs gush forth in the valleys;
> they flow between the hills,
> they give drink to every beast of the field;
> the wild asses quench their thirst.
> By them the birds of the air have their habitation;
> they sing among the branches.
>
> [Thou] makest the winds thy messengers,
> fire and flame thy ministers.
>
> These all look to thee,
> to give them their food in due season.
> When thou givest to them, they gather it up;
> when thou openest thy hand, they are filled with
>   good things.
> When thou hidest thy face, they are dismayed;
> when thou takest away their breath, they die and
>   return to their dust.

In these verses we see two things:

1. The enthusiasm and the elemental vivacity with which the Psalmist looks at nature. In enthralling procession he summons up before the mind's eye the wealth and multitude of nature's forms and configurations. One must say this psalm to oneself at sunrise in the mountains in order to realize that it is perhaps the one poem in which human speech has been able to match the grandeur of creation.

2. But there is something else that we sense in this psalm (and this is the really important thing in it that throws what has just been said into secondary importance) and that is that here it is not nature itself which is the object of worship, but rather the Creator himself. Everything has the effect of revealing him behind it, and every verse—no matter whether the subject is the winds, the waters, the birds, or the living verdure—is in reality speaking of him. The whole process of nature becomes as it were a drama in which God is acting. The winds are messengers whom God sends, flames of fire are ministers whom he appoints according to his plan. He knows them all and therefore all eyes wait upon him. When he hides his face the creatures are terrified; but on the other hand, when he sends forth his breath the face of the earth is renewed.

Therefore it is inevitable that at the end of this psalm, this nature-loving, this nature-intoxicated psalm, a statement should be made which is utterly incomprehensible on the level of nature worship. Whereas Faust finds surcease of guilt in nature and can forget the tragedy of Margaret in a realm beyond good and evil, the psalm closes with this remarkable statement: "Let sinners be consumed from the earth, and let the wicked be no more!"

Isn't that like cold water poured on all the joyful exultation in nature found in the preceding verses? In the midst of this radiant delight in God's creation this somber utterance suddenly looms up like an alien boulder. Why is it that the enchantment of sunlight, the rippling springs and streams and smiling meadows, cannot charm away this darkness of the heart, this darkness in the heart of the sinner and the wicked man?

The reason lies precisely in the fact that the Psalmist views nature as a drama in which *God* is acting. This is why he sees his holy, majestic face shining through all the forms of nature. And suddenly he realizes that in the presence of this God he is a sinner, that there is a dark spot in this lovely garden of God's creation and that this dark spot is his own heart.

In any case, there is one thing the psalmist could not have said. He could not have said what Goethe was saying: Studying nature and delighting in nature I become a pantheist and therefore I am beyond good and evil. No, what he is saying in these concluding words is just the opposite: Wherever I may be, in my work, my marriage, my dreams, or my love of nature, on mountain height or ocean strand, there I am in the presence of the holy God.

And this, too, gives us the deepest meaning of that well-loved hymn "Fairest Lord Jesus":

> Fair are the meadows,
> Fairer still the woodlands,
> Robed in the blooming garb of spring;
> Jesus is fairer,
> Jesus is purer;
> Who makes the woeful heart to sing.

Here again the woods, the fields, the sun, the stars have become transparent, and shining through them is the glory of God's Son, the greatest and most glorious of them all, the luminous promise that what shines through is not only the holy majesty of God but also his forgiving, seeking love.

We see this hand of God, gleaming and shimmering in the ground of all things, just as Gorch Fock saw it when he said that all the oceans together were only a pool in the hand of his Saviour.

All the sick, sin-stained, restless hearts, these dark spots that interrupt the stainless light of God's created world, are healed, forgiven, and brought to rest in him whom the Bible in a mysterious allusion calls "the fairest of the sons of men."

And all the crosses the church erects in the countryside, especially those on the heights of creation, the tops of the high mountains, are intended to be signs that there is one place in this world where sin has been atoned and peace is available, a place where the new sun of righteousness dawns upon a world of God in which guilt-burdened hearts and even the groaning and travailing creatures beyond the realm of humanity no longer need to be lonely spots of darkness in a world of light.

This is the Christian view of nature—and at the same time the Christian view of God's "beyondness."

VI | THE ORIGIN OF MAN

THE PRECEDING CHAPTER DEALT WITH THE BIOLOGICAL world view, and I stated that there are three points of stress in discussion of it.

The first point is the question whether Christianity turns man into a bloodless soul and wrenches him away from the organic ties of nation, family, and history. The second is the question whether the biblical message, unlike the biological view of the world, breaks down the wholeness of life by dividing it into this-world and other-world—whether the biblical message does not commit a disastrous error when it relegates God to the ghetto of the other world and thus leaves this world godless, turning it into a "vale of tears."

In this chapter we address ourselves to the third point in this argument between Christianity and the biological view of the world, namely, the question of *how man came into being*. I should like for once to state this problem in the same blunt and childish way in which it appears in the minds of many people, not only among the nasty neopagans who never tire of throwing this question at pious Christian people, but also among many Christians. And it goes like this:

Either man was created by God from a clod of earth as the Bible says; then science is wrong and man cannot have developed from prehuman and subhuman stages in the course of enormous periods of time, as the doctrine of evolution teaches.

Or the opposite is true and the idea of evolution and biological science is right: man developed in the course of time from these prehuman stages. But then one must draw the conclusion that the biblical account of creation is a myth, a legend, a highly primitive attempt by which man sought to "explain" his own origin through a miracle. Then it is an attempt which any teen-age girl can dismiss with an indulgent giggle, because she knows better. She knows that man was not created but rather evolved in a biologically demonstrable way.

Let me repeat the question once more: *either* man was created *or* he evolved. This is the either-or that haunts many people's minds.

But this questioning is not in itself important. Far more important is the utterly tragic consequence of this specious either-or, which is that many people who cannot simply shut their eyes to the scientific facts of the theory of evolution are here confronted with an insurmountable wall that prevents them from arriving at a viable biblical faith. They say to themselves something like this: "Simple personal integrity and honesty must compel us to give up a faith which, even though it may give a man strong comfort and support and some profound thoughts by which to live, can do so only at the cost of truth, that is, by twisting, suppressing, and for centuries stubbornly ignoring the assured results of scientific research. Old ladies may be willing to wear these blinders; they would believe anything, even if you were to tell them that man used to have wings like an angel. But nobody who has even some small knowledge of what is going on can do this."

But this either-or, *either* "science" *or* "faith in the biblical view of creation," can become a disastrous thing for many Christians, too. Science may become for them the bogeyman and hobgoblin of all good Christians, which would estrange us from believing in creation and lead us astray into "unbelieving" science, so that one had better keep clear of it altogether. And often the result of this is that religious people seal themselves off from life and lead an insular existence in the stream of time.

Now I must admit quite frankly that as a student I was for a long time unable to arrive at a vital Christian faith because of this narrowness on the part of many devout people. As a person who wanted to be vitally open to all truth and beauty, I said to myself, "If I can be a Christian only on condition that I deny these two things, then I prefer not to be a Christian. If the al-

leged 'King of truth,' which Christ affirmed himself to be, is someone whose life is constantly imperiled by all scientific truths and
who therefore must always be smothering these truths, then I for
one cannot honestly be a disciple of this 'Lord.' " Since that time
I have by God's grace changed in many ways, but this conviction
I still hold today; and I assume that there are many people, both
Christians and those who accept the biological world view, who
will understand this and perhaps are troubled by it in exactly
the same way I was for many years. And this is why I want to indicate how I came to terms with this question.

In the past there have been two points at which there were
severe collisions between Christianity and natural science. The
first was occasioned by *astronomy* and the questions it raised concerning cosmology, especially the discovery of Copernicus that
the earth revolves around the sun and not vice versa, and thus
that the biblical view of the world, in which the heavens are like
a glass sphere in which the stars are suspended, the earth being a
flat plane beneath it, was obsolete. This was the first collision.

The second clash was that with *biology* and *geology*. For both
of these sciences demonstrate that the origin and development
of the earth go back over tremendously long periods of time and
therefore cannot possibly be reconciled with the very limited period which the Bible assumes was the span between the creation
of the world and the present. But even more important was the
evidence of biology that the origin of the human race can also
be traced back to prehuman stages of development, and that
therefore it is utterly inconceivable that suddenly and all at once
man sprang into being as the creation story describes it. In the
seventeenth century there was published in England a work on
the chronology of the Old Testament in which a well-known and
highly respected theologian set down the results of his studies. He
said that the Holy Trinity created man on October 23 in the
year 4004 B.C., at nine o'clock in the morning. It was inevitable
that such a theology should collide with these advances in biology,
geology, and astronomy.

There were two important consequences of this. The first was
that now there is a real either-or: either the Bible is right or
science is right. One cannot serve two masters, God *and* science.
Hence one must decide for one or the other.

The second consequence can be seen from what happened in history itself: in both cases the church lost out in its decision on this form of the either-or (either the biblical account of creation or natural science). Today nobody, not even a single theologian, Catholic or Protestant, any longer doubts that the earth revolves around the sun and hence that the biblical cosmology has been corrected by science. Universal agreement on this has become so self-evident that it is hardly necessary to mention it.

But now the same applies to the assured results of biology and geology. To be sure, there is much in the results of these two sciences that is open to question, and it requires considerable study to find one's way through the jungles and labyrinths of different hypotheses and conjectures. But there is one point on which all these results agree, and that is that the present state of the earth and also the present structure of man are parts of a tremendously long process of development, and therefore it is utterly impossible that the world should have come into being as it now is in the year 4,004 or at any other theoretically datable point in time. As I have said, no serious theologian of either confession is in any doubt about this today.

But now the question that faces us is: What was God saying to his church when he allowed it to lose two such battles? Surely there must be something wrong here, for the fact remains that the church of Christ still exists, that it still continues to confess its living Lord and to receive his Word, that it still praises him and every day finds in him the only comfort in life and in death, and that still today thousands die with his name on their lips.

Actually the only logical conclusion would have been that these two lost battles should have dealt the deathblow to biblical Christianity. After all, it has been convicted of being wrong on some very crucial scientific matters! But if the church still continues to live and if the Bible, including—thank God!—its first three chapters, is still undisputedly regarded as the Book of books in Christendom; and even if it is being rediscovered and appreciated in a wholly new way, even in our own country—thank God!— then it clearly follows that those two lost battles could not have touched the heart of the Christian faith at all. Then those battles must have occurred in some outer field beyond the citadel of Christianity; or it is conceivable that these two battles may have been only sham battles. And I propose to show that this is actually what they were—sham battles! This whole warfare between Christianity and science in the forms mentioned was sham fighting. The either-or—either creation and the Bible or science and biology—is a wrong way of stating the choice in the first place.

When the church let itself in for this battle with astronomy and natural science (I mention only the names of Galileo, Bruno, Copernicus, Darwin) and itself threw down the gauntlet—in other words, when it accepted this either-or—it made some capital errors, which we see very clearly now and which also are unanimously regarded as such by both confessions today.

The first mistake of the church, namely, the acceptance of this false either-or between belief in the Bible and biology, could have arisen only if the cosmology of the Bible, and thus the concept of a flat earth covered by a glass globe, *was itself regarded as being the content of divine revelation*. That is to say, when it was so regarded, the biblical cosmology immediately became something with which faith stands or falls and hence must be defended to the death against every attack.

When Copernicus brought forward his sensational proof that the earth revolves around the sun, even a man like Luther reacted with honest alarm and regarded it as a threat to faith. Historical justice requires that it be remarked that at the point where he stood in history he could hardly have judged otherwise. The new problems raised by this changed cosmology had not yet been thought through theologically. He was still under the shock of the "first hour" of discovery. But then it was he who very soon found his way through to a view which separated the real message of the Scripture from the contemporary cosmology in which it is clothed, or at any rate distinguished between the two. (On this point his statements concerning Christ's ascension are very illuminating.) But in the "shock of the first hour" he based his rejection of Copernicus' discovery upon Joshua 10:12 ff. As you know, the passage relates that under Joshua's leadership the Israelites had fought a great battle with their enemies. But then the sun began to go down and it was impossible to continue the battle into the night. Then Joshua prayed to the Lord to cause the sun to stand still, so that they could take advantage of the daylight which was so important from the military point of view. And behold, the sun actually stood still! It was to this passage that Luther appealed in opposition to Copernicus, saying, "This fool [Copernicus] wants to turn the whole science of astronomy upside down. But as the Holy Scriptures show, Joshua commanded the sun to stand still and not the earth." From this Luther concluded that on the basis of an authoritative statement of the Bible the sun revolves around the earth and not vice versa. On the basis of this one passage from Joshua in which the author bears witness to God's wonderful intervention in terms of the cosmology of his time, Luther felt—quite understandably, as I have said—that he had to oppose a tenet of astronomical physics the purpose of which was totally different and which lay on a different level from that of the biblical author.

Now, we have already discussed at some length the significance of cosmology for our faith, and therefore we can now state this more briefly. We have seen that it makes no difference whatsoever to my faith in God the Creator whether I, the believer, think I am living on an earth which is a disk floating on a great ocean, or whether I think I am living on an earth which revolves around the sun. For, after all, it is in the framework of my particular cosmology that I seek to honor and glorify God the Creator. But this praise of God is completely independent of the framework within which it occurs.

Nor, logically, can it make any difference to me whether from the point of view of my particular cosmology I regard the divine creation of man as a sudden act, as the vivification of a clod of earth, or whether I see this creation as occurring within an evolutionary series.

Emil Brunner, the well-known Swiss theologian, has given us a fine and effective picture of what the biblical world view means for us.

"The cosmology is, as it were, the alphabet, the speech material, in which the Word of God is expressed. Just as it makes no difference whatsoever to the meaning of the word "man" whether we write this word "man" in Greek or German or Finnish, or whether we write it in small or capital letters, so it makes no difference whatsoever to the meaning of the word "God" whether we express it in the language of the ancient cosmology or in the language of modern, scientific cosmology. In this context, too, the Apostle Paul's reminder applies: "The written code kills, but the Spirit gives life."

In other words, when one makes an absolute of the biblical cosmology which is bound to its time (that is, this cosmology in the framework of which the biblical writers speak of the punishing, judging, and gracious God), then this is tantamount to asserting that one can speak of God only in the Greek language, but not in a modern language. And only when we think in this way, in this *wrong* way, does this disastrous quarrel between natural science and the church arise.

So the either-or is not: *either* the biblical message of salvation *or* modern science; but rather: *either* biblical cosmology *or* scientific cosmology. And if, faced with this alternative, we quite naturally choose the "scientific cosmology" (for no reasonable person today has any doubts about this—no one today believes that the universe is shaped like a glass bell), this certainly does not mean that we are even in the least disputing or doubting that the Holy Scriptures are the source of divine revelation. If any proof of this is needed, it is to be found, I believe, in what has been said in this book. For what we have been doing all along is to set forth the whole range of the biblical truths of salvation in the framework of a thoroughly modern cosmology, and again and again we have sought to bring these truths to bear against human errors and presumption and to apply them to modern man and his striving to be autonomous.

Not to have seen and recognized this change in cosmology to which scientific progress is subject—this was an error of the church which produced countless burnings at the stake and equally countless obstacles to faith. But I cannot say this without at the same time emphasizing that there is no cause whatsoever for anybody to turn up his nose in pride about this. For it simply took a long time before medieval man was able to adjust his thought processes to the fact that the earth is *not* the center of the universe. Just imagine the profound and painful readjustment that was required before a person was able to think his way into a completely new cosmic system and totally reorientate his own position within it. It should be clear that this was no easy thing. Once we appreciate this, we shall perhaps be more modest and humble in our judgment when we consider the stubborn and immovable attitude of refusal with which the church set itself against this cosmological revolution, and perhaps discover how difficult it is in the first moment to make a correct distinction between the unexpendable truths of faith and the expendable cosmological framework.

So the church simply needed time until it had learned to distinguish between biblical cosmology, which passes away, and the biblical truths of faith, of which not one jot or tittle shall pass away until the Lord comes.

But this disastrous mistake of the church is rooted in a second error. This is the doctrine of *"verbal inspiration,"* which means the doctrine that every word of the Bible—many orthodox would say every letter, indeed, every punctuation mark—is inspired by God and is therefore binding in character. The idea here is that the men who wrote the Bible were only passive, will-less writing instruments.

One need only to express it in this way to see that this is an absurd and, above all, an unbiblical way of thinking. For in actuality the Bible itself declares that its origin was quite different. It says that God gets hold of a man, a prophet or an apostle, and takes him into his service, a man who then is impelled, like Peter, to confess: "We cannot but speak of what we have seen and heard" (Acts 4:20). God gets hold of a man with all his faults and pride and readiness to deny (like Peter, for example); gets hold of a man who is by no means a prodigy but simply a child of his times, who therefore shares the cosmology of his times, but nevertheless has his "citizenship" in heaven (Eph. 2:19) and thus is not "of" this world which presents itself in this or that cosmology. This is how the Bible views its own origin.

According to the doctrine of verbal inspiration, however, this is not so; God does not choose a real, living person, but simply uses him as a mechanical writing instrument, to whom he dictates and through whom he gets his words down on paper, letter by letter, not forgetting the commas. This kind of thinking is utterly unbiblical. In any case, the Bible itself does not suggest in any way whatsoever that it expected to be understood in this way.

The Bible does speak of the *Spirit* of God who takes hold of a man, but it does not speak of words and letters which he causes to be set down by an automaton. The Bible speaks of living men, men with the sap of life in them, with all the strength and weakness that is inherent in men who are in need of redemption, men with the human quality we are so vividly aware of in an Isaiah, an Amos, or a Paul. It speaks of living persons, not of goose quills and penholders playing the role of automatons for the Holy Spirit.

And all of these living men who wrote the Bible know, and say in one form or another, that now they see God only in a mirror dimly but *then* face to face; that now they know only in part, but that one day they will know him fully even as he knows them (I Cor. 13:12). These men of the Bible, Paul at the head of them, all know that they are fallible human beings. They know that they are human media with all the sources of error and fallibility inherent in the human means, but which God in his grace nevertheless uses for his purposes. Paul especially never tires of emphasizing this again and again, and at certain unusually critical points in his arguments he makes a very fine distinction: in some cases he says, "This is what the Lord said," but in others he says, "This the Lord did not say, but *I* say it" (e.g., I Cor. 7:12). He knows very well that he is not a goose quill, an automatic instrument, but rather a man who is being led by the Holy Spirit, passing on the message by his command and under his discipline. The Word of God, not only the Word made flesh in Christ but also the written Word of God, has its "servant-form," just as surely as God committed his saving truth to mortal sinners and men with limited, though consecrated, capacities.

When the church lapsed for a time into this false doctrine of verbal inspiration (Luther, with few exceptions, did not succumb to it even in his day), the obvious implication was that then every statement in the Bible is equally binding. Then every statement in the Bible, because it originated in this mechanical way, is on exactly the same level; they all alike stem from God. Then Moses' ritualistic regulations concerning the ashes of a red heifer and the account of our Lord's resurrection are of equal value and therefore equally binding. In this mechanistic view it is all revealed by God. And if this is true, *then the cosmology too must* be regarded as revelation. Then Joshua must have made the sun and not the earth to stand still and, logically, one would be theologically obliged to dissociate oneself from the tenets of modern astronomy. Here one could actually play off Luther against himself, for it was he who graduated the Old Testament into definite degrees of validity and authority and attributed to it absolute bindingness for faith only in so far as it proclaims and promotes Christ (*Christum treiben*).

From all this it follows then that the battle between natural science and Christianity, between the biblical and the scientific cosmology, was possible only on the condition that one cherished a biblical literalism and thus regarded the cosmology of the Bible as being just as much revealed and sacrosanct as, say, the Christmas story or the return of Jesus Christ on the Last Day. Thus the theory of verbal inspiration constitutes the second condition that made it possible for this false either-or (either "evolution" or "creation") to arise.

Having laid this necessary groundwork, we come now to our real problem: What significance does all this have for the question of *how man came into being*?

We have already seen that the external details of the story of Paradise, which took place some thousands of years ago at a particular place in central Persia or Arabia, are a part of the biblical cosmology, which in its capacity as cosmology (not as message) has for us passed away. Today we know something about man's development out of certain primordial beginnings, however much the details of this development may still be in dispute. We know therefore that everything in the story of Paradise which has to do with cosmology merely constitutes the "letters" through which the actual truths of salvation were intended to be expressed. These cosmological details are not the truths of salvation. The truth of salvation is rather the reality that lies behind these signlike letters that point to it. So here we can proceed in the royal freedom of the children of God without fearing that this will cause us to lose our sonship.

When we say this, many people are likely to say: As soon as you break off any part of the letter of the Bible, the whole structure will collapse. But this is a false objection. Anybody who thinks in this way is not a *child* but rather a *slave* in the household of God. We are not breaking anything from the building; we know above all that Jesus Christ is the cornerstone. We are only setting up scaffoldings which are not a part of the actual building at all. The primary thing in the building itself is the *one* foundation, which Paul never tires of pointing out, namely, that God through Jesus Christ created the world and that *from* him and *through* him and *to* him are all things. What we are concerned with is only to *free* this Christ-foundation of the biblical history of salvation from misunderstandings and false hindrances to faith.

But right here is where the question that troubles most people comes in: If the biological cosmology is right and man developed biogenetically from prehuman, animal stages of evolution, is not something far more than the mere "cosmology" affected? Does this not affect the very heart of the biblical faith in creation? Does not the biological doctrine of evolution assert that man is only a more highly developed animal? And does this not actually impugn the *center* of faith in creation, the very thing which is declared to be an *imperishable* message in the first pages of the Bible, namely, that man is made in the image of God, by virtue of which he received from God a dignity that elevates him above all other creatures and therefore makes it absolutely inconceivable that he is only a "higher animal" and was thus merely gradually lifted above the zoological realm? After all, it is only this dignity, this sonship to God that makes it possible even to conceive that Jesus Christ, the Son of God, was not ashamed to call us his brothers (Heb. 2:11). If man is only a more highly developed beast of prey, if he is only an unusually noble *species* of the beast of prey, as Oswald Spengler once put it, then certainly this attacks the center of our faith, since it would mean that our being made in the image of God and Christ's being a brother of men would fall to the ground. This is the question we must now examine, and there are two points that must be made clear.

First, we must remember that man's likeness to God does *not* consist in his reason. This is true if only because, as Goethe said, man so often uses his reason "to be more brutal than any brute." We note this today in the brutalized technology which, though it is based upon reason, nevertheless cannibalizes itself, indeed, wreaks a beastly havoc in the whole structure of the world, a chaos that no lion or tiger or a whole menagerie could cause. No, the reason is not what makes man the image of God.

Rather what makes him the image of God is his character as a *person*, that is, the fact that he is responsible to God.

An example may make this clear. God put his ordained purpose (*Bestimmung*) into every living creature. He ordained that the embryo of a shepherd dog should become a full-grown shepherd dog and that a human embryo should become a man. So far the situation in each case is the same. But while the embryo of a shepherd dog arrives forthwith at what God intended it to be, going through, as it were, an "automatic" development, the situation is different in the case of man. Man has the responsible task of *realizing* his created structure, his divine determination, and—as we have seen—he can *fail* to do this. The shepherd dog is not confronted with the decision whether it is going to be a shepherd dog; but man does have to decide whether he wills to realize his determination as a man, as a child of God. And because he is faced with this decision, he can decide otherwise. And therefore he can also fall away from his determination, and even in his fall, in his sin—for the animal cannot fall!—one sees his greatness. Pascal once expressed this in an unforgettable way: Even in fallen man one can see the misery of a fallen lord, the misery of a deposed king. Only a king, only an image of God can fall so low. This is our doctrine of the image of God in man.

Second, this certitude of faith that man is created by God in his image is completely independent of the question whether man was directly created by God, or whether he was formed from the dust of the ground as indicated by the creation story, which should be read only with reverence, or whether he stands at the end of a line of prehuman developmental stages. On this question we again let the Bible itself speak, in order that we may not fall into the arbitrary, disobedient attitude of knowing better, to which we modern men are so prone.

In Psalm 139:13-16 the Bible gives us an eloquent answer to our question. It reads:

> For thou didst form my inward parts [i.e., my heart],
>   thou didst knit me together in my mother's womb.

I praise thee, for thou art fearful and wonderful.
  Wonderful are thy works!
Thou knowest me right well;
  my frame was not hidden from thee,
when I was being made in secret,
  intricately wrought in the depths of the earth.
Thy eyes beheld my unformed substance;
  in thy book were written, every one of them,
the days that were formed for me,
  when as yet there was none of them.[1]

There are two things that strike us in this passage:

a. The psalmist is thoroughly aware (and says so quite straight-forwardly) of the biological aspect of his procreation, his embryonic origin in his mother's womb, his birth; he knows what he as a biological human being has in common with other mammals.

b. But he distinguishes between this natural "formation" and his "creation": in the medium of the biological process of formation what happens is that God says, "Let there be!" and behold, there it is. There I am! He knew me, says the Psalmist, even when I was only "unformed substance"; he called me by my name and made me his own before I knew anything about him.

When, for example, Christian parents in our own day announce the birth of a child by saying, "God has bestowed upon us our first child," what they are doing is expressing their *gratitude,* not asserting that the child fell directly from heaven or that it suddenly made its appearance in the world. There is no question that they are seeing this incomprehensible divine miracle of pro-creation and creation against the background of a natural, biological process of development. Luther is doing the same thing when he says in his explanation of the first article of the Creed: "I believe that God has created me." For neither does his statement mean that suddenly and miraculously I burst into existence, but rather says: I was created—even: I was begotten and born of my parents, I was created *in* this process.

What is more natural, I ask, than that we should apply the same point of view, which is so obvious to us in our understand-

---

[1] In dealing with our problem Emil Brunner also cites this psalm in his book, *Das Wort Gottes und der moderne Mensch.* (Cf. Emil Brunner, *Man in Revolt* [Philadelphia: Westminster Press, 1942], p. 89.—Trans.)

ing of individual life and its development, to the *development of mankind as a whole?* If we acknowledge that we have been created by God as individuals—"I believe that God has created me" —and if in doing so we recognize that this miracle of creation in no way contradicts our natural descent and development through the process of procreation and birth, then what is more natural than to apply the same point of view to the origin of mankind as a whole? In other words, what should prevent us from saying, in the same sense as Psalm 139, that man in his present form goes back to prehuman forms and stages? "Thou, O Lord, didst already know him in his unformed substance, in his embryonic, original form. When he still knew nothing of thee and had no idea that thou wouldst ordain him to sonship, thou didst already see him and choose him in his prehuman form and didst call him by name; thou didst perform the miracle of making and creating man in the course of that development."

For naturally, even when we take this process of evolution seriously, the evolution of man still remains a *miracle,* a real *creation.* This is evident in the simple fact—which we must continue to hold up to biology in the name of the Holy Scriptures— that man simply cannot be explained on the basis of these prehuman, animal-like forms, even if exact proof of the existence of certain missing links were to be found. I would express it this way: the transition from the prehuman to the human stage is a mystery. It is nothing less than the mystery of creation. And this again can be shown quite simply by reference to present-day man. That is to say, we cannot explain (actually, *in principle* we cannot explain) by scientific means how it is that man, who on the biological level is a mammal and even in minute details exhibits a development parallel with this zoological realm, is at the same time something *else,* that as a *person* he is responsible to God, that unlike oxen and asses he is called by name and must give answer, and that Jesus Christ died for him. Thus here in the midst of the biological vessel there is a totally different reality which cannot be explained in biological terms.

The Bible repeatedly points to these two totally different sides of man, namely, the fact that on one side he is actually a mammal and on the other a real image of God.

For example, the Holy Scriptures speak of man's death in two ways. They refer to it in purely biological terms: man passes away, breathes his last, returns to dust, withers like a flower, he goes through the natural process of decay. But at the same time the Holy Scriptures see another reality embedded in this natural process of dying. They see in it the *judgment* of God; they see in it the fact that through death man is flung back into his own temporality and excluded from God's eternity. This confinement behind the barriers of his temporality and transience, this condemnation "to death" is God's answer to man's Promethean attempts to seize the forbidden fruit, involving him in repeated and constant falls into sin; his illicit strivings to break into the sovereign realm of God, to become a superman, to deny his limitations, and in all this to rise beyond his likeness to God and gain a forbidden equality with God. In the fact that he must die, this man who is constantly pressing toward boundlessness is shown his bounds. This is God's judgment of death.[2]

Thus in the midst of the biological process of death a completely different but real process is taking place: a personal transaction between God and man.

Here is another example of the Bible's dual way of looking at man. Man's *sexuality* is another characteristic which he shares with the mammal. But again, in the case of man, in this seemingly unambiguous biological process there occurs something totally different from what happens in the case of the animal: in expressing himself sexually man enters into a living I-thou relationship with another human being. In this act he is responsible for another person, for everything he does with the other, everything he arouses within the other, every influence he brings to bear upon the other. He can either ruin and destroy this person or he can—as the phrase from the marriage liturgy puts it— "take her with him to heaven." So here again we see the two completely different sides of man: the biological, natural side, and embedded in the midst of it a totally different reality, something which takes place in a most personal way between us and our neighbor and thus at the same time between us and God.

And now we also see what it leads to when one denies this other

[2] Cf. the author's book, *Tod und Leben: Studien zur christlichen Anthropologie* (2d ed.; Tübingen: J. C. B. Mohr [Paul Siebeck], 1946).

side, as is done in the biological world view, when one views sexuality only from the point of view of population policies or the "glass-of-water theory."[3] It leads to the dehumanization of man.

In other words one can, or rather one *must,* view man from two completely different sides: on the one hand he is a mammal and thus naturally has his descent through the mammalian animals, and on the other side he is in all this the image of God.

Sometimes this necessity of judging from both sides is true of other things too. I mention only one example, the most beautiful chorale in Bach's *St. Matthew Passion,* "O sacred Head, now wounded." When this chorale resounds, what happens on the physical level is that a number of vibrations reach our ears through the medium of the atmosphere and are there perceived as tones. But certainly it would never occur to us to say that this chorale "consists" of the frequency of vibration of particular sounds. No, these vibrations merely constitute the vessel or vehicle of the real essence of the chorale, just as in man his biological nature has only the rank of a vessel which contains the real substance of his being. In the midst of these physical vibrations an encounter between man and God, a prayer, takes place; here a man establishes contact with eternity. This is the "real thing," this is the "chorale," which here becomes an event in the midst of the operation of physical laws. These are two sides of the same thing, actually two completely different sides, totally different dimensions of reality.

This means that we have discovered a fundamental spiritual insight. Allow me to state it in two ways:

1. When we say that man is a mammal and that he developed biologically by way of procreation, birth, and death, this is not to say that he is an animal. Such a conclusion would be just as absurd as to say that the chorale "O sacred Head, now wounded" is a purely physical phenomenon, a mere stringing together of atmospheric vibrations. No, the only thing it says is that God *"created"* me, who was formed in the natural way in my mother's womb, and that he knew me before the world's foundation was

---

[3] The theory that sexual intercourse is to be regarded simply as the satisfaction of a natural hunger, as one satisfies thirst with a glass of water. (Trans.)

laid. I, who on the biological level am a mammal, can at the same time be assured that I am a child of God, created in his image, a child who has broken this image, a child who ran off into the far country and through Jesus Christ has been brought back home to the Father and the peace of the Father's house. In the midst of my natural development two miracles take place: I am created by God as a person and I am called to be his child and disciple. *Created* and *called!* These, of course, are things that no longer have anything to do with man's evolutionary descent. In the midst of my biological creatureliness occurs the miracle (the miracle which cannot be explained but only affirmed) which makes me a new creation (II Cor. 5:17; Gal. 6:15). In the midst of this development something happens which has nothing whatsoever to do with development.

2. And now we can say exactly the same thing with regard to the beginnings of the human race. Here, too, stands the fact that one day God created a man, that one day he made him aware that he was a child of God and that he had received life from his hands, and that this does not contradict the fact that this creation was preceded by an embryonic stage of development.

Edgar Daqué, the well-known biologist, whose theories I normally regard with some skepticism, once made a very discerning comment about the origin of man, referring specifically to these prehuman stages of evolution: "When all was done"—that is, when the animal world had been created—"he raised up from the animal the human form, gave it his breath." I should say that there we have a highly succinct and appropriately reverent description of the mystery of man's coming into being: in the midst of biological development occurs the miracle of God's choosing and lifting man out of the animal kingdom and calling him to himself. And more precisely, this miracle consists in his breathing his *breath* into him; in other words, in the fact that something happens to him which no development could bestow upon man and which the first pages of the Bible proclaim to us as being the basic foundation of faith in creation, namely, the miracle of inspiration with the divine breath. For this inspiration means that God gives man a part of himself and makes him the bearer of his Spirit and image. Though the story of Paradise may be geographically and historically part of a cosmology which is no longer ours, its message remains the indispensable gospel of our faith.

This affirmation that God breathed his breath into man in order to make him a man is the crux of the gospel of creation; it is "history" in the highest sense of the word, for it is actually the basis of all human history. For only by virtue of this word concerning the divine inbreathing could Jesus Christ, who bore within him intact the breath of God and is able to make men new by the breath of his Spirit, become our brother.

This brings us to our conclusion. Thomas Carlyle, says Arthur Neuberg in his book, *The World-View of Biology,* was once present in a company of scholars who were discussing the problem of the descent of man. He was asked to express his view, and he rose and said, "Gentlemen, you place man a little higher than the tadpole. I hold with the ancient Psalmist (Ps. 8): 'Thou hast made him a little lower than the angels.' "

That statement says everything that needs to be said. When he said this Carlyle was not holding up to ridicule the idea of a tadpole being a possible early stage of life and therefore of human life. He was merely saying that the divine mystery of the creation of human life cannot be understood merely by discovering the series of evolutionary stages back to an original ancestor called a "tadpole." What he was saying was that the mystery of man can only be understood in terms of the *God* who miraculously created and brought him into being by breathing into him his breath.

But in all this there is hidden still another profound biblical point of view. If we want to know what man is, we do not ask *where* he came from biogenetically—God can raise up children to Abraham from stones (Matt. 3:9); this is the ultimate relativization of the human pedigree!—but must rather ask *what* it was that God intended him to be. The mystery of man lies not in his biological *origin,* but rather in his appointed destiny, namely, that he should become a child of God and come into his peace.

Here we stand before one of the profoundest mysteries of our faith. When, for example, we want to know the mystery of *history,* we do not discover it by searching ancient documents and monu-

ments to determine how everything came to be as it is and what
the primeval history was that finally resulted in what is happening now. (Necessary as this research is, it does not lead us to the
fundamental meaning and essence of history.) Rather, when we
want to know "what" history is, we must ask what is God's *goal*
for history. That is to say, we can understand all human history
only from the vantage point of its end, when Jesus Christ will
come to judge the quick and the dead, when he will deliver the
kingdom to the Father, who then will be in all in all. *The victory
of God is the meaning and end of history*. Therefore history can
only be read backward, from the point of view of its end. Hence
when we want to know what history is, our leading question is
not "where" do we come from, but rather "whereto" the whole
course of events in which we are enclosed is going. Thus the problems "What is man?" and "What is history?" are exactly parallel
in the way the question is put and the answer that is received.

Consequently, I cannot close without casting a glance at the
figure of Jesus Christ. For all the attributes which we have just
found in man, his physical, biological existence and his existence
as a child, a "son" of God, Christ accepted from the Father in
order that he might be our brother in both of these dimensions.

At the beginning of the Epistle to the Romans Paul utters some
mysterious words to the effect that Jesus Christ descended from
the seed of David according to the flesh, but according to the
Spirit was designated to be the Son of God. Here we see that in
everything Jesus Christ is one of us. He too had, if you will permit the phrase, a biological pedigree and participated "according
to the flesh" in the natural development common to all men. He
became a child in Mary's womb. He was born into the world on
Christmas Day. He knew hunger and thirst, the cold of night
and the heat of day. In dreadful pain he shed his blood, shed it
physiologically in exactly the same way and with the same torments as any creature of the animal world, "like a lamb that
is led to the slaughter." And yet in the midst of this human solidarity with us, in the midst of his biologically parallel descent,
he was someone totally different; he was miraculously born as
the Son of the Father.

And when at Christmas we bow our heads before his crib we

are praising and adoring the wondrous marvel, the miracle which God performed here in the midst of the history of man's descent. "From Jesse's race" he comes. True, but there is something far more and totally other than "race" in that divine Child. The Saviour took upon himself both sides of our human nature, our natural body and the totally other nature which God formed within the vessel of the body. And though he thus became our brother—became, indeed, the only whole man who ever lived— we must make our own the words that Napoleon, of all people, once uttered when he thought of Jesus of Nazareth: "I know men; believe me, this was no man!"

VII | THE MEANING OF MIRACLE

WHEN WE COME TO THE PROBLEM OF MIRACLE, WHICH we shall deal with in this and the next chapter, we touch once more upon the great problem that occupied us in the last chapter, namely, the question of what is the real relationship that God the Creator has with our world, and thus with his creation.

We have already set forth two differing attitudes toward this question. Let me briefly recall the most important findings.

One attitude says that God works *within* creation; he works in it as its ultimate, animating vital impulse.

> He from *within* lives through all Nature . . .,
> Nature and Spirit fostering each other

says Goethe in his "Proemium," which I have quoted above. Once you start with this idea that God is not somewhere in the "beyond," but rather is *in* the midst of creation, then you inevitably end with the rhetorical, ironical question:

> What were a God, who, outward force applying,
> But kept the All around his finger flying?

This last, ironical statement already indicates the other attitude one can take concerning God's relation to the world. And this other attitude appears to be the Christian one, which Goethe is obviously here attacking. According to this notion of what the Christian view is, God is banished from the world; he has practically emigrated into the ghetto of the beyond.

This immediately results in the disastrous inference that with one stroke this world, nature, and history are left godless. And because there is no longer any God in the world—since God is sitting "over there" on the other side, still as a mouse—he feels compelled now and then to call attention to himself by means of a "miracle," a supernatural intervention in the world, so that men may say: Aha, he's still there after all!

Or to put it in another way, according to this alleged Christian view, miracle appears not to consist in the fact that the world is held together by a wonderful harmony, a marvellous interplay of natural laws and the forces which they guide and control. On the contrary, miracle would seem to consist in just the opposite: in the *violation of the laws of nature*. Then miracle consists, not in the meaningful *functioning* of the laws of nature, but rather in the evidential *suspension* of these laws. How else are we to interpret—we ask, playing devil's advocate for this polemic against the alleged Christian concept of miracle—the New Testament stories of reanimations of corpses or the accounts of Jesus performing instantaneous healings, which can never happen in the normal course of the natural process of healing? Are these not simply *violations* of the laws of nature? And are not these violations logically to be attributed to the fact that people no longer see God at work in the "normal" laws of nature? Is not this *super*natural and *un*natural concept of miracle a retribution for banishing God to the other world? Is not this the price we pay for banishing God from this world and forcing him to call attention to himself, as it were "artificially," by means of miracles and forced demonstrations?

To all appearances, then, we have here two extremely different attempts to define the relation of God to the world. In one case, God is *in* the world and *in* the laws of nature; in the other, God is outside the world and "now and then" acts by means of violating the laws of nature in miracles.

So we shall examine what the miracle stories of the New Testament have to say about the relation of God to the world and to our whole personal life. But before we do this, there are some other matters that must be cleared up. We must first arrive at a clear definition of terms; for when we examine the older terminology with respect to miracle we discover very quickly that there are actually three completely different concepts of miracle, which are used indiscriminately and uncritically, both in Christian and in anti-Christian literature.

What are these three concepts?

1. Imagine for a moment a native tribe somewhere in the African bush. To this native tribe comes a European trader who has an interest in getting rid of his stock of cheap merchandise and obtaining great authority as quickly and cheaply as possible. There was a time when perhaps the quickest way to gain this end was to play a record on a portable phonograph. The likely response of the natives would be to say, "This is a god! Never before has it happened that a man spoke not only with his mouth but was also able to speak out of a small box—that he is obviously able to enter into this box at the same time as he stands upright before us. This is a god!" In other words, "This is a miracle!"

Why is it that this primitive tribe should speak of "miracle" in cases like this? Simply because these people say to themselves: "This phenomenon of the phonograph has no discernible natural causes. Normally, the natural cause is that when someone speaks he stands before you and moves his lips. But we cannot discern these natural causes in this speaking box; therefore the only way it can be explained is to call it 'supernatural'; this phonograph can only be an incursion of the miraculous into life. Only gods or demons can accomplish this."

The history of mankind has shown us that at certain primitive stages of development man is inclined to speak of "miracle" whenever something happens which cannot be explained in terms of events that occur within this world, something which evidently has its origin in the invisible realm *behind* the scenes of this world and is now injecting its mysterious power into the world—no matter whether these are gods or demons who exert influence from "outside" into this world. One can probably justly say that this concept of miracle is based upon inadequate knowledge. It therefore also disappears of itself as these people gradually find out that the voice in the phonograph is produced in accord with altogether natural acoustical laws. For us modern men, what at certain primitive stages is called miracle resolves itself into a natural connection of cause and effect. And this is also the reason why the miracles of ancient times appear to us to be largely explainable, since in all phenomena we are not only inclined to look for the cause within this world, but tend right from the start to assume it as axiomatic and self-evident. Moreover, we have also developed very precise methods by which to discover these causes, and in this way have long since been oriented concerning certain phenomena which the primitives would necessarily regard as miracles.

In other words, here miracle consists only in a certain absence of enlightenment, a certain primitiveness. It is therefore only a miracle "for the time being" and resolves itself in the course of progress. Or again, here miracle has its basis not in something objective but rather in our unenlightened subjectivity.

2. The second concept of miracle or way in which the question of miracle is dealt with is that in which we say: Miracles do not consist in extraordinary, supernatural events, such as occur when Jesus heals a sick person, but rather in a very *definite way of regarding nature*. It is a form of seeing.

In order to illustrate this as graphically as possible, let me give you a fine passage from Goethe's *The Sufferings of Young Werther* in which this concept of miracle appears in very precise and significant form. The passage describes Werther lying in a lovely meadow, completely abandoned to the glory of nature, so overwhelmed by it that he cannot even move his brush to capture it on canvas. Then says Werther:

"When, while the lovely valley teems with vapor around me, and the meridian sun strikes the upper surface of the impenetrable foliage of my trees, and but a few stray gleams steal into the inner sanctuary, I throw myself down among the tall grass by the trickling stream; and as I lie close to the earth, a thousand unknown plants are noticed by me: when I hear the buzz of the little world among the stalks, and grow familiar with the countless indescribable forms of the insects and flies, then I feel the presence of the Almighty who formed us in his own image, and the breath of that universal love which bears and sustains us, as it floats around us in an eternity of bliss; and then, my friend, when darkness overspreads my eyes, and heaven and earth seem to dwell in my soul and absorb its power, like the form of a beloved mistress, —then I often think with longing, Oh, would I could describe these conceptions, could impress upon paper all that is living so full and warm within me, that it might be the mirror of the infinite God!"[1]

This passage describes exactly the second idea of what miracle

[1] *The Sorrows of Werther*, Orson Falk, trans., in *Great German Short Novels and Stories*, Bennett Cerf, ed. (New York: Modern Library, 1933), p. 3. (Trans.)

is. It consists in the fact that a particular point of reality, in this case a lovely meadow with the mist rising from it, or tiny insects or blades of grass, and thus a definite point in nature, suddenly becomes transparent and all at once we see back of it the divine formative reality that creates it all. This is what Werther is saying. He simply senses, even though nothing unnatural is happening, the wonderful "presence of the Almighty," the "breath of the all-loving One." It is not without significance that he speaks here of the "mirror" reflecting the divine in the soul: nature suddenly becomes a parable of the divine powers that lie behind it.

This is the miracle. In more precise terms, we would have to put it this way: Here in Goethe the miracle does not consist in the fact that something in the world changes, that (to employ this example for the last time) the sun suddenly stands still or stops shining, or that a stream flows upward instead of downward. The miracle rather consists in the fact that something in Werther's *eyes,* in his way of *seeing,* changes. Consequently the miracle does not take place outside in the objective reality, but rather within me, in the way in which I am touched and moved and the way in which I see altogether new things under the influence of this apprehension. In other words, the miracle consists in my personal subjectivity, in my own act of seeing.

That is to say, I see the same reality as I did before, except that now I see it differently. We can illustrate this change of vision by thinking of Werther. This same Werther, who here senses the ultimate reality, the "breath of the all-loving One," could in the next hour sit bowed over a microscope as a scientist, studying the digestive and reproductive processes of one of these tiny flies. Here instead of seeing the fly from the angle of "miracle," that is, in this instance as a transparency of the all-loving One, he could view it as a "naturalist" from the point of view of natural law. Goethe himself very definitely performed both these functions concurrently, in one case describing himself as a "pantheist" and in others as a "naturalist."

This experience of Werther is, of course, something that we can still observe in our own experience. Take this for example: We can look at a mountain peak from two points of view. We can see in it a symbol of the majesty of the Creator and in the face of such a gigantic mass we may be moved to cry out, The heavens declare the glory of God! But we can also look at the same mountain from another point of view, remembering that it is the result of certain geological processes producing a tremendous bulging of the earth's crust; that it is covered with frozen H_2O; and that from its atmospherically conditioned ultraviolet radiation are emitted certain reflections of light which can be analyzed in precise physical terms.

So we repeat: this concept of miracle says that miracles do not occur as events that take place outside in external reality, but rather within my eyes, in my way of seeing. The miracle does not attach to the object but rather to the point of view, the perspective; it relates not to the reality but raher to my *attitude* toward the reality. In this connection there is one very important fact which must not be overlooked. This way of seeing requires a certain aptitude, a certain form of religious genius. If miracles occur only within our own subjectivity, then logically it would require a particular disposition of one's subjectivity in order to allow them to come into being—in other words, in order to "see" a miracle. A person who did not have this gift would be quite matter-of-fact about it and see in the mountain mass only a complex of upheavals of the earth's crust, whereas another person, the so-called "religiously gifted" person, would see in it a liturgy of creation, a geological doxology to the Creator in his majestic glory.

Again and again in life we encounter this twofold way of seeing and hearing. In music we have exactly the same situation. Undoubtedly there are unmusical people who hear only a sum of tone vibrations when they listen to a Mozart sonata, and the experience means nothing to them except that it is terribly boring. And a Bach fugue can actually make a dog howl with pain. On the other hand, there are musical people who are equally aware that these are physical sound vibrations, but also know that through them Mozart is expressing some very profound things about life which stir them to the innermost depths. Thus here, too, one can listen in this twofold way.

So once more: this kind of "miracle" consists not in a change in the reality of things, but rather in a change in my own eyes. It is a process that takes place *within* me.

3. This clears the way for the third concept of miracle, the one

used by the Bible. We see now how differently people talk about these things and how necessary it is at the very outset to reduce this Babylonian confusion of language to some kind of order.

We need only to look at a few of Jesus' miracles and we shall immediately discover in them an essential characteristic which distinguishes them from everything we have said so far about miracles. In biblical thinking miracle is in every case something done by God, and therefore an "event." *Something happens.* True, the New Testament accounts also give us a clear impression of the effect these sudden and objective events had upon people. They could be literally shocked by them, actually fall to the ground in amazement; but in every case they are compelled to make a decision with regard to them which affects the very center of their being. So something "happens." And this above all is the important point. In other words, the biblical miracle is in no case limited to my eyes, to the act of seeing. It is rather an act which becomes an event in the outside world through the sovereign creative power of God.

When we proceed to examine the various forms in which these miracles were accomplished, we find that there are really only two such forms.

a. The miracle may be such that it takes the form of an act by which God directs the laws of nature in such a way that his action has the overwhelming and convincing effect of compelling me to confess: Here God has spoken; here he has acted in my life or in the life of my people. The Book of Job gives us an impressive example of this. Job, a good God-fearing man, received in one day three calamitous messages. First a gigantic fire broke out and destroyed his cattle. Then the Chaldeans raided the country and slew his servants. And the third messenger reported that a hurricane had blown down the house in which his children had gathered, burying them all. Job is left a poor man, a man without children. And Job's response to these messages is this now famous saying: "The Lord gave, and the Lord has taken away; blessed be the name of the Lord."

Now, what is the miracle here? The miracle is that God acted here, and acted in such a way that Job had to say: God has taken away; he is the acting subject behind it all, and this concourse of

natural events was only the *means* through which he acted; over
against the divine subject they have only the rank of a predicate.
Naturally Job did not doubt that his servants were slain by the
Chaldeans in a perfectly "natural" way. There may have been a
quarrel, one side provoking the other, and the result was a free-
for-all. The servants were overwhelmed by the superior force of
the Chaldeans; a very simple and quite natural consequence of
the proportion of strength in the two groups. And certainly Job
would not have doubted, if he had any meteorological knowledge,
that the hurricane which destroyed his house and buried his children was the result of perfectly natural atmospheric conditions.
But he also knew this: he (the Lord) has fashioned the course of
these events in such a way that he himself is literally coming
straight at me, so that I can almost feel his hand upon me. And
there is nothing else to say but this: Not fire, not hurricane, not
Chaldeans; no, the *Lord* has acted through the fire, the hurricane,
the Chaldeans.

In other words, the miracle consists in God's so directing the
natural course of things, the *laws of nature,* that certain things
happen to me. Here God acts in the medium of the laws of nature.

Perhaps I may permit myself to illustrate this by means of an
experience of my own. Some years ago I was paralyzed and medical science was unable to do anything further for me. At that time
the head of a well-known university hospital gave it as his opinion
that I had only a few months to live. Then in these months—actually a short time before the doors were to close, as I was approaching the end in full consciousness of my condition—the news
suddenly arrived that a new medicine had been discovered which
could cure or at least keep within limits this illness, hitherto beyond control. This was the medicine that still keeps me alive, and
which at that time suddenly restored a doomed cripple and
turned him into an able-bodied man. You will understand how
deeply I felt at that time that "this the Lord had done," and you
will appreciate that such an intervention in one's life, or better, in
inevitable death, does not pass by without leaving its mark. What
had happened? I was critically minded enough to say to myself:
This thing happened quite naturally; this was just a matter of two
chains of causes happening to cross each other. On the one hand

my illness was advancing with iron necessity to its terminal point, and quite independent of it another chain of cause and effect was proceeding on its course somewhere else in Germany. For, you see, somewhere else in Germany there was a researcher who knew nothing whatsoever about me, feverishly at work in a laboratory to combat this disease. And at the decisive moment, that is, the *last* moment, these two chains of causality intersected. I have never contested the fact that nothing supernatural happened here at all. Two very normal processes were running their course here, except that in this totally incomprehensible way they intersected in me and my "case."

I could only say, "The Lord hath done this"; he disposed these chains of causality in such a way that they had to meet at this specific moment. And I count it one of the greatest joys of my life that I and the discoverer of this medicine and the head of that hospital are in agreement on this, and that all three of us are in a common bond of faith—that we simply stand in reverence before this "miracle." We shall discuss later the special problems which this poses for the critical view.

b. Now the *second* form of miracle in the Bible. We have seen that the first form was embedded in the laws of nature. The second form of miracle in the Bible actually consists in the violation of the laws of nature. When Jesus says, "Rise, take up your pallet and go home" (Mark 2:11), and in that instant a paralysis simply vanishes, this certainly is no natural process of healing. Then at the very least the claim is being raised that something utterly extraordinary is happening here, and not happening by way of the immanent autonomy of natural processes, but that here, rather, a reality has broken in "from the outside." The same applies when Jesus raises a person, the young man of Nain for example, from the dead. So what is being claimed here is that this is a real irruption of divine power into the world.

I now pose three questions:

First, does not belief in miracles—at least in this last very drastic form in which we are obliged to speak of supernatural interventions—belong with an outworn biblical cosmology? After all, we have said that there is such a thing. May not miracles too, at least in this drastic form, be a part of this cosmological, and therefore peripheral, framework? And would not even Jesus Christ himself be more human to us—or to express it more theologically, would not his incarnation be more essentially understandable—if we got rid of this idea of miracle which is so hard to digest, and freed ourselves of this "ballast," which is all that it seems to be?

And the *second* question: If, however, we must be convinced that these miracles, including the healing of the paralytic or the raising of the young man of Nain, are an integral and indispensable part of our faith, how then are we to interpret them? I do not mean that we can claim (God defend us from this) to "explain" them. This would mean that we were making ourselves the measure of all things and raising the monstrous claim of stripping the living God of his right to mystery. Nevertheless, as honest men we cannot believe that two times two equals five simply on command. Nor can we be commanded to believe that here something happened which is the opposite of what we normally regard as a precise operation of natural law. Consequently, at this point where we must insist that miracle is an indispensable part of faith, we must simply seek together for a way in which we shall see how this kind of miracle is related to the natural law with which we are normally familiar.

And the *third* problem consists in the question of what really is the deepest purpose of the biblical accounts of miracles; of what the *message* is that comes to us through them. This central question we shall deal with in the next chapter. Here we shall briefly discuss only the first two questions in preparation for the third.

Now the *first* question: Is miracle really an integral, indispensable part of our faith, or can we be Christians without believing in these things?

To begin with, in a very general sense I must accept without any reservations the last mentioned form of miracle. Without miracle our prayers would simply become meaningless. Prayer would be degraded into a monologue and we should have to assume right from the start that God could never answer our prayers or intervene in our lives. Then there would literally be no more prayers, neither petition nor intercession. For logically we can pray to God for specific things only if we assume that everything has not been fixed and that the future is not unchangeably settled, in the way

expressed in the Mohammedan term "kismet," a mechanically unalterable fate.

There is a particular view of nature—in the history of philosophy it is called the Kant-Laplace theory—according to which
everything that happens in the world is simply fixed and established by the iron necessity of cause and effect. Laplace, a younger
contemporary of Immanual Kant, expressed this in a famous statement which I should like to quote here. He said,

"An intelligence [by this he means a supreme intellectual being, a divin-
ity] knowing all the forces acting in nature at a given instant, as well
as the momentary positions of all elements in the universe, would be
able to comprehend in one single formula the motions of the largest
bodies as well as of the lightest atoms in the world, provided that its
intellect were sufficiently powerful to subject all data to analysis; to it
nothing would be uncertain, the future as well as the past would be
present to its eyes."[2]

Since this statement is not easily understood at one reading, I
should like to explain it. Laplace thinks of the course of things
as being absolutely fixed now and in all the future by the law of
cause and effect. Consequently, the whole course of events can be
deduced, at least theoretically, from the present moment and pro-
jected into the future and the past. I need only to determine the
causes in the past and the effects in the future in order to know
from the situation in the present moment the whole course of the
world, since according to this iron law of natural necessity everything is fixed. In order to arrive at these determinations of cause
and effect only *one* condition must be fulfilled, namely, that I
must know absolutely all the causative factors. The reason why
the future is practically unpredictable lies therefore not in the
fact that it actually is accidental and irrational but rather in the
fact that it is practically impossible to determine *all* the causes.
That is to say, if even a single cause is not determined, immediately an unpredictable disturbing factor enters in and renders any
prognosis impossible. So at this point Laplace, too, resorts to the
mythical construction of a supreme "intelligence," which, unlike
limited human beings, has an unbroken knowledge of the totality

[2] *Essai philosophique sur les probabilités* (1816).

on air but will rather fall to the floor, and we do so not only in technology but in everyday life.

But this natural law, and thus the regularity with which certain effects follow certain causes, can be explained in a way that is different from Laplace's explanation. This could be a matter of empirical laws; in other words, one may have ascertained on the basis of the law of great numbers that this experience is a clear rule and then stated it in the form of a law. Two simple examples will make this immediately clear.

If I cast a die on a table six times in succession, I cannot expect that a different number will turn up each time, that is, a two, a three, a four, and so on. Rather the result will be quite irregular, erratic, and accidental. This is what makes a game of dice fascinating; otherwise it would be simply boring. Every time a different number comes up. But if instead of six times I throw the die 120,000 times, I can with great probability reckon upon it that the number one will turn up about 20,000 times, number two 20,000 times, number three 20,000 times, and so on; and hence that in actuality all six numbers will turn up with a high degree of regularity. Thus what in the individual case is pure accident suddenly becomes a law when the law of great numbers is applied.

Another example of the same fact. Think of the incidence of suicide. Somewhere in a small town a suicide occurs. People become excited and say, "This has not happened here in ten years, it's terrible." And they discover very specific motives to explain why it happened. But now, though we know that the dreadful act of suicide can be traced back to some very specific tragic circumstances in this individual case, the statistician, the man who operates with great numbers, finds that the national average number of suicides in the year has remained fairly constant. What makes this so terrible when we hear it for the first time is that it appears to be a kind of law of nature that so and so many people must snuff out their own lives. So what is a shocking "incident" in this individual case in a small town, which can be explained only by the utterly personal motives of the suicide himself, suddenly becomes a statistical "law" when the law of great numbers is taken into account.

Then, too, from this point of view we know in a very mysterious

Then our *second* question. Though I have no intention of presenting a lecture on physics (if for no other reason than that I myself am a layman here), it ought nevertheless to be of the highest interest to us to cast a glance at the attitude which modern physics takes toward Laplace's world view, which is still very commonly held among us. I am thinking primarily of the scientist Max Planck.

I want to be as brief as possible, but yet I think that for many people it will be a kind of liberation to learn that for modern physics even Laplace's approach to the question is wrong. That is to say, that supreme intelligence which knows the relationship of all the world's elements to one another, and thus can calculate the future exactly, cannot exist at all, because there are no such things as elements. For Planck has shown us that matter does not consist of solid atoms whose relationship to one another could be calculated even theoretically (as Laplace proposed to do); but rather that according to the modern view matter appears to resolve itself into energy. A modern physicist has gone so far as to employ this epigrammatic formula: matter "is" not (i.e., it does not consist of solid materials), but rather "happens." Thus it is quite impossible to go back to solid and tangible elements. According to this view, therefore, the ultimate entities are not of a physical nature, not "atoms," but rather *energies*. And this of course immediately nullifies Laplace's scheme. For now it is impossible even in "theory" to determine the course of the world in the past and the future, because the ultimate constants, i.e., the ultimate tangible constituents of material, do not exist at all and hence the basis for such a calculation is lacking. Modern physics therefore faces a great crisis with respect to natural law.

Now perhaps some may object and say: All that I hear today about these developments in the thought of physics may be true; I have no way of checking it; but the fact still remains that wherever we look we see these iron, predictable laws of nature in operation. We take care, for example, not to set down a soup plate on thin air instead of on the table, because by the law of gravity it will shatter on the floor. This we *know*. So this talk about the unpredictability of the laws of nature is not very serious after all. We still go on reckoning with this natural law that a plate will not sit of all causes. To such an intelligence the course of world events is absolutely fixed and is therefore predictable.

We can illustrate this view by taking the example of a film story. When I see a motion picture on the screen, then, no matter how I may wish it to turn out, I know that the story is simply fixed and that it will go on unreeling exactly as it is recorded on the film. Unforeseen incidents and sudden turns which have not been included in the calculation of causes simply cannot intervene—as they actually do in real life.

Something like that is the way that Laplace envisioned the course of events in this world. In this view of the world, which is very widespread among us, there can be no such thing as an unforeseen incident, and naturally this also means that there can be no intervention of God, either in the familiar sense of his breaking the law of causality (as in the case of the healing of the paralytic) or in the sense of his directing the laws of nature (as in the case of Job or in the example of what happened in my own life).

It is quite obvious, then, that on this level prayer is out. From Laplace's point of view, prayer is merely a weak and foolish attempt to appeal to God to change something in the necessity of things. For this he *cannot* do. Characteristically, therefore, Laplace describes him as an "intelligence," a merely passive and theoretical "onlooking" being. He could never describe him as a "will" or even as "Creator." Consequently, in dealing with this world view we are really facing a question that is fundamental to our faith.

The choice we face can be expressed as follows. *Either* natural science compels us to regard the course of events in the world in the same way as we watch the unreeling of a film, and then prayer is part of an outworn cosmology which we cannot honestly accept. *Or,* if the opposite is true, if we can really count on there being a power which is higher than this necessity, a power which is able to grasp me with a fatherly hand through everything that would come between us, a power that leads and guides me in the sense of Paul Gerhardt's hymn, "Commit thou all thy griefs and ways into his hands," then Laplace's picture of the world cannot be correct; then it is not only an "error" in the scientific sense, but also "false doctrine" in the spiritual sense.

way that two completely different worlds are intermingled with each other. On the one side is the world of my own personal freedom; if I take my life, this is my own responsible act. I cannot say to myself that I am under compulsion to complete the number of suicides necessary to make up the national average; it is my act, my "free" act. On the other hand, there is the other, totally different, factor, namely, the law of great numbers, according to which the suicide rate remains fairly constant. The point of intersection between the line of our freedom and the line of the law, which annuls this freedom, cannot be objectively determined, any more than we can see the "point of debouchment"—as Reinhold Schneider once put it—where what we do meets with the superpersonal plans of divine providence within which our acts are embraced. Kant has long since shown that one cannot "discover" freedom, that is, that one canot discover a hole or break in causality. Consequently, the possible objection of the scientist that he can see only laws, and that he does not know how there can be room for freedom within these laws, is in the strict sense of the word "invalid" and just as irrelevant as Virchow's statement that in all his pathological investigations of the human organism he had never yet discovered the soul.

In any case, what we generally think of as the conflict between science and faith in God could only have arisen on the basis of Laplace's philosophy, that is, in a situation where one is convinced of the autonomy of a mechanical law of causality and consequently regards natural events as being a dead process which cannot be influenced by any act of will; which simply goes on mechanically unreeling like a motion picture film, and which cannot be changed by any God. Instead of this, according to this new view in physics, what we have is a mysterious, "energetic" process which has a certain similarity to the processes of the human will.

Karl Heim, who concerned himself especially with this question, quite justly pointed out that this new quantum physics also throws a whole new light upon the miracles of Jesus. That is to say, when we look at the miracles of Jesus, say, the healing of the paralytic, our impression is certainly not that here a mechanically functioning machine is being stopped for a moment in order that Jesus can make some repairs on it, but rather with all his miracles our impression is that here a conflict between two wills is taking place. The one will which is on the battleground is the power of destruction, disorder, and apostasy, the empire of demons, which is asserting its claim to dominion and is holding in possession these sick and sinful people. The other power, which opposes the powers of destruction, is the manifestation of the will of the in-breaking, restorative dominion of God.

Today there are also significant statements in medical literature which indicate a whole new understanding of this matter. There are leading medical men who do not regard illnesses as mere organic, or perhaps even mechanical, processes, but rather see diseases in relationship to the whole person and thus likewise relate them to the powers of the human will and the areas it affects. Then, accordingly, medical treatment consists not only in physical "repair," a few injections or pills, but also in a personal encounter in which the physician opposes the healing will to the patient's will and unconscious mind and thus to those powers which manifest themselves in the phenomena of illness.[3]

In any case it is a promising sign that at many points medical thinking is re-examining the ultimate foundations of the processes of illness and healing, engaging in a kind of thinking which, if I am not mistaken, is turning more and more to the New Testament and is therefore also attributing a value to miracle which is quite different from the derisive attitude that medical schools in the past thought they could adopt. Nor is it altogether exceptional these days that a leading scientist, like Max Planck, should express himself on the question of miracle and make his knowledge available for an understanding of it in a way that was unheard of in earlier times.[4]

Miracles are therefore *acts of power*. Jesus Christ is struggling with demonic powers, the power of disorder and chaos. And only because he is in an ultimate oneness with the will of God, only because he is in conformity with this will, can he perform these acts of power.

Altogether different is the situation with his disciples. Because

[3] Cf. especially the books of two Swiss physicians: Theodor Bovet, *Die Ganzheit der Person in der ärztlichen Praxis* (Zurich: Rascher Verlag, 1939); and Paul Tournier, *Krankheit und Lebensprobleme* (English trans., *A Doctor's Casebook in the Light of the Bible* [New York: Harper & Row, 1960]).

[4] It should be noted in passing, however, that I have some fundamental theological reservations with regard to Planck's theory of miracle.

again and again they lacked this ultimate consonance with the will of God, because the greatness of their faith never equalled a grain of mustard seed, they were constantly failing when such acts of power were demanded of them. This explains their remarkable question in Mark 9:28, "Why could we not cast out [this spirit]?" Jesus' answer was cryptic, but nevertheless one that points to this lack of oneness between the will of the disciples and the will of the Father: "This kind cannot be driven out by anything but prayer."

We may sum up our conclusions concerning the first two concepts of miracle in three statements.

1. Miracle is in fact an indispensable component of our faith. We must simply recognize that God reigns and that he is really the Lord who gives and takes away and whose name is to be praised. Therefore, for faith it is intolerable to think that the course of this world is fixed by law and therefore constitutes a parallel with a film that simply unreels mechanically without any possibility of intervention of any kind. The view of Laplace, which assumes this, does not have the status of a scientific *cosmology*—as such it is obsolete, as we have seen. It rather has the status of a world view, an ideology; it is an assertion of a closed, self-sufficient finitude; it banishes God from the world and is basically a logically consistent atheism.

2. But at the same time, we have seen the sense in which and the degree to which modern physics makes it possible to think in terms of miracle. And when I say this I certainly do not mean that this makes miracle "explicable." It retains the status of mystery, simply because what Paul said applies to everything that God does: it is what "no eye has seen, nor ear heard, nor the heart of man conceived." If God were to ask me to believe that two times two equals five, if this were in the Bible, then I should have to ask whether the God of truth, who, as Luther said, gave me "my reason and all the faculties of my mind," could really have said such a thing. Undoubtedly he *cannot* have said it. But when God performs a miracle, when he marvellously guides and directs my life, so that I am compelled to say, "God meant it for good"; when Jesus says with authority to a sick man, "Rise, take up your pallet and walk," then to be sure all this is hidden in the mystery of his

counsel and I cannot ask, much less answer, the question of Nicodemus, "How can this be?" Jesus himself refused to answer it. But at the same time I can learn that this miracle is not "unthinkable" (as the statement that two times two equals five is unthinkable for me), because I see that here God is directing the elements of reality and marvellously subjecting them to his will.

3. Miracle in the biblical meaning of the term is therefore not a "way of seeing," not a mere process in my inner eye (as it is thought of in Goethe's *Werther*). Rather it means the objective guiding and forming of my life by God, so that I am compelled to say: The Lord gave me to be what I am and can be, he gave me what I have; the Lord has taken away, and though this is dreadful to me, blessed be the name of the Lord!

This concludes our preparatory line of thought. All that we have said so far has been only an overture for the *real* message of miracle. In the next chapter we shall face the central question: What is the *message* Jesus is proclaiming to us in his miracles and what does it mean to us, in utterly practical terms, that you and I can live our lives in the name of a miracle?

But this much we can say here: Jesus Christ is not a "teacher," but rather a "doer." The kingdom of God which he proclaims does not consist in talk but in power and deeds. This means that Jesus does not "teach" us by means, say, of a book, that there is a loving Father or a Shepherd who watches over life and keeps it in order; no, Jesus *acts*. He does not "teach" us that God can forgive sinners; but rather he speaks a word of effectual power which in the very utterance of it is already an act: "Your sins *are* forgiven!" He says it to us in a way—a way which still today is expressed in the Lord's Supper—that actually brings this forgiveness to me, so that I can *touch* it with my hands. When Jesus comes to a man he *acts*, he *does* something. And it is in exactly this sense that the miracles testify that Jesus is one who acts, that even his words have the character of deeds—effectual, operative actions. "For he spoke, and it came to be; he commanded, and it stood forth." This is the living, acting word, this is miracle.

And further, in the New Testament sin, sickness, and death are an unnatural incursion into God's creation. All this is like a spell that hangs over mankind. We saw in Laplace what it means when such a spell—guilt, suffering, and death, but also the spell of fate and causality—lies upon the world. And this is precisely the reason why Jesus was not only the pastor of souls, who helps a man to get straight with his conscience, but also the physician, who heals real wounds, even physical wounds; to whom one can trust even one's body, even external things. But everything he did in miracles and in words, healing and forgiving, all these were only individual signs. Even in that day millions of people walked the earth and never heard of Jesus of Nazareth. Millions of people—before Christ and after Christ—have suffered and gone down to utter grief and death, and only a few did he heal. Individual signs! And these individual signs the New Testament says are the lightning of the kingdom of God on the horizon, lightning that proclaims the *day*, the reign of *God*. And in that kingdom that still stands beyond the horizon and seeks to come to us, guilt and suffering will cease, and even death will be no more. So when things grow hard for us, when the dark descends upon us, when sore fate comes down upon our life, when we no longer know how we shall get through the coming night and the following day, then we are to look to this *kingdom,* which is already making itself known in the lightning flashes of Jesus's miracles. God's hand is effectually at work. And that's the gospel message of miracle: the message that tells us of lightning flashes in the deep of night when darkness confuses and I grope about with sightless eyes. This is the gospel message that tells us that when these things come we need not run for cover.

No, when all these things come, then "look up and raise your heads, because your redemption is drawing near"; for the lightning flashes of miracle are the heralding of that lightning which comes from the east and shines as far as the west and is a parable of the coming of the Son of man (Matt. 24:27). This is the message of miracle.

IN THIS CHAPTER WE SHALL TRY TO WORK OUT THE
central message of miracles. Let us begin with that exceedingly
characteristic miracle story to which I have already referred, the
story of the healing of the paralytic in Mark 2:1-12:

> And when he returned to Capernaum after some days, it was reported
> that he was at home. And many were gathered together, so that there
> was no longer room for them, not even about the door; and he was
> preaching the word to them. And they came, bringing to him a paralytic
> carried by four men. And when they could not get near him because of
> the crowd, they removed the roof above him; and when they had made
> an opening, they let down the pallet on which the paralytic lay. And
> when Jesus saw their faith, he said to the paralytic, "My son, your sins
> are forgiven." Now some of the scribes were sitting there, questioning
> in their hearts, "Why does this man speak thus? It is blasphemy! Who
> can forgive sins, but God alone?" And immediately Jesus, perceiving in
> his spirit that they thus questioned within themselves, said to them,
> "Why do you question thus in your hearts? Which is easier, to say to
> the paralytic, 'Your sins are forgiven,' or to say, 'Rise, take up your
> pallet and walk'? But that you may know that the Son of man has
> authority on earth to forgive sins"—he said to the paralytic—"I say to
> you, rise, take up your pallet and go home." And he rose, and immedi-
> ately took up the pallet and went out before them all; so that they were
> all amazed and glorified God, saying, "We never saw anything like this!"

The subject of this healing story is an incurable cripple. His
friends were carrying him, and it is definitely indicated that they,
and not only the paralytic himself, were believers. The event as it
is narrated falls into two acts, the first act in which Jesus forgives

113

his sins, and the second in which he heals the sick man of his incurable illness.

We begin with the first act. When Jesus said, "Your sins are forgiven," all who were present may well have looked at him, expecting that he would then relieve the sick man of his suffering. The fact that this was precisely what he did *not* do undoubtedly caused disappointment in all who were there. But above all it must have been a disappointment to the sick man himself, for it would seem to him that, is Jesus heard his prayer for healing at all, he must have heard it as something different from what he meant and hoped for. So he had to undergo an experience with prayer to which all of us have been subjected and which we were promised that we would have. This is the experience of finding that God apparently does not answer our actual petition at all (a petition, for example, that he may free us from an illness), and then helpfully intervenes at some other point quite different from what we expected or even desired. The burdensome thing in this kind of answer to prayer, as we all know, is that at first we can discover no relation between what we prayed for and what God is now pleased to do *de facto* with our life. Neither did the paralytic see any such relation, and undoubtedly he was disappointed when Jesus, instead of healing him, proceeded to talk to him about his *sins*. He still did not see that in a subsurface sense his illness had a very real connection with his sin, his discord with God, and that Jesus was attacking his illness at its deepest root when he began by settling the problem of guilt in this broken life.

In other words, to all appearances there was nothing left but resignation for the paralytic: "He did not hear, he did not answer my prayer."

But also the bystanders who peopled this scene in great numbers, especially the representatives of the church, who in those days also represented the medical profession, may well have been estranged and disappointed when Jesus instead of performing a miracle administered forgiveness of sins; or better, seemed to administer forgiveness (for the act of forgiving sins is hidden from everybody else and therefore cannot be verified). I can imagine them saying, for example, "Just look at him, he's making a cunning move to dodge the issue; instead of performing a visible healing, he's taking cover in the inscrutable realm of a spiritual, metaphysical process. This wonder-worker is evading precise diagnosis by taking flight into metaphysical assertions that cannot be tested. Obviously he is so anxious to retreat that he is even willing to risk the charge of blasphemy in order to escape the disgrace of being a feckless miracle-doctor. That's easy, that's cheap."

This is what they were thinking. But Jesus himself, we are told, divined all these secret conjectures and suddenly cast this pointed question into the evil operations of their thoughts, "Which is easier to say . . . , 'Your sins are forgiven,' or to say, 'Rise, take up your pallet and walk'?" Naturally, the first thought of the bystanders is that it is *much* easier to say, "Your sins are forgiven," because this is something that cannot be verified; so the other is infinitely harder. Then Jesus said, "That you may know that the Son of man has authority on earth to forgive sins . . . rise, take up your pallet and go home." And it was done.

When we allow these two profound actions to have their effect upon us, I think our first impression will be that the object of the miracle in this story seems to be to furnish a sensational, convincing practical evidence of what took place in the preceding act of forgiveness of sins on the level of the invisible and unverifiable, which therefore could be doubted. That is to say, after the first act of the forgiveness of sins one might have seen some long faces, doubting, mocking looks, and perhaps also a look of depressed disappointment on the countenances of those who were on the side of the Nazarene. But after the corroborative miraculous act the situation was suddenly changed. What we see now is general consternation, a tremendous shock-effect, and we hear people breaking out in songs of praise and spontaneous exclamations: "We never saw anything like this!" What we are witnessing here, these people are saying, is an absolute exception, a tremendous manifestation of authority which cannot be doubted (after all, we are actually seeing it).

So once more we say: here the object of the miracle seems to be (and this, of course, is in harmony with the popular conception of miracle) simply to translate the invisibility and therefore doubtfulness of divine things into the visible, and thus make it certain. Or, to put it in another way: Whereas the first act, the forgiveness of the man's sins, is in no way clear and convincing, the miracle of healing the paralytic is something that can be medically observed and tested because now the means of diagnosis are at hand.

So in this miracle Jesus seems, so to speak, to be seeking to get hold of a medical attestation. If he succeeds in securing this clear evidence, he will be officially accepted as a miracle-worker and therefore proved to be the Messiah.

Just think of this for a moment, translated into the present and thus in terms of the best form of illustration. Imagine that the medical faculty of some great university had decided on the basis of careful scientific and medical diagnoses to attest the genuineness and credibility of all of Jesus' healings and raisings from the dead. I suspect that this would have an extraordinary effect. All the talk, all the discussion about this Nazarene, as to whether he is of Aryan origin or a Jew, whether he is a heroic martyr or an unworldly bankrupt—all this would stop.

But at the same time we recoil from the thought of a medical faculty doing this, not only for the external reason that we know very well that this would never happen. Rather it is above all an inner reason that makes us feel uncomfortable about this idea, for we perceive that, if all the students who heard this medical diagnosis began to applaud and broke out in cheers for the wonder-worker of Nazareth, somehow this would really be missing the meaning of miracle, and even the enthusiasm of these students would have nothing to do with the reality we Christians call "faith." Why not?

I have purposely drawn the extreme consequences of the generally prevailing conception of miracle so that we might have a clear contrast between what we normally conceive of as miracle and what the Bible means by the miracles of Jesus. There are three considerations that prevent us from thinking of miracle as a "proof," a datum for medical diagnosis. (Here we are approaching from still another angle the thought discussed in the last chapter, namely, that miracles are "conceivable," but cannot be "proved" and thus stripped of their "mystery.")

First, if miracle were to be understood as "proof," this would mean that Jesus, by performing miracles, was putting *sight* in the place of *faith.* And in this story it would mean that one must simply *believe* that the forgiveness of sins took place, simply *trust* that Jesus had the authority—taking his word for it; whereas the healing of the paralytic could be *seen*.

Hence, if miracle had the significance of "proof," this would mean that one would no longer need to *believe*, but could rather *see*.

Now actually we do know that the hour will come when faith will end and will see what it has believed. And the hour will come when unbelief, too, will end and will be *compelled* to see what it has *not* believed. But we know that this moment of sight will be the last moment of history, the moment when Jesus Christ will come back at the end of history to judge the living and the dead. Now, however—and this is the central teaching of the Bible—it has not yet been given to us to see God face to face, now we are still in the state of faith and pilgrimage, still in the state of waiting for that moment, that *last* moment when we shall lift up our heads. Hence it would be completely unbiblical to think that the function of miracles is to substitute sight for faith. We are still in the forecourt of that sanctuary of final fulfillment where God will be "all in all."

Second, if the function of miracle is to make faith unnecessary by providing visual evidence, then we should have to regard it as a very cheap propaganda act. We should have to say (and, quite frankly, I would not know what to reply to this) that the message of Jesus, his person, and his actions do not convince people by their power and authority. But, after all, we demand of every thinker and writer that he convince us, not by means of political and military power or some other nonintellectual means, but rather that he compel us to agreement by the weight of his arguments. So this would be to assume that Jesus had *not* succeeded in convincing us through his inner authority. Then because Jesus does not convince through his intellectual authority and thus cannot prevail in this way, he is compelled to resort to miracle. And when anybody has to resort to this cheap propaganda method, this certainly does not argue well for his authority.

Then there is the other, equally aggravating, factor that at best miracles can have a convincing effect only upon one who is present to experience them and thus receives an immediate impression. For all who were born later, like us today, these miracles quite automatically cease to be proofs, for, after all, we did not witness the miracles; we have only reports of them and the reports can be false. Our relationship to them therefore is very indirect. "It is one thing to experience a miracle; it is quite another thing merely to receive a report about a miracle." So said that great and honest skeptic Lessing.

In other words—and this can summarize our second point—mere corroborative miracles, mere miraculous proofs whose purpose is to substitute sight for faith, are more likely to undermine the authority of the message than to vindicate or even to enhance it.

Third, this is in fact Jesus' own attitude toward his miracles. All through the Gospels we can observe Jesus fighting a passionate battle against the popular concept of miracle which is still widespread among us. We recall the well-known story in Matthew 12:38 in which the people come to Jesus and say, "Teacher, we wish to see a sign from you," the implication being that if he performed a sign they could believe in him. Jesus refused in the most blunt and brusque way and said, "An evil and adulterous generation seeks for a sign; but no sign shall be given to it except the sign of the prophet Jonah"; and that was the end of it.

It is very interesting that here in response to a demand for a sign Jesus should refer to the "evil and adulterous generation" which is inclined to hanker after miracles, and that he should thus in a very drastic way denounce the inner attitude of those who have a mania for miracles. What does he mean by this rebuke? I believe that in order to understand this remarkable saying we can turn to another saying of Jesus, namely, John 7:17, "If any man's will is to *do* his will, *he*"—and *only he*—"shall know whether the teaching is from God or whether I am speaking on my own authority"—in other words, whether I am the Christ or whether I am speaking in my own name and thus am only a charlatan. Only he who *does* the will of the Father will ever find out—nobody else.

And this means that only he who places his whole life at God's disposal and surrenders to his will, only he who comes to him in the right *attitude* discovers who Christ is. Only he approaches God and Christ from the right angle; only he stands at the point where he can see him. When, for example, I do not know what to do with Christ, when I am assailed by every possible doubt, then the thing for me to do is to *do* something for him, in his name help another person whom otherwise I would not have helped, or forgive another person something that is terribly hard to forgive, something that is hard for natural man to do. I should "do" this for once "in his name." Or for once I should in his name speak out for him in a company where this may bring down scorn upon me. I should "do" all this for him, "as if" he were already my Saviour. I should stake my whole life on him, "as if" he really mattered. And then, when I do his will in this way, I will find that, strangely enough, my doubting thoughts will also be set at rest. Faith is a matter of *life,* not of *thought.* If for once I try *living* for him, try carrying out and translating into reality the kind of thing we have just mentioned, then my thinking, too, will be set to rights.

So he who acknowledges God and acknowledges him in actual deed, also knows him. And *that's* the order in which it comes about.

We can also express it this way: What is repeatedly preventing us from arriving at a clear and certain faith is not reasons, arguments, and intellectual doubts, but sin. That is to say, we all by nature have an interest in not letting ourselves in for an encounter with God. Accordingly, our reason obliges us by furnishing us with reasons, doubts, and intellectual scruples. Every pastor who has ever had even a little glimpse behind the scenes knows that behind most of the questions of doubt that are brought to him there is something rotten in this person's life that makes him want to keep God out of it. Jesus is alluding to this when he says that only he who *does* the will of his Father in heaven will find out who he is. Or to put it the other way around: anybody who refuses to submit himself to this will of God will never get anywhere by thinking, reflecting, brooding, or even by a Faustian search for meaning; he simply treads water.

Now perhaps we suddenly understand that passage about the

people who demanded a sign. When Jesus administered such an abrupt snub to that demand—"An evil and adulterous generation"—he was saying, "You people who demand a sign belong to this type of person who will not surrender their lives, and therefore will never find out who God is and who I am. And precisely because you will not surrender your lives, you want a very cheap proof of Christ. You want me to play a few tricks, turn stones into bread, defy the law of gravity, or something else that never happens otherwise, to prove to you that I am something out of the ordinary. And after I have done it you will say, 'Yes, there must be something to this man.' And then you would go back home as if you had attended a variety show and go on living just as you did before. And as you know, no man has ever yet been transformed by a variety show."

So Jesus sees in these people who demand a sign a peculiarly nasty, craven type of human being who does not take the Christ question seriously. Jesus is known only as a man stakes his life on him, that is, in faith and in deed, or he is not known at all. Therefore he also rejects the cheap proof of God provided by miracle, because you can calmly accept that kind of proof and still remain the same old scoundrel you were before. In other words, Jesus rejects miracle wherever people use it to escape personal decision and to shirk putting their own faith into action. He abstains from any cheap miracle propaganda whatsoever, because he knows that with this kind of propaganda you never win people at the ultimate center of their lives. When something like this happens they stand there for a moment in astonishment, but then the spiritual fireworks subside and the shadows of night close in again about the heart. But Jesus wants men's faith and heart, he wants the *center* of a man's life, his utterly personal decision. Only so can he become our Saviour. That's why he rejects any kind of cheap impression made by miracles, for this reaches only the extreme outer defenses of the soul, and perhaps not even that but only the nerves. In any case, he certainly does not intend to render superfluous the innermost act of faith by employing a miracle that appeals to "sight," a demonstration that simply overwhelms.

And the conclusion that follows from this is that the healing of the paralytic, despite all superficial appearances to the contrary, was *not* intended to reinforce the invisible act of forgiveness by a visible act of healing. There *is* no proof, or better, there dare not be any. This should now be clear to us.

But if all these purposes of the miracle are out, then what is the purpose of it?

Let us examine carefully what Jesus says in the *first* act of the story of the paralytic, namely, the forgiveness of the man's sins. What does he say, or rather what does he not say with regard to sin? Characteristically, he does not say: "Now listen, you paralytic, we men are all sinners and God is a judge. But in certain cases he can allow grace to be reckoned as righteousness. And it is conceivable in your case too, my poor man, that God may make an exception and allow you to be healed." Now, if Jesus had said that (but of course he did not say it), then he would have been merely enunciating a general doctrine about God. He would have been saying that in the last analysis God is identical with the moral order of the world, with the law of guilt and retribution— "all guilt is avenged on earth"—and God is the executive officer who carries out this retribution, this avenging. But occasionally he makes an "exception." If Jesus had said this, he would have been stating a "doctrine" of God, he would have been a teacher, a theologian, a savant; and there have been many such at all times who have set forth their theories about God, fate, judgment, and the moral order of the world. He may even have had a *higher* idea than that of all previous thinkers, but still it would have been only a "good idea."

But the fact is that something happened in this story that was totally different from anything that ever happened before in the history of ethics, philosophy, or religion. That is to say, the moment Jesus said, "Your sins are forgiven," he was not "teaching," but "acting." He says, "Your sins *are* forgiven." And in more precise terms this means: "It is true, of course, that God visits the iniquity of the fathers upon the children; it is true that the principle of retaliation prevails in the world, and also that God applies this principle of retaliation in the punishment of the guilty; it is true that the law of guilt and punishment obtains. But look, my poor man, now you have met *me* and I have the authority to take your hand and put it back into the hand of the Father. By my word I can open the closed door of the Father's house for you; look, it's opening now. I say to you, it's opening, and you are God's child again."

This is what Jesus does. Or, to put the stress differently, this is what he *does*. With a mighty arm he grasps the spokes of that gigantic crushing wheel of guilt and retribution that rolls like a juggernaut over us all and brings it to a stop precisely before the man who looks upon Jesus with believing eyes and who trusts that he can do this. Albert Schweitzer, the great theologian, physician, and artist, once expressed this in vivid imagery, saying that Jesus himself still hangs on Golgotha, a mangled corpse caught in the spokes of the world's wheel, which he has brought to a stop.

So we insist, Jesus does not *teach* the possible forgiveness of sins, he *accomplishes* it, he *enacts* it. Jesus does not *talk* about the chains of guilt and does not deliver an ethical lecture on what is good and what is evil; he *bursts* the chains so that they fall clattering to the ground.

Let me take the Lord's Supper as an illustration of what happens here, for in this sacrament there comes a moment which constitutes an exact parallel of all that has been said. After the minister has asked in the confession those who are participating in the Communion whether they "truly acknowledge, confess, and lament" their sins and they reply "Yes," he makes this declaration: "As a minister of the church of Christ, and by his authority, I declare unto you the entire forgiveness of all your sins: in the name of the Father, and of the Son, and of the Holy Ghost." Don't you see, in this tremendous moment of the Lord's Supper the minister does not talk about there being such a thing as forgiveness in the world or a "loving God"; he *declares* this forgiveness in the name of Jesus Christ. This Word spoken from the altar is not just *teaching;* it is an *effectuating* Word. And whenever in the liturgy of the Lord's Supper I am privileged to utter the words, "the forgiveness of all your sins," I want to add in thought, " 'Rise, take up your pallet and walk.' Now you can really go away a new man, now something has really happened to you, something that wasn't there before. I have not merely been teaching and instructing you as we do on some occasions. Rather now something has broken into your life. Now you can 'go home,' really born anew and in the name of this miracle, this new beginning which God has bestowed upon you."

In taking this look at the Lord's Supper, you must not think we have been digressing. On the contrary, this is the point from which the miracle of the paralytic really becomes clear. In this miracle, this miracle of healing, Jesus is not trying to validate and prove his power to forgive sins; rather through this miraculous act he is saying: *When I call a halt to this disease, this is an authoritative intervention in the course of natural law; and in exactly the same way, it is an authoritative intervention in the law of guilt and retribution when I say, Your sins are forgiven.* So here it is very clear that both are *acts*, both are *interventions* in the iron forces of law; here a "stronger one" (Luke 11:22) is at work; here the Son of God is in the fray. *That's the meaning of this miracle, that and nothing else!*

So, if we may reduce what we have said to one succinct sentence, this is what we must say: The purpose of this miracle is not to "prove" and therefore be something "more" than the Word, but rather to *expound* and *interpret* the Word. It expresses the fact that the Word of forgiveness is not a matter of teaching and docrine, but rather of an *act*: Your sins *are* forgiven! Rise, take up your pallet and walk! Both—the forgiveness of sins and the healing—are two sides of the same thing.

We have had to take some time and labor to arrive at this decisive point. But it is also the strategic point from which we can now view and deal with the whole problem of miracle. Everything else follows almost of itself.

Now at one stroke an important characteristic of all the New Testament miracle stories becomes clear to us: by no means are these miracles intended to coerce and force men to intellectual capitulation. This, of course, would have to be the case if they simply put sight in the place of faith. All of us have eyes in our heads, and if miracle were only a matter of seeing, a matter which is subject to diagnosis, then every person who sees it would simply have to capitulate; then even the most crass and frivolous scoffer would simply have to bow and submit.

Instead of this, what we observe in all the miracle stories is just the opposite.

The first thing we observe is this: *these miracles do not relieve*

*a person of the necessity of making an altogether personal deci-
sion with regard to Christ, but actually confront him with that
decision.*

And here again I refer you to an extremely interesting and remarkable passage. In Matthew 12:22-32 we are told the story of
the blind and dumb demoniac whom Jesus healed. The reaction
to this miracle is quite the same as that in the story of the paralytic: universal amazement. The people were perplexed and nobody, not even the strongest, could deny that now the man could
actually *see* and that he also actually *heard* and *spoke* and was
inwardly liberated. Nobody could deny this; we are left in no
doubt about that. But now, just when one would think that everybody was convinced, the Pharisees made a very characteristic
assertion. They said that this Nazarene had driven out the demon
by Beelzebub, that is, by means of a superior demon. Expressed
in modern terms, this means that the fact that he performed this
healing miracle is no sign at all that he is in league with God. No,
he is in league with the devil; he has sold himself to Mephistopheles. So this "perfectly unambiguous" miracle did not convince these people at all, but actually drove them into extreme
opposition. For all the unambiguousness of its performance cannot conceal the deep and dubious ambiguity of the sign under
which it is performed, and therefore it does not relieve man of
the hazard of a decision, but actually thrusts him into it and thus
remains entirely within the realm of the Word, which likewise
compels decision.

We see the same thing in other passages, in Matthew 21:23, for
example. There the people say to Jesus, again after a perfectly
straightforward miracle had been performed, "By what authority are you doing these things, and who gave you this authority?"
In other words, they do not doubt the fact that a miracle has
occurred, but they do doubt that it has been done by *divine* power.
They consider it possible that it was performed by some demonic
or occult or fakir's power. This is the question of authority which
is constantly being presented to the miracle-worker. And in this
story we have perhaps the very clearest indication that miracle
is not intended to be a visible, verifiable proof. For here again
we see two things very clearly.

First, the miracle demands of people a completely personal decision. That is to say, they have to decide for themselves what they are going to do about the person Jesus Christ. They, the Pharisees, the skeptics, and all who were there, just as we today, have to decide whether this Jesus is really in a special, unique connection with the higher world. They have to make up their minds (in a word, "decide") whether they want to see in him the Lord to whom all power in heaven and on earth has been given, so that he can command the elements and break the powers of fate and destruction. They have to make up their minds (in a word, "decide") whether they want to see in him the lightning of the coming kingdom, that kingdom in which there will be no more mourning, no more crying, no more death. They have to make up their minds whether they are going to see in him the representative of this kingdom or whether he is a magician, a cunning spiritual operator who deals with dark, occult forces.

This entirely personal decision which we must all make, and of which no miracle can relieve us, cannot be evaded by means of an exact diagnosis of miracle and therefore by scientific observation. For no matter how incontrovertible the miracle may be (the people of that time, especially these ecclesiastics and physicians, were not exactly such fools, either, as to let themselves be bowled over by any fakir who came along; they too had a good measure of perception and skepticism in their make-up) the real question of decision still remains: Is this miracle of God or of demonic powers —Beelzebub and Mephistopheles? By what authority does he do this? Who is this man? Still we face the awful question: Shall we call him God or the devil?

This is the critical question to which we men are driven by miracle, and we cannot escape either to the right or the left. This decision really goes to the depths of a man's personal life. And men, you and I, will be able to decide that the miracle is of God only if we are willing at the same time to acknowledge this Jesus of Nazareth as *Lord,* and therefore only if we surrender to him the burden of our personal sin, suffering, and care. If we are not willing to do this, then naturally we immediately have an interest in discrediting every miracle, that is, in declaring them to be demonic tricks and hence not binding upon us.

Accordingly, Jesus is not trying to *prove* anything by his miracles; his purpose is rather through his active, effectual Word to compel us to personal decision. And therefore his miracles are by no means intended to have the effect of *propaganda*. That is, they never have the effect of simply bowling over the spectators and compelling them willy-nilly to applaud. Rather in all the miracle stories we observe the bystanders immediately separating into two parties.

Upon one group the miracle has the effect of illuminating the previously spoken Word, and therefore they must capitulate when Jesus says, "Rise, take up your pallet and walk," because now they must acknowledge that what he said before, "Your sins are forgiven," was not merely a "word" but a "deed." They recognize that here someone is "acting" with authority and that his Word has the character of an act.

Upon the other party the effect is just the opposite, namely, obfuscation and stubborn rejection. They are looking into darkness instead of a marvellously lighted landscape. "Seeing they do not see, and hearing they do not hear, nor do they understand"; and they simply make excuses, "It was nothing but a fakir's trick," or "He is in league with the devil." Thus they evade Jesus' claim. In other words, the miracle does not surpass the Word, but rather expounds it. And therefore miracle shares in every respect the same fate as the Word: it is not unambiguous but hidden, it is subject to misunderstanding and challenge, and it demands decision.

This brings us to a *second* point. Because miracle is not intended to be a "proof" of the Word, but rather shares its fate in every respect, it possesses a very important characteristic, for which we may use the rather awkward term "mistakableness." That is to say, the Word and miracle are never unmistakable and unambiguous. One can, for example, "mistake" the Word of God for the religious emanation of a particular race, such as the Jewish–Near East race. One can say this is the intellectual expression of an alien culture. Or one can mistake the Word of God for a general doctrine about God, like those of the philosophers. The Word of God is defenseless against all mistaken ideas. And the remarkable thing is that it *wants* to be defenseless, for God does *not* want to force us to repentance, to bow the knee to him. God does not shout down from heaven with loudspeakers simply to make us stop, listen, and conclude that this is a "different" voice from that which we ordinarily hear in the world. He speaks to men in all quietness and calls them to decision.

And so it is exactly with miracle. A miracle can be mistaken for a fakir's trick, for example, or for demonic and occult practices. Miracle is likewise defenseless, and it makes itself defenseless against misinterpretation. Miracle likewise is not intended to coerce men and overwhelm them by the force of its demonstration. On the contrary, it leaves men, all of us, the freedom of decision; indeed, it literally forces it upon us. The story of Paradise is the clearest sign of this. There is only one compulsion miracle would exercise, and that is to use our freedom to stop and make our decision about what we are going to do with Jesus. And as a matter of fact this is the effect it has. Not one of us can read or listen to the healing miracles of the New Testament without making a decision. Either you say, "My Lord and my God, I too am sick, I too am sinful, I too am one who walks to death where no man can help us across, I too need you. The great wheel is in your hand, my Lord and my God." Or you say, "Depart from me, you magician"—even if this is expressed only by a shake of the head or a shrug of the shoulders, or the words, "I don't know what to do with such things."

This is what we mean by the "mistakableness" of miracle; it exposes itself to misunderstanding. I believe that we modern men understand this very well. When it comes to any miracle that happens in our life today we are in exactly the same situation, except that we moderns are not so likely to mistake the wonderful providences of God in our lives for demonic, diabolical powers, but rather for natural laws or fate or accident or fortune.

In any case, however, this "mistakableness" is evident here too. May I recall just once more the example of what happened in my own life, that miraculous healing by means of the medicine which was discovered just in time to save my life? That was a miracle, don't you agree? All I could say was, "This the Lord hath done!" But at the same time it is quite clear that logically this miracle consisted in a remarkable coincidence of several chains of causality and that therefore I cannot prove to anyone that it was a miracle. From any human point of view it could just as well have been "luck" that caused these two sequences of events to intersect. In other words, modern man is always "mistaking" the miracle, mistaking the hand of God in our life for "luck" and "accident," just as the people in the New Testament mistook it for the finger of "demons."

One thing is certain in any case: whether we see God at work here or a completely *natural* process with its coincidences, does not depend upon whether we are somewhat "religiously" inclined or whether we are cold and objective, with no antennae for "metaphysical things." No, it depends upon something altogether different. We can recognize God in his miracles, in the guidance of our life, for example, *only* if we are willing to *submit* ourselves to his guidance and really *be* children of this Father. Here again it is true that only if we are willing to "do the will" and surrender our whole life to him will we know whether these acts and guidances and miracles are of God. Only then! Only he who is of the truth and lives by the truth hears the message of miracle; nobody else. But if he does so and thus hears the message, then it makes very little difference whether he is religiously inclined or is the sober, realistic, unimaginative type. God finds his children in all camps, among all types and characters. In his house are many mansions and provision is made for change. So here, too, it is not a matter of a dead system but rather of the most vital kind of life.

Not only the Word, not only miracle, but Jesus himself exposed himself to misunderstanding and "mistakableness." You can mistake him for a wandering preacher, a founder of a religion, or a very noble man who in the end suffered shipwreck for his idea. He can be misunderstood, and he is—or rather he *makes* himself —defenseless against the rhetorical question: "Can anything good come out of Nazareth?"

Twice in his life Jesus was confronted with the tempting opportunity to cast off the covering mask of his servant form and his "mistakableness" and stand forth in an overwhelmingly clear and demonstrative way. The first time was when the devil took him to a high mountain in the wilderness and offered him the kingdoms of this world. If Jesus had accepted the kingship of the kingdoms of this world, accepted them perhaps with the noble purpose of Christianizing them, he would no longer have been mistakable; he would have to be recognized as the king of the world, who has absolute power and will not tolerate abuse; for what king would ever suffer himself to be "mistaken" for a beggar? He would have become the king of the world in a clear and unmistakable way and the disciples would have shouted for joy over the banners and emblems of his sovereignty, the clear, unambiguous signs of his kingship. This was *one* temptation.

The other was on the Cross when the people cried out, "If you are the Son of God, come down from the cross. If you come down now, if you mobilize twelve legions of angels, then there is no man living who can say a word against you. Then you will have publicly proved yourself to be the Son of God and everybody will be compelled to capitulate."

Both times Jesus rejected the temptation.

What would he have achieved if he had acceded? Well, if Jesus had indulged in that kind of prodigious, miraculous demonstration of power, he would have produced only a cheap, wholesale Christianity for the great masses. People would have flocked after him, following the law of least resistance, as they have always followed after the great wielders of power in the world, without really making any personal profession. Because Jesus did not want this, he went about incognito, wearing the mask of the servant form, and this is why, as Luther expressed it, he resorted to the concealing cover of the Cross. And now the only ones who can find him underneath the mask are those who meet him in personal decision and say: Here I am and here you have me; you have won! Nobody finds him on the street, nobody experiences an earthquake that miraculously blows his life apart, nobody is overpowered by the marching tread of twelve legions of angels. Only he knows him who stops and stands quite still before him, holding the sacrifice of his own life in his hand. For him he miraculously emerges from the incognito of the Crucified and Reviled and suddenly stands before him as the King with sickle and crown and the Physician who is able to heal his wounds. Jesus Christ is not to be found just anywhere on the streets, nor his miracles either;

he wants to be sought by those who are willing to stake their life on him. Only he who seeks him so will find the track and trail of his miracles, in his own life too.

> God walks through waters dark and deep,
> His path runs through the tide's long sweep,
> His foot may fall you know not where.
> So, too, in life's great sea of cares
> His secret path he never bares,
> To make us seek and find him there.[1]

Seek, seek him with all your heart! For God assures us: "You will seek me and find me; when you seek me with all your heart" (Jer. 29:13).

---

[1] Stanza three of hymn by Heinrich Arnold Stockfleth (1690), *"Wunderanfang, herrlich Ende,"* based on Ps. 77:19. (Trans.)

FATE AND PROVIDENCE | IX

WHEN WE CONTEMPLATE THE SUFFERING AND THE DEV-
astation in this world of ours and ask what God's will is and what
his goals are, cherishing the hope that we shall receive an answer
to our question, we find that in the last analysis his purposes are
hidden from us. As natural men we never escape the vicious circle
of thought in which we ask whether God could not achieve his
ends in some other way and how in a war, for example, he can
allow both the sanctuaries and the gin-mills to be reduced to the
same hideous ruins. For the same reason the Cross of Christ has
always been for disciples and worldlings of all times either a crisis
or a manifestation of faith: Could not God have achieved his
great goal of reconciliation in some other, less bloody way? Why
do we always have to go through blood and tears to reach the
divine shore?

These questions lead us directly into the problem of providence and history, which is again a part of the great complex of
the doctrine of creation and therefore of the first article of the
Creed, which is the basic theme of this book.

Luther's classical explanation of this first article of the Creed
in his *Small Catechism* begins with the idea that creation is not
something in the past, not merely a unique, nonrecurrent act at
the beginning, which is concerned only with the ancient figures
of Adam and Eve, but rather that creation is an ongoing, constantly recurring event of immediate concern to me. A quick review of his explanation will make this immediately clear.

I believe that God has created me and all that exists; that he has
given and still preserves to me my body and soul, with all my limbs and
senses, my reason and all the faculties of my mind, together with my

raiment, food, home, and family, and all my property; that he daily provides me abundantly with all the necessaries of life, protects me from all danger, and preserves me and guards me against all evil; all of which he does out of pure, paternal, and divine goodness and mercy, without any merit or worthiness in me; for all which I am in duty bound to thank, praise, serve, and obey him. This is most certainly true.

That statement declares that there are two ways in which God's act of creation is related to me and the present:

1. *I* was created by him—and therefore not only my "first parents" Adam and Eve, so that the act of creation touches me only through the mediation of all the generations preceding. No, I am directly related to my Creator.

2. God continues to preserve my life, which he created, by providing me with all the requirements for existence, including everything from "reason and the faculties of my mind" to "raiment" and "food." But in saying this about "me," Luther is regarding me as representative of everything that happens in the universe, over which God here and now holds his sustaining and directing hand.

And that applies, in the first place, to the *historical* sector of this total life of the world. Nobody can show us this better than the Old Testament historians and prophets, who differ from all the other historians in world literature in that they constantly and rigorously relate all historical events (victories and defeats, birth and death) to God, the Subject of history. God alone is the unconditioned Actor.

But in the second place, this also applies in exactly the same way to the realm of *nature*. Psalm 104, for example (cited earlier on p. 71), describes the processes of nature not as a self-contained, autonomously functioning mechanism, but rather as a drama in which God is acting at every single moment; and without his sustaining preservation and intervention the world would immediately collapse and, to speak in modern terms, the laws of nature would disappear.

> Thou makest springs gush forth in the valleys . . .
> From thy lofty abode thou waterest the mountains;
> the earth is satisfied with the fruit of thy work . . .
> When thou hidest thy face, they are dismayed;
> when thou takest away their breath, they die . . .

> When thou sendest forth thy Spirit, they are created;
> and thou renewest the face of the ground.

In the eyes of this ancient contemplator nature can be described, so to speak, only in prayer, only as we address the Creator who is acting. He can describe nature only by describing the Thou who creates and sustains it. But even this he cannot do in the form of an objective description, but only as he addresses him. We can talk about the mystery of the world only on the basis of an immediate and personal I-Thou relationship to the Creator, that is to say, only on the basis of *faith*.

Now the question arises how Luther, and before him those ancient historians and psalmists, arrived at these convictions concerning God's providence and preservation of the world. Did they arrive at them through observing life? Did they look at life and find there a just and meaningful apportionment of the burdens of life between the good and the wicked? Did they find in actual life that the good prosper and the wicked always lose out? Did they see, therefore, that a just and meaningful will rules life, to which one could apply the term "providence"? In everything that happens, whether it be the earthquake of Lisbon, the destruction of cities in war, or a poor widow's winning of the lottery, can we say what reasons and purposes of fate are to be found in them?

By no means!

When we look at *history,* no matter whether it be the history of the world or of our own life, viewing it with our natural eyes, it appears to be an inextricable tangle of sense and nonsense, and it would seem to be only a matter of temperament or other background which of these two elements I see more emphatically, the sense or the nonsense.

Hegel, the philosopher of idealism, saw in history a self-unfolding of the world-spirit and thus also thought it possible to find an inner logic in the course of history; therefore in all its stages —thesis, antithesis, and synthesis—it has meaning and purpose.

The opposite pole in the interpretation of history is represented perhaps by the Jewish philosopher of history, Theodor Lessing, who in the twenties wrote a book with the title, *History as Giving Meaning to the Meaningless.* In this book he presents the thesis that what we call history is only a conglomeration of accidents and thus a confused chaos without reason, goal, or meaning. It is only the man who observes this chaos of historical raw material, or even attempts to describe it as a historian, who performs in his thinking an organizing function upon this raw material and forms from it a meaningful structure. But, mark you, this meaning does not lie *in* history, so that we might objectively lift it out of it; the meaning is rather brought to it from the outside and introduced into it.

A remarkable intermediate position between these two views is one that Schiller could sometimes take, for example in his well-known passage: "Know that the sublime spirit" (meaning the man with a great mind) "puts the great things *into* life; he does not seek them there."

So different, therefore, can be the impression that history makes upon the observer that these two extreme interpretations are possible. Nor is there any objective arbitration that can decide between these two possible interpretations. The fact is that for the natural eye meaning and meaninglessness lie indistinguishably side by side in history.

It can also be expressed in this way: history contains within itself the most extreme *contradictions;* at one time these contradictions suggest the conclusion that there is a providence fashioning meaning in this world; at another time (perhaps even the next moment) they make us doubt it all over again.

As an example I give you two such contradictions.

First pair of contradictions:

Proposition *a.* We all know the proverbs: "Pride goeth before a fall," or "Honesty is the best policy," or "Lies have short wings."

All these proverbs, which have come out of observation of life, are statements about certain laws which obtain in the world and which we cannot violate with impunity. In the last analysis they point to a kind of "moral world order" which sees to it that lies are unmasked and maintains the value of honesty. And here it is not absolutely necessary to identify the moral order with a "personal God"; it is quite possible to think in terms of a world economy that regulates and keeps itself in balance. This economy weeds out all disturbing elements. This view also constitutes a fair outline of the metaphysics of classical German tragedy.

These observations of life then suggest the conclusion that there is a meaningfully operative *providence*. And Bismarck, starting from a similar point of view, said that the revisions of history are more exact and precise than those of the "Prussian Chamber of Audits." Every crime, every injustice, and also every stupidity in historical action—he was saying—must be paid for. But this is just what seems to bring *meaning* into history and to give us a glimpse of something like *providence*.

Proposition *b*. In contrast to these observations there is the observation that completely meaningless and incomprehensible things happen in this world. I have already referred to what we saw happening in the last war: sanctuaries and gin-mills collapsing indiscriminately to the ground. It can happen—and to my knowledge, did happen—that of two neighboring houses, one belonging to a greatly esteemed citizen who had lost three sons in the war and the other to a shameless speculator and profiteer, the home of the decent citizen is destroyed by a direct hit while the other is left unharmed. Staggered by such occurrences, we feel we have to say with Schiller, "Haphazard strikes the lightning," and conclude that there is no providence either.

When we compare these two points *a* and *b* with each other we see at once that they cannot be resolved into a smooth formula, but rather stand in irresolvable contradition to each other. Hence it is impossible for our natural observation to break through to an assured, demonstrable concept of providence.

Second pair of contraditions:

Proposition *a*. People say, "Every man forges his own fortune," and correspondingly also his own misfortune. Here again the assertion is that fortune and misfortune are not accidental but are the result of a very meaningful and just apportionment, namely, the individual's ability to "forge," my own energetic efforts, my ability, and my singleness of purpose.

Proposition *b*. On the other hand, our generation has experienced in full measure the kind of "fate" that circumscribes or even strangles all our own will and action with relentless, overwhelming power. The tragic poets of Greece can tell us dreadful tales about that, and the Germanic religion had its Norns, spinning the fabric of fate at the spring of Wyrd. And like the Greeks, the Germanic peoples also knew that in the end even the gods are subject to the doom of fate, and are even now approaching the twilight of the gods.

In our own day perhaps Oswald Spengler has most impressively set forth the laws of fate that govern peoples and cultures, laws by which even the macrocosmic realms of national and racial civilizations have "their time" and are helpless to prolong their reprieve by any exertion of will or effort. Fate seems to be completely unaffected by our "forging," our merits, and our passing away. Even the greatest of the world's strong men are subject to it (just as are the gods in the Germanic religion) and they rattle their chains in vain when their hour comes. Goethe expresses this with reference to the fate of Napoleon in his drama *Epimenides*.

> Who boldly from the abyss arose
> May, by a fate severe and stern,
> On half this earth his will impose;
> But to the abyss he must return.
> Fear even now boils to the brim,
> In vain will he that dread forestall;
> And all who still would cling to him
> With him to rack and ruin must fall.[1]

Thus Napoleon, who rose like a meteor from the depths of obscurity and flashed brilliantly across the sky, must fall precipitously to his ruin. Neither genius of will or of mind can alter in the least this parabola of fate: "to the abyss he must return."

Again the result is that these two statements, *a* and *b*, namely, that every man forges his own fortune and that, on the other hand, fate pitilessly tramples upon his ambitions and achievements, cannot be reconciled and thus foredoom to failure any conclusion that there is a governing providence at work. We can phrase this result as follows:

History has in it *too much sense* for us to be able to regard it as a gigantic playground of the forces of blind chance.

History has in it *too much nonsense* for us to be able to deduce from it a purposeful providence that guides it.

Thus history lies in a strange twilight which we must explore further. In any case, it is not clear and transparent in the light of

---

[1] Goethe's *Des Epimenides Erwachen* ("Epimenides' Awakening") has not to my knowledge been translated into English, and the reader must be content with this effort. (Trans.)

God (at this point this is the most important thing to realize). It is obvious that still other factors are at work here.

So already at this point we realize that when we Christians talk about "providence" this cannot mean that in every event we are able to ascribe the cause to God. The case of the destruction of churches instead of gin-mills would forbid that conclusion. Nor can we discover any formula in which the contradictions of history are resolved. On the contrary, if at this point we are ready to use the word "God," we find ourselves repeatedly confronted by the *hidden* God whose ways we cannot fathom.

And here we run into the deepest mystery of the problem of providence. Expressed negatively, it consists in the fact that there is no such thing as providence in the sense of a "moral world order" or a self-balancing metaphysical world mechanism. At the place where we look for this mechanism stands the Father of Jesus Christ. It is this *personal God* who "provides," "foresees," "determines," "resolves."

The mystery of the world, therefore, is not resolved in a formula, but rather in a personal decision or decree.

This is an extraordinary shift in our thinking. Let me try to make it easier with an example.

Two countries find themselves at war with each other. The general staff of one of the two countries knows exactly what are the principles of strategy of the other general staff. Moreover, their agents are able to furnish them with the other party's plan of deployment, which has been worked out in precise accord with these principles of strategy. So they know the formulas and principles as well as the practical directives for carrying out these principles. Thus the situation is clear and predictable.

But the situation is immediately changed—really changed and not merely so construed—when the strategic plans are not simply fixed on paper, but rather have their source in the *decisions* of the commander-in-chief, which as such are not "predictable," because the commander-in-chief can always make use of freedom and resort to improvisation. The strategy is therefore no longer a calculable system but rather a matter of personal decisions. But as soon as we enter the personal level, we can no longer determine beforehand what the next step will be. Nor can we explain at first many of the reactions of the enemy commander-in-chief, and at first many of his maneuvers appear to be meaningless. In other words, I cannot explain for the very simple reason that I do not know what he has in mind, what he is thinking. And often he may even try to conceal his thoughts, so that at first we cannot discern any congruence between his strategic plan and the externally visible realization of it.

All examples, all comparisons are imperfect, especially when we come to illustrate the problems of God's governance by reducing it to earthly proportions.

Nevertheless, the situation is roughly what this example shows: There is no such thing as providence as a "system" of world order any more than there is a battle plan which is set down on paper and intended to be followed in *purely* mechanical fashion. Providence is rather contained within the "higher thoughts" of God that determine his personal decisions. The world and our destiny lie in a "hand"; they are laid upon a "heart" that is concerned about us. So there is profound significance in the fact that here the Bible and the church always have to resort to very "personal" words.

From this there follow two consequences to which we must give further consideration. In concluding this chapter we merely indicate what they are.

1. Providence cannot be reduced to an *objective* formula which would simply solve the mystery of what happens in the world. It rests upon the *personal* decisions of him who "provides" (in the literal sense of that word, which means "to foresee").

2. But then, logically, the only way I can get at the mystery of providence is to enter into a personal relationship with him who "provides." And because I learn to know his heart in Christ and because I trust him, I am no longer irritated by the dark and impenetrable parts of his providence. So we understand the attitude of the author of Psalm 73, who does not get at these dark passages by seeking and finally discovering *reasons* behind the mysterious leadings of God, so that he can then say, "Because of such and such, God did this or that." Rather he confesses and declares (and does so in the face of impenetrable *darkness*): *"Nevertheless,* I am continually with thee"; in thee the darkness is made light, and therefore, if only I have thee, "there is nothing upon earth that I desire besides thee."

FAITH IN PROVIDENCE— CHRISTIAN AND SECULAR

WE MAY SUMMARIZE THE CONCLUSIONS OF THE PRECED-
ing chapter as follows:

No unambiguous clue for the existence of a providence can be found in experience.

Providence lies in God's "personal thoughts." We have access to his providential hand only as we become his *children.*

Christian faith in providence therefore is always faith in spite of appearances to the contrary. It is armed with that defiant "Nevertheless," and stands shaken before the fact that there is no discernible plan and thus no perceptible hand that governs the events of history, but notwithstanding lives in the name of that hand and in the name of that plan, because it knows the Father of Jesus Christ.

Paul Gerhardt's hymn "Commit thy way, confiding" is a classic precept showing how one can understand and withstand this hellish trial of temptation. This hymn is by no means a mere simple "Christian optimism"; it expresses all the hells of tension and distress that come from faith impugned. It speaks of Satan's forces that resist God's plans and every conceivable demon, even of the terrible silence of God:

> Should Satan league his forces,
>   God's purpose to withstand;
> Think not their rage and curses
>   Could stay his lifted hand.
> When he makes known his pleasure,
>   The counsel of his will—
> *That,* in its utmost measure,

Will he at last fulfill.
'Tis true, that for a season
He may his gifts restrain,
And leave thee room to reason
If all thy trust be vain;
Or, while thy hopes shall waver,
And fears and griefs prevail,
To ask, "Must then God's favor
And all his mercies fail?"[1]

Faith in divine providence has to go through all these fiery
furnaces of satanic challenge. And the hymn then rises to a mighty
crescendo in the words: "Blessed be thou, thou child of faithfulness!"

And that already indicates how the Christian overcomes the
onslaughts upon his faith. It does not say: Blessed be thou, thou
thinker, thou philosopher who with thine ingenious mind hast
found the cosmic formula that resolves the enigmatic and tormenting mysteries of the world. Paul Gerhardt knew that worldly
wisdom never catches sight of this formula and therefore never
finds the comfort of providence. Instead he addresses man as the
"child of God," the "child of faithfulness" who clings fast to his
father. Only in this personal, childlike fellowship with the Father
will he get through the dark forest with its frightening specters,
its threatening gullies and pitfalls, and its pathlessness. To become a child of God is the only solution of the world's enigma.

So faith is never something "finished," which one "has" once
and for all and could smugly boast of possessing. No, faith is always traveling a definite way, a particular road. We can characterize the starting point and the terminus of that road by saying
that it is a way that leads from the trial of doubt and despair to
the praise of God. It is the faith of the church militant which, like
that of the writer of Psalm 73, is always in danger of foundering
on the dreadful incongruities of this world, the undeserved fortune of the wicked and the equally undeserved misfortune of the
good. It is the faith of that company of people who, like Job, want
to curse the day of their birth, because the meaninglessness of life

---

[1] Stanzas 5 and 9 of *"Befiehl du deine Wege,"* translated by Henry Mills.
(Trans.)

—especially in times of catastrophe—overwhelms them and forces them to fight their way through to the "Nevertheless" of faith.

But this road to faith goes farther still. For this *Nevertheless* is topped by something that happens on still a higher level: by the songs of praise of the church in glory which has passed from faith to sight and now surveys the depths and wonder of the impenetrable mystery of God's governance of the world.

So faith is really a pilgrimage, a journey on a road from "trial" to "praise" and from "faith" to "sight." Faith is not a self-assured possession (so that one need only to have swallowed a dogma once and for all) but rather the *hope* that praises the day in the midst of might; it is a *waiting* that looks for the coming of the Lord in the midst of the crumbling of all human hopes. Faith in providence is not something you sit on, but rather something you reach out for.

I have already suggested that the popular idea of providence as it is frequently expressed by many people, great and small, wears an essentially different face. It is usually defined by two characteristics.

First, the people believe in a hidden scheme of things that gives order to the world: "God will not allow the wicked to enslave the good," or "The good cause will win out in the end." Schiller expressed the problem in a brief formula when he said, "The world's history is the world's judgment." That is to say, the cosmic economy, by virtue of its inherent autonomy, constantly restores the balance; it eliminates disturbing elements and recognizes the good by giving it abiding value.

But we have already shown that this scheme of world order breaks down, that the good are constantly being "enslaved" by the wicked, and that the heavenly "chamber of audits," of which Bismarck spoke, seems not to function very well (at least within the limited time of a human life, which is all that we are able to survey). Thus the popular notion of providence is constantly leading us into absurdity and ends in meaninglessness.

The *second* characteristic of the popular belief in providence is this. Man has a way—especially one who reaches the pinnacle of human affairs—of imagining that providence is on his side, or even of thinking that he himself is the chosen instrument of

providence. Julius Caesar, and perhaps more impressively Napoleon, believed in their "stars." This was an expression of their
conviction that their individual destiny was interwoven with the
operation of higher cosmic laws. This was why they believed that
no power on earth could topple them or stop them from accom-
plishing their task. As long as they were dependent upon their
own will and their personal initiative, one could still conceive
that a combination of other hostile forces of will might rise
against them and finally overpower them. In other words, one
could then imagine a revolutionary force triumphing over them.
But such a triumph becomes *inconceivable* the moment Napoleon
or any of his modern successors persuade people that they are
the executors of a God-given, providential world plan. For naturally, no human arm can be raised against the law of providence
and its human instrument.

Hegel gave expression to this view of things in his doctrine
of "world-historical individuals." He said that the world-historical
individual, as distinguished from the ordinary individual, does
not live by his own strength but is rather the instrument of the
world-spirit and therefore describes his life-curve with all the
mathematical certainty of a constellation (hence, too, the recur-
rent imagery of a star!), and no human arm can prevent it. In
other words, that which in the last analysis does not depend upon
an individual but is rather accomplished in the name of providence also cannot be hindered by any human individual. Thus
when Hegel looked out of the window of his study in Jena and
saw the Emperor Napoleon on his horse (which doubtless caused
metaphysical thrills to run down his spine), he said, "I have seen
the world-spirit riding by."

*Why did Napoleon and his "world-historical" fellows of yes-
terday and today believe in their stars?* They did so because they
were convinced that their star would be *serviceable* to them. So
thoroughly were they convinced of themselves and their mission
that they believed that the stars were looking at them and that
the heavenly constellation must serve their ends. This perhaps explains the tendency of many of these world-historical individuals
in the past and today—we need only think of Wallenstein and
Hitler—to occupy themselves with astrology. For astrology seems

to be particularly adapted to strengthen them in their belief that their individual life is not limited to the circle of their individuality but is rather a part of the sublime and immutable laws of the macrocosm.

So what we have here is basically a faith in oneself, a piece of self-worship which employs belief in one's star in order to surround oneself with a cosmic aureole; even the stars must serve the great man.

Immanuel Kant, that very prudent man, said with reference to this attitude of world-historical individuals: "The intention of all of them is to manage to their own advantage the invisible Power which presides over the destiny of men."[2]

Here we must pay very close attention. The attitude of these "world-historical individuals" toward providence and the laws of the cosmos is by no means that of obedience and humble subordination, but rather that of arrogant endeavor to make these laws serve their purpose. At its greatest heights (these highest representatives of mankind have shown) humanity betrays its most secret tendencies, namely, rebelliousness, the desire to be at the center of the world and to degrade God to a mere function of its own desires—even when all this is disguised in sham humility, as if they were acting in accord with a "higher mandate." Nietzsche saw most deeply through this fundamental attitude of man when he suggested that every one of us wants to be more than everybody else, but most of all, to be God himself.

In view, then, of this attitude toward providence, a very definite law of history seems to come into operation, for the boundless assurance which the world-historical individual receives from the certainty that he is the instrument of providence and that his life has been given a metaphysical planetary orbit leads him, in accord with the primal law of all tragedies, to that *hubris,* that pride, which "goeth before destruction." According to Goethe's poem, Napoleon had to return to the abyss from which he rose, and this path of Napoleon is only one of many that have been followed in the world's history—and are still being followed today.

But then with this inevitable downfall of the world-historical

[2] *Religion within the Limits of Reason Alone* (New York: Harper Torchbooks, 1960), p. 164.

individual there comes the *collapse of faith in the star and in providence*. The last act of such interpretations of history is resignation and a *plunge into meaninglessness:* the journals of the lonely man on St. Helena furnish eloquent testimony of that, and Shakespeare's *Julius Caesar* does so, too.

So for this human, autarchic faith in providence there comes with deadly certainty the moment when the cosmic order, which one thought one could discern and to which one gave the name of providence, collapses before one's eyes and its place is taken by blind, meaningless, cruel *fate*—the moment when nihilism celebrates its triumph. The end of *this* kind of faith in providence is always belief in fate.

Thus we can draw a sharp line between the Christian and the secular faith in providence:

The *Christian* faith, grounded upon personal trust in the Father of Jesus Christ, leads from doubt and despair to praise. The *secular* belief leads from self-security to resignation.

The *Christian* belief in providence leads from despair over the invisibility and imperceptibility of God to the "Nevertheless" of faith. The *secular* leads from belief in providence to the darkness of fate.

This brings us, then, to the point where we can tackle the question of *providence and history*.

One thing at any rate we have discovered, and that is that providence is not simply the *cause* of everything that happens in the world. If it were, then logically it would be possible to derive all events in history from this cause. In other words, everything that happens (from the birth of an infant to a bomb attack, from a lost war to an examination successfully passed) would be logically explained and clearly discernible as to cause, meaning, and purpose, at least theoretically and for an intelligence which brought to it the necessary prerequisites (Laplace).

But the fact that divine providence in this sense is by no means the cause of everything becomes immediately clear when we keep in view the following two points:

1. In the face of certain events in history we are simply inhibited from regarding God as the author and doer of these acts (for example, the bombing attacks in the war). We know only

too well that here it is not *God* but rather *man* who is at work. It is not God who rains down phosphorus and dynamite; it is man who has drunk from the intoxicating cup of mad destruction and vengeance and is thus destroying himself. With the aid of technology, one of the peak achievements of humanity, the gigantic work of self-destruction goes on. God allows all this to happen, manifestly in order to let mankind find out for itself where it gets to when it ceases to be a family of children bound to God, and when nations and individuals insist upon living their own autonomous lives in separation from God and in distrust of each other.

But the very fact that we express it in this way, the very fact that we say that God "allows" all this to happen means that here God has, so to speak, withdrawn into a state of silent and almost passive permissiveness, of just letting things happen. From the Bible we know that when God leaves man to himself and the destructive instincts with which he has broken away from his child-relationship, this can be the most dreadful judgment of all and therefore the most hidden kind of activity of God. In any case we know only too well (and this is expressed in our use of the term "allow"), that there are other forces at work and that God had permitted them a certain latitude of action.

We would completely misunderstand the mystery of divine judgment if we tried to explain the terrors of the world simply in terms of God as being the "cause." Psalm 104 gives vivid expression to the mystery of God's allowing things to happen in the verse that says: "When thou takest away their breath, they die."

2. When we allow the biblical story of salvation to pass before our eyes we repeatedly meet with events and figures shadowed by a dark enigma. I mention only two examples: "Adam's fall" and that somber figure "Judas Iscariot." It is impossible for us simply to attribute Adam's fall to divine providence. This we are taught by the story of the Fall itself, in which Adam attempts to fix upon God the blame for being the cause of his fall; for there he says, "The woman whom thou gavest to be with me, she gave me fruit of the tree." In other words, "You yourself, God, are the real seducer; *you* used the woman as your instrument." We know how far God was from agreeing with that and how Adam was

compelled to accept his own responsibility. And in the same way Judas Iscariot was not exonerated by the fact that God had included the betrayal of Jesus in his plan of salvation. Judas himself, who hanged himself and thus pronounced judgment upon himself, knew only too well that he had acted, not in the name of God, but rather in the name of dreadful opposition to him.

In these two examples, which could be multiplied indefinitely from the Bible and from life, we perceive not only how impossible but also how impermissible it is to attribute all this to providence. For such a monstrous attempt would make us guilty of assigning to God the responsibility for all the evil that has ever happened. We would be accusing God of what the aged harper says of the gods in Goethe's *Wilhelm Meister:*

> To earth, this weary earth, ye bring us,
> To guilt ye let us heedless go,
> Then leave repentance fierce to wring us;
> A moment's guilt, an age of woe.

In other words, even when we say that this or that has been "allowed" to happen, we are admitting that there is a sector of life in which we simply cannot apply the concept of providence as a cause, not only in the sense that we do not recognize it as the cause, but also in the sense that it would be blasphemy to designate it as such. We are admitting that there is a sector in which we must rather speak of our *opposition* to the Father, or at least of a certain autonomy of human life.

This sector of life we call "history." History is the place where the divine, the human, and the demonic are at work in a mysterious intermixture.

But when we go on to ask precisely what history is, we cannot be so bold as to define it in a few words. We still have some long thinking to do about it.

Let me begin with a fact with which we are all familiar: history is usually in contrast with *nature.* There is a certain justification in this, even though—from the biblical point of view—it does not bring out the central thing in history at all. Nevertheless, from the point of view of method this distinction may be helpful to us; for *nature* is the realm of law, of "natural law," and therefore the realm in which the predictable sequence of cause and effect prevails.

History, on the other hand, is the realm of *man.* But man is in some way distinguished by the fact that he is free, or that he was originally free, but paradoxically, by the very use of this freedom, finally lost it again and prescribed for himself the fate of an enslaved will. In earlier chapters in which we discussed the image of God in man we have already considered the deep creative purpose of God which is expressed in man's original freedom. God did not desire impersonal marionettes which would dance at the flick of his hand; he wanted the "man" who stands over against him in free responsibility. But in doing so, he takes the risk that man may break away from his fatherly dominion. And this precisely is part and parcel of what it means to be a man, namely, that he *can* break away and that therefore his fellowship with God is an expression of his free child-relationship to God. We have coined the phrase: man, the risk of God. And this risk and this freedom also characterize the human realm of life which we call history.

So history is the place where God's providence rules and at the same time the place where (in a mysterious way and within the framework of this providence) man is given a certain independence. And because of this independence which is an inseparable part of the concept of man and his history, the Bible again and again speaks in terms of a *history of rebellion.*

The history of rebellion actually begins with the Fall, with the fact that man did not remain *under* God, but wants to be *as* God and thus play his own role. This is the reason why we feel when we read the first two chapters of the Bible that the paradisal state is something "without history," or better, something "beyond history." It was on the same ground that Schiller came to utter his blasphemous saying that the Fall was "the most fortunate deed in the history of the world," because it was only by this act that freedom was realized and history came into being. In any case, however, there is one thing that is right in that statement: history exists only where there is guilt. This is clearly expressed in literature. One can, for example, look upon a drama or a tragedy as "concentrated history" in which all the features of life are gathered and concentrated as it were in a concave mirror. But it is precisely this concentrated life that is characterized by the fact that it always revolves around guilt and thus always has behind it man's urge toward rebellion. We understand, then, what is meant by the statement that in the biblical view history is always rebellious movement and that therefore, as Erwin Reisner says, it moves "from the Fall to the Judgment."

From the *individual* separation from God that occurred through our first parents, history then went on to *collective* guilt in the building of the tower of Babel, where mankind sought to disengage the whole foundation of its life from God and to build an autarchic, independent construction *without* God.

In this attempt an elemental law of life again manifests itself: man does not find the independence he seeks, but rather falls into the slavery of a terrible bondage. Jesus sketched the outlines of this process in the parable of the Prodigal Son (Luke 15). The son wanted to get away from dependence on the father and the parental home in order to stand on his own feet in the world and fashion his life autonomously. But instead of gaining the freedom he expected, he fell into the toils of his sexual urges, into dependence upon men, his vanity, his hunger, his homesickness; and finally ended in the pigsty, a dreadful symbol of this servitude into which the formerly free child fell. Whenever men throw off the bond that links them to God, they fall into the bondage of idols and demons. There is no such thing as a free and neutral state of suspension between the two, of the kind man looks for, and Geibel's proverbial saying is confirmed: When God is driven out of the door the specters come in through the window. It is always the ancient choice, which cannot be evaded by any neutrality, the choice which Paul said was that of being either a "child" or a "slave." There is no third choice. And hence there is profound meaning in the fact that the last book of the Bible shows mankind's history of rebellion ending, not in the sought-for freedom from God, but in a hideous servitude to demonic powers that goes to the depths of horrible excess.

How different is this biblical picture of history from that, for example, of Gotthold Ephraim Lessing, the philosopher and dramatist of the Enlightenment! In his *Education of the Human*

Race he observes that mankind does need dependence upon God and his guiding hand for a time. And he sees the justification for the biblical revelation in the fact that it was needed "for a time" in order to control and guide men. But the purpose of all education is to make itself unnecessary and the pupil gives poor thanks to his teacher if he always remains a pupil. So at the end of mankind's journey Lessing envisions a conscious and God-approved *liberation* from divine tutelage. At the end he sees the eternal, pure gospel of reason, the autonomy of man, and therefore freedom from the divine educator.

So different are these two ways of viewing history: on one side the movement of separation from God ends in freedom, on the other the movement of rebellion ends among the demons. Only one of the two can be true? Which is it?

In any case, for biblical thought history is an event between God and Satan. It lies in the dark twilight between these two, and even Goethe had some inkling of this when he called history a struggle between "faith" and "unbelief."

But however great may be the leeway that the satanic power possesses in history (and who is not conscious of this today!), however strong may be the rebellion and the opposition, the fact still remains that in the ultimate reckoning even this opposition is included in God's plan for the world and is being guided by God to a goal which the demons themselves never sought. Luther summed up this experience in the rather startling phrase that even the devil is still "God's devil" and must be subservient to his higher goals because God is *his* Lord, too. When the apocalyptic horsemen storm across the earth and the world shakes beneath their hoofbeats, when war, pestilence, famine, and terror lay waste mankind, then we must remember that it is *God* who allows even these powers of destruction to ride, that it is he who waves them on and he who can check them with a flick of his sovereign hand.

This is the hidden structure of providence and God's governance of the world, and it is there even when God has abandoned men to their own self-destruction and seems to be doing nothing but "letting things happen." This is the ultimate comfort of the Christian faith in providence when God is silent and history grows murky and dark.

XI | FREEDOM AND BONDAGE IN HISTORY

IF IT BE TRUE, AS I ATTEMPTED TO SHOW IN THE PRECED-
ing chapter, that history is the realm in which man has freedom,
and often enough even the freedom to rebel against God, then
we must also point out on the other hand that he is by no means
left to do entirely what he pleases. On the contrary, we have seen
that, according to the biblical view, the man who has "freed"
himself from God is always subservient. Jesus made this clear in
the parable of the Prodigal Son, who likewise was eager to slip
off the bonds of the father's house and have his freedom. We see
how dependent he is upon his urges and his ambitions, and how
he ends up in the pigsty as a slave. The man who separates himself from God is always in bondage. Man belongs *either* to God *or*
to the devil, and according to the Bible and according to Luther
he is far less a rider than a horse that is being ridden. And in this
sense we also see two dimensions in history: one in which man is
bound and another in which he is free. I propose to discuss these
two forms of life in the light of the Bible.

First the dimension in which man is bound.

Every one of us is set down in a very definite place in history
which we cannot avoid or escape. For example, we are all con-
temporaries in a very definite epoch. As Oswald Spengler put it,
we are all living in the century of wars, Caesars, and dictators.
We live in the age of world power politics and power struggles.
It is no use for a person to think he would rather be living in an
idyl of Biedermeier or rococo; it would no longer suit his type
anyhow. He has to stick it out *here*, in *this* age, and no matter how
"artistic" and sensitive he may be, no matter how distasteful it

may be for him to have to live in these crude times, there is nothing he can do about it. He has to go on sailing in the same boat with these rude companions; he cannot step out of it. When we say a person is "old-fashioned" or "behind the times" there may be at least a spark of justification in our irony when a person's "old-fashionedness" in appearance, behavior, or views is a sign that he is unwilling to let go of the "good old times," that he is trying to hang on to them artificially, when this is impossible anyhow and every new age puts us in a new situation which we cannot evade but must rather accept. If he is trying to retreat into the age of his youthful habits and customs because he does not like the fact that time moves on, we sense in all this a false attitude toward life.

Jesus once pointed out in a very significant context how infinitely important is the *place* in history where we stand. He was speaking of the people "before" and "after" himself. Thus he once said to the bystanders, "I tell you that many prophets and kings desired to see what you see, and did not see it, and to hear what you hear, and did not hear it" (Luke 10:24). What Jesus is saying is that the people before Christ and after Christ are bound into an entirely different situation. And in this condition of being bound is expressed not merely a *gift* (the fact that it is a blessing to live after Christ), but also a *task* or responsibility.[1] For now all who are born after Christ must come to terms with him. Anybody who lives after Christ and knows of him is simply confronted with the question: What am I going to do about the sin in my life? Hitherto he was not confronted with this question in the same unconditional way. Now that he knows something about peace and reconciliation with God he must ask: What about *my* relationship to God? Everybody must come to terms with him; he can become the hidden torment of men and the rock on which their lives are shipwrecked if they deny him. Even Pilate had to take a position with regard to him, though he was a Roman, and suddenly he found himself, of all places, in the Creed. Herod the king likewise had to take a stand—with all the consequences that this had for the course of history and his per-

[1] The original German here has the familiar play on the words *Gabe* ("gift") and *Aufgabe* ("task"). (Trans.)

sonal life. Some are broken upon that rock (and this army of the wrecked and ruined is headed by Judas Iscariot); others gain all things, and, like Stephen, even in the torments of stoning they look up and see the heavens opening: "Lord Jesus, receive my spirit." But take a stand all of them must—because they live "after Christ." He has fallen like a boulder into the water of their lives and now they must see for themselves how they are going to contend with the waves he causes. He has kindled a fire on earth and they all have to go through it. That's how important the fact is that they are all bound to this situation "after Christ" and cannot get away from it.

Today we are all beginning to realize that it is actually true that we shall never get away from this bond we have with the unrepeatable historical fact of Christ. There are many people who would like to break away from this *post Christum* bond; who would like to revise history. There are neopagans who are trying to get back to a position "before Christ" because they consider the whole history of Christianity in the West a mistake. In other words, they would like to undo these millennia, turn time backward, and step out of history. And in the attempt they make a recommendation that one would have to call downright silly if it were not so tragic. They recommend that, instead of saying "B.C." and "A.D." we should say "before and after the era." As if simply ignoring a fact changed anything; as if the suppression of this shocking Name were not in itself an utterance of it; as if this foolish avoidance did not actually emphasize and proclaim the Name. The fact is that he is the watershed between "before" and "after," he is the "center of history." No, we cannot step out of this chronology "after Christ," for this Christ has fatefully divided the line of time and there is no getting around that fact. We cannot begin a chronology wherever we please, and we can never reverse a line of history. For one thing is sure: the line from Ragnarok and Olympus to Christ cannot be reversed—the old gods are dead.

This road can only lead to nihilism, to an attitude of complete emptiness, beyond which not only Christ but also all the gods have vanished—whether this nihilism be openly acknowledged or whether it be carefully disguised with the paper flowers of a synthetic mythology in order to make it philosophically palatable.

Here we have a basic example of how we are bound up with our history and therefore cannot divest ourselves of the Christian West as one would discard an old dress. We cannot break away from our history. This is what we call the dimension of bondage. We are bound to our history and thus to our historical hour.

Take a *second* example of this bondage. I can never undo or reverse anything that has once happened, a sin, for example, or even a missed opportunity. Every period of my life—and the same applies to the larger history of nations—possesses as it were a door which I can open as I please. Every day, for example, I go through the door of my morning awakening. But once I have entered, it slams shut behind me. This is the mystery of time, which a person who is growing older is more aware of than the young person. I cannot undo anything; time is irreversible. The symbolism of the circular dial of my watch deceives me, for as the hands revolve they give me the illusion that time recurs in a circle; it acts as if time were constantly beginning anew. It begins at one and ends at twelve, only to begin again at one. And this is a lie. For the fact is that my life runs in a *line* and not in a renewing circle. On New Year's Eve, a birthday, or other milestones in our life we note that the period of time that lies behind us is *past*. Even when the clock strikes twelve on New Year's Eve the year does not begin afresh; it has gone on and passed away, and inevitably we find ourselves drawn closer to eternity. Time is a one-way street on which one never returns. In the parish hostel in Korntal there is an inscription: "Time never says 'Until we meet again.'" It compels me to go on and forces me to leave it behind.

And therefore this also means that I must assume all the guilt of my past. It is not as if with time my sins grow old and pass away, as if the weeds grow over them or are eaten away by the "tooth of time"—or whatever other stock phrases we may use to take the sting out of the fate of time. No, they stand before me as an everlasting accusation; I must assume responsibility for them. I cannot undo the past, for this would mean that I could open the closed door again. And that's why the Psalmist prays, "Remember not the sins of my youth!" (Ps. 25:7). And he goes on to say, as it were between the lines, that these sins are *not* subject to revision, but rather, since they are points on the continuing line of time, they continue to have the force of something that is permanently present.[2]

Not until we realize this fact that the tyranny of the time victor compels us to go on do we begin to appreciate the significance of the doctrine of justification taught by the Apostle Paul and also by Luther. For here is where the background and also the deepest meaning of this doctrine comes out. This doctrine of justification tells me that God, by forgiving me and making me his child, opens up a new future for me, a future in which I no longer need to drag along with me the mortgages of my past, because they have been taken away from me: "He has borne our griefs and carried our sorrows" (Isa. 53:4). Christ cancels our *past* and gives us a new *future*. The whole doctrine of justification can be expressed in this one sentence: God cancels our hopelessly stranded history and in its place puts *his* history. Now the history of sonship begins and the history of slavery is ended. And now we can really say (but only here!) what would be a lie anywhere else: "The old has passed away, behold the new has come" (II Cor. 5:17). "The old has passed away"—this means that now the sins of our youth are gone, now the mortgages of the past cannot rise up to accuse us. No more can they torment and mock me; they are wiped away; they are cast into the depths. Or better, they have been laid upon the shoulders of a Lord who accepted them— as a stronger brother helps a weaker—and who was content to die beneath this load. All things have been made new, I have a new future. The Christian always lives by the *future;* more precisely, by the last hour, the last day, the coming again of his Lord. The past is strangely unimportant, and the mystery of life and history lies only in the Coming One. So enormous is the role that time plays in biblical thinking.

In any case, however—and this is what concerns us here—apart

[2] Not until I was reading the proofs of the first printing of these chapters did I come upon the outstanding book by Oscar Cullmann, *Christ and Time: The Primitive Christian Conception of Time and History*, Floyd Filson, trans. (Philadelphia: Westminster Press, 1950). Here the Christian concept of time, which I have only indicated, is discussed fully in terms which the non-theologian will find very readable.

from Jesus Christ we are bound in the bondage of history. And history is irreversible; time runs on in the one-way street that is allotted to it.

But we are bound in still another way. This becomes evident, not so much when we think of history in longitudinal section, as we have been doing so far, but rather in cross section. We find ourselves, for example in a definite state or position in life. And when I say "we find ourselves in," this does not mean that we have "entered into" it. We *are* in it. We are the children of very definite parents, whom we did not select ourselves. We are also either men or women, again something which we did not choose ourselves, and this binds us to the destiny of our sex. (At certain times this can take on a tremendous significance, especially when there is a disproportion in the number of one or the other sex, as in the case of the surplus of women after times of war.) Or we belong to a particular nation. This, too, we did not choose for ourselves. Or we belong to a particular race. And precisely in an age of racial struggle and tension we begin to realize what a fateful significance membership in a race can have.

All these are things that bind me, bondages into which I have been "thrown" and in which I find myself existing.

They also repeat themselves in human *society*: in social position we are either "high" or "low," or to mention a particular form of bondage in the environment and language of the New Testament, we are born slave or free.[3]

Naturally, I cannot think of these various forms of natural and historical bondage in any other way except that it was *God* who set me down in them. And then from this point of view Luther's statement "I believe that God has created me" acquires a profound and graphic acuity. For when I say, "God created me," this means that he created me as a man or a woman, a Greek or a Jew or an Aryan—just as *I* am with all the multiformity of my natural and historical relationships. He caused me to be the child of these particular parents. I receive these bonds and ties, which I did not myself choose, from his hands.

And so because I know that I am bound to my own historical

[3] Cf. the Letter to Philemon.

place and time, I also know where this hour and where I myself come from: from God the Creator. All these bonds we have mentioned pose the question: Whence? *Whence* did I come into this particular place—into this historical hour in the twentieth century, into my biological structure, into my position in life?

So this is the *first* of the two historical dimensions, the dimension of "bondage"; and it confronts us with the question, *Whence?*

The *second* dimension of history is the dimension of the *freedom* required of me.[4] That is to say, on this level which is fatefully determined by my historical situation and my historical hour I now have imposed upon me a certain room for freedom, a certain radius of action.

Let me illustrate this at once. As one who is thus a man or a woman, "slave or free," a child of this or that time, I am now asked what I am going to do about this, what I am going to make of it, and what purpose I will let it serve. In other words, now this is *my* affair, my concern. How am I going to come to terms, for example, with this time of troubles into which all of us have been born? Am I going to take this time of troubles as an excuse to lapse into a paralyzing pessimism or futile fatalism? Or will it serve to make me a gambler, rashly teetering for a while longer on the rafters of a collapsing age and trying to work my way through in order to be among the survivors? Or will I settle with it by accepting it from the hands of God?

What am I going to do with it?—this is the question my *freedom* addresses to me. That I am the child of particular parents, over this I have no control; but what I do with this fact, how I behave myself toward my parents, this is the realm of my freedom and my responsibility, and this is therefore also the realm that is claimed by God's command: "Honor thy father and thy mother . . . " Or to take another biblical example, I have received some definite talents, for example, a very definite gift, of a mechanical or intellectual, secular or spiritual kind. But here again I am asked what I am going to do with this my talent, my gift, my skill; whether I

---

[4] In what follows we do not go into the theological problem of freedom *in extenso,* but rather view it only from one very special point of view; nor do I relate this point of view to the various concepts and cases connected with the idea of freedom.

am going to invest my talent (Luke 19:11 ff.; Matt. 25:14 ff.) or play fast and loose with it, in other words, how I propose to deal with it "in freedom." Freedom has been assigned to me.

Here we see the two dimensions, that of bondage and that of freedom, expressed in clear, sharp contours. We can also express this in another way which brings us to the really central question of this chapter.

The dimension of *bondage* addresses to me the question *Whence?*—whence came my historical time and place, my whole "being as it is"; whence came the totality of those factors over which I have no control, yet which determine me in the profoundest way? The fact that I am bound addresses to me the question *Whence?*

In the second dimension, the dimension of freedom, however, I am asked "to what end" am I here, what do I intend to do with my gifts, my hour, my manhood or womanhood, what am I going to use them *for.*

Thus we see how very really our actual life is determined by these two questions: *Whence* am I what I am, and *for what purpose* am I here, what I am going to do with myself and my "being as it is"? My life, my history, swings between these two poles.

We can put this in another way. God the Creator is by no means merely the "original beginning of life"; he is by no means merely that entity to which only the question *Whence?* pertains, even though it is true that ultimately this question is aimed at the "original beginning." Rather God is at the same time the one who has a definite *plan* and a goal for my life, to which he desires to lead me; he therefore tells me *why* I am here, *to what end* I exist.

It is therefore very characteristic, after that tremendous review of history developed in the ninth, tenth, and eleventh chapters of Romans, that Paul should break out in the hymn: "From him and through him and to him are all things." There really is no other way to describe history except to allow oneself to be led by the question *Whence?* (from God) and the question *Whither?* (to God) to the two poles between which all historical life is enacted. Only he understands his life history aright who considers both: whence he comes and why he is here.

These same key questions apply also to the larger history of the

nations: they were "called" into life by the Lord of history and at
the same time they were "called" to perform a historical task, to
fulfill a mission. Anybody who does not see these two questions
really sees no history at all. In the realm where history should
occur and be seen, he sees only a miserable, meaningless, boring
conglomeration of facts and dates: that a man was born, vacci-
nated, sent to school, arrived at puberty when his voice changed;
that he may have written an important book, and after a long
series of significant and insignificant events died of a heart attack,
and was buried on such and such a day with so-and-so many
wreaths on his grave. This is a pretty insignificant series of accidents and processes of biological laws (which later could be
studied more practically and adequately outside in nature). This
can be illustrated by a police record. The police official would
never claim that he is writing a bit of "history" when he records
a series of events. What he does has only the rank of a chronicle, a
report of facts. "History" comes into being only when I know the
Whence and the *Whither,* the incorporation of an event in an ultimate context of meaning. Friedrich Rückert expressed this with
reference to each man's individual history (though it could apply
equally to the striving of nations toward the realization of their
destiny and their mission) in these well-known words:

> In every man there lives an image
> Of what he ought to be.
> As long as he is not that image,
> He ne'er at rest will be.

In other words, even from an altogether non-Christian point of
view, Rückert is aware of this goal.

In our own time this has perhaps been most beautifully expressed by Joseph Wittig in his small book "On Waiting and
Coming."[5] He says that if one wants to write the story of a man's
life, one must not begin with his *birth,* but rather with his *death.*
Only when the finished life lies before me, only when I can contemplate it as it were from its *goal* (from its goal achieved or un-
achieved), do I see that each individual stage of that life was not
merely "accidental" but rather purposeful and therefore meaningful. Everything moves toward this finished state of a fully rounded

[5] *Vom Warten und Kommen.*

and completed life. Therefore, says Wittig, a life story is not there until death comes, that is, when I can survey it all the way to the end. The objection, which can be raised immediately, that for human eyes even the life which is "completed" in death still remains largely incomplete—because only God sees a man's real life history in its shipwreck or its fulfilment, or in both at once—need not confuse us here. Here we are concerned with the fundamental recognition of the point of view which looks to the *Whither* of a man's life and which Wittig has vividly described in this example, this inadequate example, of the death of a man.

This looking at life from the point of view of its end is a thoroughly biblical idea, for the Bible turns our thoughts not only to the individual human life, but also and above all to the total history of mankind. The Revelation of John is basically nothing else but a prodigious survey of human history in tremendous pictures. And it is altogether characteristic that this survey of world history begins, not with the primordial age or the primitive cell or with Adam and Eve, but with the image of the end of history, the moment when Christ is about to come again. Then this overarching light falls upon the whole of history, including its "worldly" and secularized areas, which—despite their own self-understanding—are all ordered in relation to him, even though his name has here been erased and he himself is hardly an open secret any more. Only as we see this, namely, that all lives end in him and that he stands at the vanishing point of the whole world perspective, do we understand history, understand it in faith. This is the way we understand our own history with its troubles and catastrophes— again, of course, only in faith in that end at which the coming Lord stands. This also explains why it is that in times of great historical distress the church of Jesus Christ has always gone back to this Book of the Revelation of John, often very ineptly but yet always with a right instinct. It does so because all human explanations fail in the face of such epochs of decline when the times are "out of joint" (Hamlet) and the world is in upheaval, and because it knows that we must look to the end in order to lay hold of the directional constants of this seemingly directionless time that is lost in nothingness. This example makes it clear that history can be known only from the point of view of its *goal*.

If I were to translate into Christian words what Rückert says about the image that is to come into being within us, and the rest and peace of destiny fulfilled, I would say: In every man there lives a thought of God, a thought of what God intends him to be, and this he must now make an actuality within himself, and as long as he does not do so he lives in dissension and discord.

Now it is characteristic that, on the one hand in Rückert (and incidentally also in Goethe), and in the Bible on the other hand, we should find a completely different concept of history. In Goethe, for example, his view was such that he said that man is by nature a seed, an entelechy, a "minted form" which "develops as it lives,"—which, as it were, must develop. Our life then is nothing but a development of this "minted form," this seed which is implanted in us. And therefore the goal of my life history is "to become what I am," that is, to bring out of myself and allow to mature that which has been put in me in germinal, minted form. Only when I "become" what I "should become" will I be at rest, at peace. And here "peace" means that I find myself in accord with myself, that there is no longer any contradiction between what I am and what I ought to be. This is Goethe's view, and Rückert's is similar.[6]

The biblical view of history is completely different in that the Bible sees man only in relation to *God* and therefore says that only when man comes to *God* does he also come to *himself*. According to this it would be simply absurd (in what follows I am purposely exaggerating and drawing a one-sided conclusion from Goethe's ideas) for me to begin "becoming myself" by asking what are my innate characteristics, in which direction do my intellectual talents lie, and so on, in order then to develop them in living. This is not the way it goes. Rather, the biblical view says that when I come to God, I come to myself. I am a child of God and precisely for this reason I can realize my destiny as a child only by being with my Father. Only when I come to *God,* therefore, do I come to *myself.*

In the view of the Bible, man is not to be seen at all as an indi-

[6] Cf. Goethe's *"Urworte: Orphisch."* (A prose translation of the "Words of Ancient Wisdom: Orphic" may be found in *The Penguin Book of German Verse,* Leonard Forster, ed. (Baltimore: Penguin Books, 1959), pp. 229 ff. (Trans.)

vidual in isolation, but only as a child in relationship to his Father. And therefore he attains his image, his appointed goal, only when living contact is re-established with the Father, when he is again enclosed in the divine circuit.

The difference between the two views is characteristically expressed in the way in which each interprets the word "peace." Goethe and Rückert interpret peace to mean harmony with oneself, my being what I ought to be. An artist, for example, gains "peace," according to this view, only when he is able to live out his artistic self and thus achieve his appointed destiny, and he remains in conflict and discord with himself when for economic reasons he is obliged to become, say, a truck driver. "Peace" means harmony with oneself.

In the Bible, however, "peace" really means "peace with God"; it means that real peace has been concluded between two entities, between God and me. "The awful feud is ended." And now that objective peace has been concluded between these two entities, all the tension and rebellion ceases and is brought to peace in sonship. Thus the subjective peace of a man's heart is related to an objective "treaty of peace"; it is dependent upon his finding his proper order under God. Hence this peace of heart cannot be attained by *direct* attack; I cannot find it, for example, by directly striving for it, by autosuggestion or some other "self-deceiving" training which I undergo in order to find peace of mind. No, the prerequisite of real peace is that I put my own personality right with God, instead of trying to harmonize it with itself; then this harmony results as a by-product of this new relationship.

These two examples show that Goethe's concept of history and that of the Bible must necessarily develop differently.

We insist, then, that according to the biblical view man comes to himself and finds peace only when he is called by God and when he responds to this call.

This could be shown in many examples, for instance in the story of the calling of an Isaiah or a Jeremiah or an Ezekiel. In that these men were called to God they also came to themselves. This is where the real "Isaiah," the real "Jeremiah," actually came into being. It is not that I become someone else when I make God my Lord; on the contrary, I really become "myself"; then the orig-

inal image of what God intended me to be emerges. We see this in
the encounters of men and women with Jesus: when the woman
"who was a sinner," when the publican, when other disreputable
characters met him, something entirely new was kindled within
them and they were mysteriously changed. And yet when we look
more closely, this was not really a transformation in the sense that
they "developed away" from themselves; rather they were going
back home in the deepest sense to their real selves by becoming
once more the "children of their Father in heaven."

We can round off the course of our thinking in this chapter by
saying that *all history is in the last analysis history of meeting and
being called*. It takes place between *two* entities (God and man)
and is therefore anything but a mere "development" of innate
abilities (the Goethean "minted form"), which could take place, at
least theoretically, within the solitary individual. Only in meeting
with the divine Thou, and thus indirectly, do I also come to "myself." I never come to myself by seeking and aiming at myself
directly. Jesus's saying, "Whoever would save his life will lose it,"
is applicable here too. For this "self" which I want to attain and
realize lies in my becoming a child. And how could I become a
child again without the Father?

But all meeting with God has two aspects. First, I accept as from
the hands of God the realm in which I am bound (my place in history, my sex, my talents and abilities, etc.) and here the question is
whence I came. And second, I accept from him the realm of my
freedom in order that I may be assigned my task, my destiny in
life, and here the question is *whither,* to what *end* am I here.

Only by starting with these two questions can the mystery of all
human history be fathomed.

THE REALITY OF THE DEMONIC | XII

HISTORY, AS LUTHER PUT IT IN MANY A STRONG ILLUS-
tration, is a contest between God and antigod, or—as Goethe once
expressed it—a battlefield between faith and unbelief. And this
confronts us with the question of the demonic powers.

It is not easy to speak about the reality of the demonic. For this
cannot be dealt with merely by stringing together a number of
Bible passages. As long as we proceed merely in this statistical
fashion we are not facing the *reality* of the demonic. For then it
may still be "mythology," the universal idea of evil dressed up in
the ancient costume of myth, an idea of evil of which we are conscious but which does not confront us as a *power*. It is, after all,
quite possible calmly to philosophize about good and evil. The
demonic, however, is that which is utterly menacing.

How simple it is to talk about "evil"! One can think of it as a
par of that power which "always desires the evil and always produces the good." One can laud the outbreak of evil in the Fall (as
Schiller did) and call it a fortunate event because it created the
possibility of freedom. One can (as the philosophy of idealism
does) extol evil as the productive counterpart of the good, the
only means by which life is given creative tension and generative
power. And finally one can even (as Nietzsche did) make it the
"highest good."

But this harmless way of looking at evil from an objective
bird's-eye point of view ceases the moment we begin to talk about
the demonic. Here the armchair philosophizing ceases; here we
are personally affected and touched.

It is the same with talk about *God*. Paul says in I Corinthians

163

2:11 that no one knows the thoughts of God except the Spirit of
God himself. That is to say, God is never the object of our human
knowledge, but only the object of his self-knowledge. And we
Christians can say something about God only because we have the
Spirit which is from God (2:12) and therefore can share in God's
self-knowledge. Revelation means nothing more nor less than our
being honored with participation in his self-knowledge and thus
being called out of our own hopeless inadequacy.

But just as we cannot speak of *God* from the standpoint of disinterested objectivity, so we cannot speak of the *demonic* in this
way. We can speak about the demonic only as we are touched and
afflicted by it, that is, only as we discover the demonic reaching out
for us and also become aware of something within ourselves on
which it can take hold. Hence we can speak of the demonic only
on the basis of the horrified realization that we actually possess a
secret capacity that makes it possible for us to understand it. "If
the eye did not have something of the sun in it, it could never see
the sun." And if it were not diabolically infected, it could never
recognize the diabolical. So Luther, too, did not merely "excogi-
tate" his drastic dicta concerning the devil—by mythologically
and symbolically rigging out, as it were, the speculative dualism of
his cosmology with a devil. No, he stood in the open jaws of hell,
he carried on a real, almost physical struggle with the real tempter
—and that is why he threw his inkwell at him.

I said that we can talk about the demonic only as we are
touched and afflicted by it. And if all the signs are not deceiving,
we are living today in a time when we are peculiarly aware of it.

There are times which are especially out of joint (in Hamlet's
phrase) and are therefore lacking in order, even though the external order of dictatorship prevails. The demons of power, lust,
destruction are let loose and man ventures to reveal himself
openly and without the constraint and the mask of his cloaking
ordinances. This situation occurs especially in times in which man
autocratically overturns ancient ordinances in order to set up new
ones. In such times he wishes to be only the subject, but not the
object of order, and thus is himself disordered in the ultimate
sense and is left defenselessly exposed to the powers that descend
upon him. The fact that we appear to live in such a time may ex-

plain why there is a new appreciation of the Revelation of John. For in this book is described the *homo inordinatus* of the time of the end, the man who is unordered and therefore at the mercy of the powers of the Antichrist, offering them one point of vantage after another. Our time is beginning to discover in itself a hidden correspondence with the historical situation which is portrayed in the biblical Apocalypse.[1]

It is probably equally characteristic that our time has produced a number of books which speak with especial appropriateness of the reality of the demonic and the gods. I mention only the two books by Friedrich Alfred Schmid-Noerr, *Dämonen, Götter und Gewissen* ("Demons, Gods, and Conscience") and Walter F. Otto, *Die Götter Griechenlands* ("The Gods of Greece"). One theme that is common to both books is that when we are dealing with gods as well as demons we are not dealing with anthropomorphism but rather with real powers. Schmid-Noerr says that "enlightenment" is always a powerful protection against demons, but that "the mind that refuses enlightenment or the curiosity of modern man is *defenseless* against the demonic powers."

This essay of Schmid-Noerr is content to define the true state of affairs with regard to demons, "to warn against speaking about the demons and gods carelessly, in other words, to set up a danger-signal: Look out! High-tension!"

The fact is that the general defenselessness against demons in our "enlightened" time is all too apparent. We can observe so-called "intelligent" people, intellectuals to whom we must concede sanity, broad-mindedness, and other serious qualities and who yet have not the least understanding of the mystery of the course of events today, either with respect to its background or to very obvious diagnoses and prognoses—an astonishing degree of delusion and blindness to what is going on.

They see in everything that is happening merely struggles for power which are being settled according to the purely mechanical law of superior strength. In all the lawlessness and sadism let loose among us they see only "excesses," that is, more or less unavoid-

[1] My thesis that there are signs of a new understanding of the biblical Apocalypse is naturally not affected by the fact that now as always it is being subjected to numerical and every other kind of speculation.

able departures from the normal; so in all this they see not the manifestation of an "essence," but merely the manifestation of the inessential and incidental. They do not see a "necessity" expressing itself here (that is, the "necessary" symptom of man's being out of God's order and at the mercy of the powers), but merely accident and incidental deterioration. "No sun without shadow," they say, and try to look calm when they say it. They believe in all seriousness that men make history and that history is therefore the autobiography of great individuals blown up to macrocosmic proportions, whereas these men actually live in enslaved subjugation and, what is more, are most often carried where they do not wish to go.[2] Thus the "enlightened" men of secularization become blind to demons and are therefore incapable of recognizing one of the fundamental factors in history and thus incapable of discerning history as a whole. *Anybody who would understand history must be in possession of the category of the demonic.*

Now, naturally, one cannot talk about the demonic simply by stating that it exists "outside" of ourselves in the world, that the great Babylon rules "outside," and then listing its symptoms. No, we find all this within ourselves; the vigorous gods and demons of our heritage—to mention only these—maintain their heartfires in *us.* It is not at all as if the onslaught of these gods and demons simply came to us from the outside. No, the mystery of this assault lies in our vulnerability, that is, in the fact that we are unresistant to them from the outset and actually oblige them with points of vantage. The voice of the "old Adam," to which these powers address themselves, is heard within *us.* It was not without reason that, again, Luther (who had perhaps the deepest knowledge of these things) said that this Old Adam must be daily "drowned" within us. He is actively at work in us, like an enemy agent in the interior of a country, giving information by radio to the hostile power and directing it to the weak spots in the front.

So neither from this viewpoint can we speak about the demonic power in disinterested and objective fashion. We human beings cannot talk about theology (or, naturally, demonology either) the way angels can. Our theology is always theology of temptation

[2] It should be noted that this chapter was written in 1943.

(Anfechtung) theology in the face of the open jaws of hell that would swallow us up. We can theologize only from within the "mighty fortress" of the church, to which is given the promise that the gates of hell shall not prevail against it.

Therefore we must not look *outward* but *inward* into our own heart. C. F. Meyer saw this aright and gave it expression in his well-known work on Luther:

> Two aeons warred and fought within his soul;
> No wonder, then, that he should demons see.

1

We begin by defining the personal power whom the Bible calls *Diabolos* or *Satanas,* and I preface our comments with this basic statement:

With respect to the demonic power (the devil) theology must not claim to "explain" evil but only to "describe" it. The demonic power is fundamentally connected with the concept of sin as servitude. But since this servitude of the world and man is the theme of all demonology and not merely of speculation about the devil as such, we may lay down this principle: *Diabolum cognoscere est maleficia eius cognoscere,* to know the devil is to know his evil designs.[3]

The fact that we cannot "explain" evil, and also that the Bible makes no effort to do so, is connected with this personal element, the figure of Satan, which lies behind all "neuter" concepts of evil. In order to understand this we have only to think of our encounter with human persons. When I say, for example, that I "understand" another person or I seek to "understand" him, this also does not mean that I can "explain" him. I can determine his environment, his biological derivation, his motives, but I always find this this causal nexus never fully explains him. The idea of accountability and responsibility in law is based entirely upon this fact that man is not explainable on the basis of biological structure and environment, and that he is *not* fully explained by the

[3] This statement is patterned on Melanchthon's famous dictum concerning Christ, *"Christum cognoscere est beneficia eius cognoscere (Loci communes* of 1521, Introduction).

causal nexus by which he is conditioned. Otherwise he would be nothing more than the causally conditioned product of the factors we have mentioned; then we could not hold him accountable for his own actions, but would have to assess them as well as him as the mechanical products of these factors. But then man would not be responsible for his deeds, one could not punish him for them; then the most one could do to neutralize the human elements of decay and destruction would be to confine such dangerous subjects (or rather "objects"!) in rubber or concrete cells. But the criminal law of all countries simply assumes that the lawbreaker must be punished, and therefore presupposes that he is responsible and hence also not to be derived or explained.

Accordingly the assertion that one can "understand" a person by no means implies that one can also "explain" him. "Understanding" goes back to a personal encounter with the other person in which it was communicated. "Explanation" is based on an impersonal stance (a di-stance in which there is no community) from which I regard the other person as *one* object among others and therefore, like *all* objects, a causally determined "thing."

This distinction between personal "understanding" and impersonal "explanation" proceeds from the following reflection:

When I give an account of another person and try to make him "understandable" to a third person, I do not present the latter with a logical formula of him, nor does it occur to me to represent him as the product of such and such factors. (True, I can mention these factors; but when they have hardly more than the significance of an emphasis and commentary.) Rather, when I give an account of a person I describe to the third person my *encounter* with him, I describe the effect he had "upon me," which sides of his character he showed me, which are therefore understandable to me in either a positive or a negative way, and which sides of his character remain obscure and unknown. Thus in encounter I get a picture in perspective rather than a geometrical, causal phenomenon which is flat and superficial. This is also the reason why everybody has a different picture of everybody else. The greater, the more demonic, and the more of a genius a man is, the more clearly apparent are the limitations of what I say about him on the basis of my meeting with him; for here it becomes evident that only a very limited part of his personality is being shown to me, and that a correspondingly larger part of its volume is turned away from me, not entering into the encounter, and remains blurred and indistinct in a background which is inaccessible to me. When I describe the other person (especially a great person of genius) I am describing only the reflex he caused in me. But this means that every person who meets him describes a different reflex. And the several images can never be made to coincide.

One example will serve to illustrate this: the biographies of Luther written in both camps, which, despite a genuine intention to be historically unbiased, are widely divergent and incongruent. Or think of the diametrically opposite attitudes toward great living personalities. But the way in which they meet me and deal with me determines how I see them. All the objective statistics concerning their reprehensible or their great actions, all recollection of their inherited structure, environmental factors, etc., do not cause me to believe in them or reject them, but only confirm my recognition or rejection of them, which occurred in the encounter. Persons are not deducible; they cannot be deduced from these factors.

So it is that I also cannot deduce evil. For when I encounter evil I likewise encounter a personal power, the *diabolos*. I cannot deduce it; it is *there*. Nor can I establish it objectively; I can only encounter it. Characteristically, Adam and Eve learned to know good and evil only in the moment when they encountered evil and fell victim to it. Before that moment of contact evil was not even within their range of vision. In the same way a person first experiences the evil in sexuality (not that sexuality itself is evil!) when his physical maturity makes an encounter possible. Previously it had no existence for him.

So in the encounter with evil we are constantly meeting with the personal category. In any case it cannot be grasped in the objective category of causality. This is shown by the common saying: "To understand all is to forgive all." We need only change the word "understand" to "explain" in order to make that clear. When I do this I am treating evil objectively and resolving it into its several causes, so that then the evil itself disappears, evaporates as it were into nothing. This means that when I deal with evil impersonally and in analogy with an object—in other words, when I "explain" it—it does not appear at all; it becomes a mere trifle, a nothing; and thus everything which at first looks like evil is actually to be forgiven and declared null and void. But when I understand everything (that is, when I see through the other person in an encounter), by no means do I forgive him (at any rate not simply as an automatic concomitant of understanding); rather then his guilt appears perhaps for the first time in the right light. God understands us men utterly and completely. But for this very reason he does not simply *forgive* us, but is at first our judge and accuser. The fact that he wants to forgive us and be a gracious Father to us is certainly grounded upon facts that are entirely different from the mere circumstance that he "understands" us.

To sum up, the more impersonal a thing is—and the most impersonal of all is perhaps the mathematical formula—the more able I am to speak of it in terms that are general, timeless, and detached from myself. But the more personal something is, the more I must limit myself to describing only my encounter with it: I am thinking, for example, of my attitude toward works of art or toward historical personages. The very word "attitude" is in itself characteristic. Since evil always has a personal background, and because when we are dealing with evil we are dealing with the devil, I can perceive it only with the category of the personal, that is, in *encounter*. I cannot deduce it.

This presents us, then, with the following important thoughts:

1. In the first place, when we start here we understand why in the Bible not a word is wasted on the origin of evil, why evil is simply "there." The Bible is aware that evil is personal and therefore that it is nondeducible. Accordingly, its approach is completely different: it faces this brutal and physical fact that *the enemy has broken into the land.* I stand in utmost peril. This is no place for me to philosophize; here I must fall to and fight. This is an emergency that leaves no time for reflection. *Mea res agitur!* After all, when a bomb threatens to strike in my vicinity the idea does not occur to me to stop and consider who manufactured it or to regard it as real only if we have been able to identify its weight, explosive effect, and method of fabrication.

How different is this attitude from that of idealistic speculation which says that evil is the creative negative element in life! From this point of view, how unserious this seemingly earnest intellectual endeavor appears! The fact is that there is not a moment in my life when I can withdraw in this fashion into a detached bird's eye view of things in order to "consider" the phenomenon of evil *sine ira et studio* (without anger and partiality). How can I behave *sine ira et studio* when the hostile power of evil is full of *studium et ira* and seeking whom he may devour? Anybody who opposes a spiteful and cunning enemy in an attitude of calm objectivity and lazy lack of interest in the enemy's disguises only proves that, despite his objective perceptions (which the one who throws himself into the fight and strikes back immediately may *not have*), he has disastrously mistaken and misjudged the enemy. Thus, biblically speaking, we have a real knowledge of the demonic power only in so far as we see in it the enemy and enter into battle against it. True, this attitude may overlook many things about the enemy, because it has "no time" for peripheral observations; but it does see the central and important thing. So here again we have an altogether personal attitude, namely, the attitude in which one meets an *enemy*.

2. Then there is something else which shows us why we cannot even ask the question of the origin of evil: the reality of the demonic cannot be perceived with our natural eyes. For these natural eyes are themselves darkened and it is precisely the demonic power that darkened them. It is not for nothing that the Bible calls it the "power of darkness." Putting it in more modern terms, one might say it is the "power of obfuscation." One of the mysteries of sin is that it cannot see itself, but becomes manifest only in the light of God. In this respect it is not unlike stupidity. Stupidity likewise cannot see itself, for this "seeing" would in itself require a proper degree of intelligence. Stupidity is too obtuse and devoid of standards to see itself. In order to be able to say, "I know that I know nothing," one must be as great a genius as Socrates. Stupidity becomes manifest only in the face of intelligence. Similarly, the power and nature of the demonic becomes evident only in the light and the glory of God and his Christ: Isaiah becomes conscious of his unclean lips only in the face of the glory of

God (Isa. 6); and Peter realizes that he is a sinful man only when he is confronted by the superhuman miraculous power of Jesus (Matt. 16:16). And the demons, too, do not become aware of themselves, as it were, until Jesus Christ walks the earth and they sense in him the ultimate threat to their existence.

Why is it that sin cannot see itself? Simply because it is a relational concept. It can be defined only as a particular relationship to *God,* namely, a separation from him, a denial and a rebellion. In the same way the satanic is a relational concept: it is that which is severed from God.

It seems to me to be of primary importance that this be clearly seen and stated. For only so will we be saved from the Marcionite misconception that Satan is an independent antigod and thus that Christianity has a basically dualistic structure. Actually, the satanic can be defined only "negatively," as that which is in a "negative relation"—it is that which is separated from God, that which has entered into opposition to God.

And this is just the reason why we also cannot speak in terms of that hypothetical dualistic structure. This would mean, after all, the existence of a region of reality which is exempt from the all-embracing relationship to God. But there *is* no such region. This is evident in the fact that the devil can be defined *only* in relation to God. Here Luther goes so far as to speak of the devil as still being "God's devil," in order to indicate that, even though he is pure negation, he is nevertheless included in the whole sphere of God's dispensation.

We repeat: only in God's light does the demonic power reveal itself, and only there can its existence and nature be understood. And what is more, it not only discloses itself here but here it also reaches its highest potentiation: confronted by the Christ who walked the earth, all the demonic powers gathered themselves together in one last effort. This applies not only to the evil spirits of the possessed (cf. the New Testament accounts of demons), but also to demonic men—such as Herod and Pontius Pilate—who despite their diverse intentions and characters closed ranks and became friends in an ultimate negation of the Christ. Note the *negation* again! The eschatological vision of the Apocalypse also gives a similar picture of the potentiation of evil in the face of the

Second Coming of Christ. The unmasking and the potentiation of evil naturally belong close together, for the more concentrated and demonstrative the negation of God becomes, the more powerfully it emerges and the more difficult it is to fail to see it. And yet one will fail to see it even in its most patent form as long as one closes one's eyes to the light and glory of God. Only so are we to interpret the strange statements of the Apocalypse that in spite of all the demonic irruptions at the end of history men become increasingly unrepentant and imperceptive.

So here again we see that the demonic power never comes into view as the object of a neutral approach which is interested in its causation, but only *in actu*, that is, in the moment when we come to grips with it, the moment I make my utterly personal decision for or against the personal God. The point is that in these relationships everything depends upon the category of the personal.

How, then, does the Bible describe the demonic power more precisely? We begin with the term *diabolos*, in which we find all the points which we have mentioned and only alluded to. *Diabolos* comes from the verb *diaballein*, which means "to throw into confusion," "to upset," "to set at odds," "to put asunder." *Diabolos* separates, puts asunder God and man.

The Book of Job clearly shows how he does this in two ways: first as *accuser* and second as *tempter*.[4]

To begin with, as *accuser* he is a member of the heavenly court which God convenes from time to time. Here he exercises the function of a heavenly public prosecutor, that is, he doubts God's optimistic opinion of his servants. Thus he discredits God's "servant Job" with the argument that he is devout and good only because hitherto things have gone well for him and therefore his piety and goodness were "profitable." But the moment God breaks this transparent correspondence between reward and punishment Job will renounce him. In the New Testament this function of accusation and discrediting is represented in the term "adversary," *antidikos* (Luke 18:3; I Pet. 5:8).

But this metaphor of public prosecutor and accuser does not

---

[4] Cf. the comments on this by Gerhard von Rad in G. Kittel, ed., *Theologisches Wörterbuch zum Neuen Testament*.

altogether fit. For he does not seek to prove his accusation by showing that Job has actually deserted God; he proceeds first to *provoke* this desertion in order that he may maliciously offer it as evidence to the divine Judge as soon as it occurs. This is very clearly his strategy in the Book of Job. Thus he is not only the accuser but also the *tempter*. He is less a public prosecutor than a Gestapo, which seeks to provoke an offense it considers a victim capable of committing, in order to secure an alibi for its procedure.

I should like to say that again we are not interested in these characteristics for their own sake any more than we are interested in the devil for his own sake. All this interests us only in relationship to what all this says about "me." Just as in Christology we should not, according to Luther's counsel, keep goggling at the mystery of the person of the Son of God, but rather think in relation to salvation (*salubriter cogitare*), so in our thinking about the *diabolos* we should think "ponerologically," that is, in relation to "the diabolical subjugation of our existence."

In this respect, however, there is one thing that accusing and tempting have in common. Both the tempter and the accuser address themselves and appeal to a weakness that exists in me. The diabolical serpent in Genesis 3 was able to accuse and tempt our first parents only because it could be sure to find a vulnerable spot in them. The same is true of Job. At the moment when the accuser makes his prophetic accusation that Job will react thus and so, he is already certain that there will be in Job points of vantage which evil can take hold of. The seduction that follows is then nothing but a demonstration of this prophecy, a factual exploitation of this weak spot. On the other hand the *diabolos* finds no purchase, nothing to take hold of, in Jesus either for his accusing *or* his tempting.

The examples I have just mentioned can show very precisely the relationship between temptation and temptability, between seduction and seducibility. A very inexact, wrong proverb says, "Opportunity makes the thief." The proverb is so wrong because the truth would seem to be exactly the opposite: "I *am* a thief." That is the reason, and the only reason, why I can be (a) accused and (b) seduced. The "opportunity" merely exploits an existing tendency to steal, nothing more. Temptation merely means that a potentiality within me is made into a reality. I am open to temptation, and therefore I can be tempted.

The secret of man, therefore, does not consist in the fact that he *faces* temptation, but rather that he *is* vulnerable to it. Because I have sin *in* me, I give the *diabolos* a claim upon me. He can appeal to it. And however true it is that in its influence upon me a necessity and a servitude is working itself out, this power of the tempter by no means has the character of a *coactio,* an external coercion, but rather that of a necessity, an inner necessity inherent in our nature.

This biblical view of man is also apparent in the fact that in the Ten Commandments God addresses me at the point of my temptability. The predominantly negative formulation of the commandments, which ingenious worldlings have thought they had to explain as being a supposedly Jewish negative attitude toward life, whereas Western ethics makes positive ideals the object of its imperatives—this predominantly negative formulation has in it the sense of a protest against man as he actually is: You shall *not* kill, you who *are* a murderer; you shall *not* steal, you who *are* a thief.

The point is that right from the start the *diabolos* can be certain that he has a foothold on the terrain of our soul. It is not at all as if our heart were a thing apart and the tempter stood outside:

> . . . all man's Babylons strive but to impart
> The grandeurs of his Babylonian heart.[5]

According to Gerhard von Rad, it is also on this basis that the strange designation of the *enemies of Israel* as "satans" (adversaries) is to be understood:

With Jahweh the enemies of Israel have a special function, they are the accusers of Israel and therefore correspond to an indictment of the people of God. This important conception gives us the right to interpret the "satans" whom Jahweh raised up against Solomon—Hadad the

---

[5] Francis Thompson's sonnet, "The Heart."

Edomite, Rezon the Aramaean—not simply according to the general basic meaning of the word "enemies," but to surmise that here the term also has a specific juridical sense: according to the Deuteronomic historian, Solomon had sinned, and now the "satans" who arose during the course of this king's reign are related to this sin. . . .[6]

This idea of the devil's "foothold" also expresses the deepest meaning of bondage—the New Testament calls it *douleia*—to the accuser and tempter. I belong to the demonic power not simply in the sense of belonging to an alien master against my own will. Rather I belong to that power in the sense that *I belong to myself*. That is to say, I cannot plead that it simply has control over me and that because of this coercion I incur no responsibility. No, this demonic bondage exists only as I belong to *myself*, to *my* ambitions, *my hubris, my* self-assertiveness, *my* passions. So decisive is this theological concept of the foothold: the devil lives in the medium of *amor sui*, love of self. I do not love the devil by name (who has ever made such a declaration of love or heard anyone else making it!), rather I love *myself* by name—and precisely in doing this I deliver myself over to him. In other words, I am never the object of demonic action in the exculpating sense that it is merely applied to me "from the outside"; rather I am always a *subject*, too. When the *diabolos* employs the *Zeitgeist* or the anonymity of the crowd (*das Man*) to lead me astray, I can never plead this as an excuse. I myself am one who has the *Zeitgeist* within him and helps to constitute it; I am never (never!) a merely passive victim of the spirit of the times. I cannot dissociate myself from it; it is "the lord of my own spirit." As we have already noted, this is why Adam cannot excuse himself by pleading that Eve exercised inner coercion, and why Eve cannot throw the blame upon the serpent. In the judgment of God they seek in vain to play the role of the "object."

Thus, even though I am here dealing with *myself*, it nevertheless becomes clear that in the very act of doing this I am dealing with *another*, simply because I cannot break the bond in which I am held, and am, so to speak, forcibly bound to myself. I see a powerful spell hovering over this bondage.

[6] Von Rad, in Kittel, *op. cit.*, II, 72, pp. 1 ff.

It is only against this background of the biblical image of man that the doctrine of justification also becomes intelligible. For justification is intelligible when I know that my acts, my "works," cannot free me from this spell that keeps me in bondage. On the contrary, my deeds only draw me deeper into its toils. In that I appear to be fulfilling all the commandments of God I may fall victim to Pharisaism, "security," and pride. *Amor sui* can appear in the most disguised forms. And it is not at all as if the *diabolos* always approached me "head on" in an objectively comprehensible way and took the form of a concrete sin. No, he is also capable of becoming nonobjective and of coming at me from behind. (This is where the sins of Pharisaism, *hubris,* etc., mentioned above would come in.) This dual strategy of the tempter can be illustrated by reference to the two tables of the Law. The second table with its individual commandments relates to the objectively comprehensible *diabolos,* to concrete individual sins which I can clearly recognize and against which I must be on guard. Now, it may be theoretically possible for me to keep all these commandments to the letter and by careful examination of conscience cleverly escape all the snares of the Adversary. And yet in the very act of doing so I may fall into secret pride before God ("God, I thank thee that I am not like other men, . . ."), and thus sin against the first table of the Law, which commands me to give glory to God *alone* and not allow myself or any other person or any other thing to be "other gods besides him."

Thus I never get free from this bondage through actual deeds of moral decision; it comes about only as a decision is made about me: the power of the *diabolos* cannot be broken by men, but only through the power of another Lord to whom I must enslave myself. The devil cannot be conquered by men, only by God. But I am God's. In the last analysis human life is only a question of allegiance, of who is going to be our liege lord. So all Faust's talk of "in the beginning was the Deed" and that therefore the only thing that counts in the end is man's "ever-striving effort"[7] is pure twaddle. "For," as Reinhold Schneider said, "the doers will never conquer heaven." This also explains why it is that the Lord's

[7] Goethe, *Faust,* Part I, Scene 3, and Part II, Act V, Scene 7. (Trans.)

Prayer does not make a *prohibition* of the question of temptation, but rather incorporates it into the prayer, "Lead us not into temptation." In this petition we call upon the only Lord who is able to challenge the pseudo-lord. Christ has the battlefield, and I belong on his side.

Satan, the other designation for the devil, means "enemy," "adversary." As such he is the head of a great host of demons. The word "demon" appears repeatedly in the plural. Satan has under him the angels of darkness. To this extent there is here an exact parallel with the heavenly host of angels. In Satanology in general and in Antichristology (Rev.) biblical thought revolves around the spirits of darkness who rule the world (Eph. 2:2; 6:12), and its ultimate thought is that these spirits culminate as it were in a personal being (Satan, Antichrist).

And here again, in order immediately to be safeguarded against dualism and to understand that the power of darkness is exclusively related to God, the concept that Satan is a fallen angel appears to me to be very important. Already in Job he is a member of the company of angels. The two classical passages for this are II Peter 2:4 and Jude 6: ". . . God did not spare the angels when they sinned, but cast them into hell and committed them to pits of nether gloom to be kept until the judgment." "And the angels that did not keep their own position but left their proper dwelling have been kept by him in eternal chains in the nether gloom until the judgment of the great day."

Just because the devil is a fallen angel, he is also privy to the strategy of the kingdom of God and he seeks to work against it. Because he knows the angels so well, he is able to disguise himself as an angel of light. *He has all the passion and the inside knowledge of a renegade.* Thus he performs miracles like Christ himself (II Thess. 2:9; Rev. 13:11-13). Likewise his "blasphemies" are not simply anti-Christian tirades like those poured forth from a soapbox, but rather are an attempt to appear religious and to talk like God (Rev. 13:1). In everything he does and the way he does it he is the imitator, "the ape of God." And the ability to play this role is based upon his remembrance of his former greatness.

In this downfall of the demonic angel there is the operation of a basic law of the kingdom of God, namely, that everything demonic and anti-God, whatever its negative rank may be, points back to an original greatness. This applies to men as well as to ideas.

As concerns man, a beast could never have fallen so low as has man who was created in the image of God. And in the great corrupters of mankind we still detest something of the inner dignity which they once possessed or to which they were destined. In the system of co-ordinates operative in the kingdom of God the negative degree of fall is always proportionate to the positive degree of determination: the higher the actual rank the lower the fall. Therefore the animal cannot become demonic, but man can. Nothing is so corrosive as corrupted greatness. And the worst scoundrels of mankind have always been capable of becoming its greatest exemplars. Man's misery is the misery of a great lord, the misery of a dethroned king, says Pascal. This is the lost image of God—not merely a reversion to the animal, as the naïve spirits and the Pollyanna philosophers would have us think. No, it is the image of God in man, squandered and lost, nothing else.

The Revelation of John gives repeated expression to this basic law of the downfall of the highest into the demonic depths in its pictures of the falling of the stars: heavenly beings which are separated from fellowship with God are plunged to the earth and here—precisely because of their divine rank—they lead a peculiarly demonic existence severed from God. This applies especially to the tremendous picture in Revelation 12:2 ff., in which the great red dragon appears in the heavens, sweeps down a third of the stars of heaven with his tail, and casts them to the earth. Who is not reminded by this—noting that Hellmuth Frey has given profound expression to it in his exposition[8]—of all those history-making powers whose divine origin we perceive, but which are fallen powers. One might think, for example (naturally only as illustrative examples and not in the sense that here the Revelation of John is setting forth concrete prophecy) of how certain great *ideas* are also subject to this catastrophic fall. The great ideas and ideals of humanity, which may be of divine origin, are

[8] Hellmuth Frey, *Weg und Zukunft der Gemeinde Jesu* (Stuttgart: Calwer Verlag, 1940), p. 13.

changed into their opposite the moment they are separated from their divine source. We need mention only the ideas of the true, the good, and the beautiful which, disengaged from God, become "presuppositionless" science without God, empty attitudinal morality without God, and pure estheticizing art-for-art's-sake art with all the decadent phenomena that are so apparent today. The same applies to the ideas of liberty, equality, and fraternity. It is certainly not too bold to say that all three ideas were originally biblical. But once they are transplanted from their place of origin and separated from God they acquire all the qualities of disintegration—and today they have become the watchwords of Marxism. We could go on and cite a whole list of terms which betray the same Luciferian fall. I mention only the word "obedience"; what means liberation when it is connected with God, without him becomes slavery and murder of conscience. This is proved by all the dictatorships that exist by obedience and submission. We see therefore the profound working of an immutable law which lies hidden behind this seemingly bizarre conception of the devil as the fallen angel, the toppled Lucifer.

2

And now to come back at once to the picture in Revelation mentioned above: stars falling to the earth. Here they carry on their demonic existence. This shows that what is meant here is not an abstract principle of evil (in the sense of a concept that is merely "prevalent" but does not "exist" in morality). Rather what is meant is a *power*, a power that lays hold upon this earth, this aeon. "He" is the *archon tou kosmou, tou aionos toutou* (the ruler of this world, this aeon—John 12:31, 14:30; 16:11).

As such a cosmic power it is at the same time something that profoundly governs the structure of this aeon. In actuality it is not so simple as was thought, for example, by Ritschl, who localized supra-individual evil (e.g., in the form of original sin) in environmental factors and regarded it here as being in a process of gradual and yet avalanchelike growth.

The very great extent to which the demonic *exousia* (power) goes beyond the sphere of mere environment and affects the real depths of the nature of the world itself can be seen in the New

Testament concept of the state. (Unfortunately, the discussion of this question in our context would lead us too far afield.)[9]

The state is a proper paradigm for such an observation for the very simple reason that it is in a very special way representative of "this aeon" with all its essential characteristics, and therefore quite consciously comes into repeated conflict with the coming world of God. We have only to think of the encounter between Jesus Christ and Pontius Pilate, or of Paul's statement that God will destroy all authorities, principalities, etc. (I Cor. 15:24). In his *Commentary on Genesis,* Luther expressly contrasts the state with the original state of the world by saying that in the original state of mankind before it had fallen, God ruled men *uno motu digito* (with *one* movement of his finger).[10] When sin came, inner rebellion came into the world—and with it the threat of chaos. Then God was obliged to institute orders of force which would hold the menacing chaos in check. These orders of force are represented by the state. And thus the state itself becomes a representative of this aeon, which, precisely because it is a *fallen* aeon, requires force. And thus we may also assume that, in so far as the demonic power is really the "ruler of this world," this dominion will find expression particularly in the area of the state.

We limit ourselves in this connection to a few observations.[11]

According to Romans 13, the earthly state is actually one of the "powers" *(exousiai),* that is, it belongs among the angelic and demonic powers. This is generally overlooked because in most interpretations of Romans 13 it is too quickly concluded that its purpose is only to set forth the divine authorization of government. It is true, of course, that this authorization is there, but yet in a very qualified sense; for the authorization is only for the order of the *fallen* world. The *exousia* which the state represents is therefore not simply a reflection of the divine *exousia,* but rather a reflection of those intermediate powers for which God makes

[9] Cf. my essay *"Von der Grenzen der Fürbitte"* (*"The Limits of Intercession"*) in *Theologie der Anfechtung* (*Theology of Temptation*) (Tübingen: J. C. B. Mohr [Paul Siebeck], 1949) .

[10] Luther, *Commentary on Genesis,* WA 42, 79, 7-19.

[11] Cf. the more detailed chapter on this in my book *Geschichte und Existenz: Grundlegung einer evangelischen Geschichtstheologie* (Gütersloh: C. Bertelsmann, 1935) .

provision in the fallen world. So besides God's direct will there is this indirect will of God which accommodates itself, as it were, to the fallen world and meets its actual condition.[12]

Once this relation to the fallen world and to the *exousia* of the intermediate powers is understood, however, the statements about governments in Romans 13 and the statements in the Revelation of John 13 concerning the demonic power-state as being a beast from the abyss are not so far apart as they may at first appear. The concept of *exousia,* that is, the relation to the angelic and demonic powers, binds both statements closely together. It is therefore not accidental that the authority of the state, which is borne by human rulers and yet is entirely independent of these individual persons, being as it were suprapersonal, is called *archai kai exousiai* (rulers and authorities). It is significant, says C. L. Schmidt, that Werner Foerster in his article on *exousia* in Kittel's *Wörterbuch,* despite the circumspection and caution with which he veers around Romans 13, nevertheless is almost drawn by the mention of *exousiai* there into the realm of angelic powers and thus into that of the intermediate powers.[13] Probably in dependence upon the rabbinical term *rem'outh* (Rom. 13:2 ff.; Col. 1:13), *exousia* denotes the dominion of the state (Luke 23:7) *as well as* that of the realm of spirits (Eph. 2:2; Col. 1:13).

Thus the state has two aspects. In one it is the representative of the world order which God wants and which Caesar realizes through his office, and thus within certain limits must be obeyed. At the same time, however, there is in the state the demonic tendency to become overweening; the beast of the abyss lies in wait

[12] This is perhaps most clearly expressed in Jesus' prohibition of divorce in Matt. 19:1-12. God's real will is that man and wife remain inseparably together. A certificate of divorce was allowed by Moses (naturally in God's name) only because of "Your hardness of heart." Both divorce and marriage therefore have a relationship to the will of God, and yet in both the will of God is expressed in a completely different way. One could say that in one case it is direct and in the other indirect; in the case of the certificate of divorce the alien element of the fallen world has intervened. The situation is similar in the case of the relation of the state to the will of God: as it is now, it is not a direct expression of the will of God, but rather exists and is permitted to exist, as it were, because of men's hardness of heart.

[13] C. L. Schmidt, "*Das Gegenüber von Kirche und Staat in der Gemeinde des Neuen Testaments,*" *Theologische Blätter* (1937), I.

within it. And overweening also brings with it the danger of self-destruction. The state, especially at its highest potentiation (the totalitarian state), inevitably manifests its provisional character and its vulnerability to the demonic.

Hence one might say that the state is the point of intersection of two movements, one that comes from below and one from above.

The movement from *above* is that which is given in that God vouchsafes to man, who in his "hardness of heart" keeps edging toward chaos, the grace of the order and constraint of the state in order that the world may be preserved and the saving providence of God may be available until the Last Day. The movement from *below* is that which is given in that the state at the same time contains within itself a concentration of all the human forces of rebellion; in a really *mysterious* way it at the same time represents a self-organization and self-entrenchment of this aeon. For all the destructive forces that lurk within the individual appear as it were in macrocosmic magnification in the state *(polis):* the urge to suppress and expand, the lie in certain strategems of diplomacy and in espionage, the passion for power instead of justice, and so on. The state as it were compels the one who exercises the power *in* it and *through* it to conform to the structural laws of this aeon. Thus Jochen Klepper has Friedrich Wilhelm I say that kings must sin more than other people. The simple fact is that the more a man gives up his real self, the more he is drawn into this dominating vortex. The great tyrant in Werner Bergengruen's novel says, "Here lies one of the great contradictions and imperfections of our world, that clean hands are not strong hands and strong ones are not allowed to remain clean."[14]

From this point of view light is also cast upon the state's urge to absolutize itself. It falls back as it were to its dark side. The dynamite of its *exousia* character explodes. The powers from below surge titanically against the divine will to order from above. Perhaps there has never been a time which more unmistakably demonstrated these laws than ours. The demonic power-state of the last times in which the beast is unleashed means nothing other

[14] Werner Bergengruen, *Der Grosstyrann und das Gericht,* p. 233.

than this, that the powers of the abyss are able with God's permission to achieve a temporary triumph over God's will to order—or to put in less misinterpretable fashion, that God leaves the world to its own demonic, chaotic tendencies, "abandons" it to itself. In any case here we begin to realize that the demonic power is really "power," and that as a hidden "ruler of this world" it is waiting for the open establishment of its dominion. The hand of this "ruler" is at work in the very depths of the structural laws of this aeon. The paradigm of politics makes this clear.

3

Up to this point we have had to conclude again and again that the reality of the demonic is not simply a principle but a real and personal power. Now we must add to this conclusion this further point: the demonic power always seeks to remain *anonymous*. We have already seen that it hides behind the divine mask as an angel of light and conceals itself in the temple of God. Even in the story of the Fall in Genesis 3 it appears not in its capacity as the devil but rather in the name of divine curiosity ("You will know good and evil") and in the name of the intoxicating upward development of man ("You will be like God"). And in the temptation of Jesus it by no means appears in its capacity as the devil, but rather in the name of a plausibly rational principle of employing politics for the benefit of Christianity: How would it be, Christ, if you were first to accept the whole earth and power over its peoples in order to "Christianize" them? The idea is plausible and impressive, like all the devil's ideas. And if there is one thing one can know for certain, it is that he never hands you his visiting card.

This is manifested in the tactics of any tempter. For a tempter will never say, "Come now, I'll teach you a sin." "I'll give you something evil." No, he will always say, "Look, I'll show you something interesting, something pleasurable, something that will enrich your life." *Anonymity* is therefore an indispensable mark of the demonic power. The New Testament expresses this anonymity by speaking of powers which exert their influence as spirits of the air from out of the dark, hidden background of the world (Eph. 2:2; 6:12). Hence they are as life-determining as the atmosphere and just as imperceptible. An example is the so-called

"*Zeitgeist*," the spirit of the times. Who can determine where he himself ceases and the *Zeitgeist* starts! The *Zeitgeist* is so much in the atmosphere around us that we think it is we ourselves who hold its opinions and prejudices. It is true that we as subjects help to sustain the *Zeitgeist*, but it is also true that here we are being held under the spell of an anonymous power which is not ourselves but only acts as if it were ourselves and were expressing our own thoughts. Its anonymity lies precisely in the fact that it cannot be objectively grasped, but rather surrounds us in a nonobjective way. Therefore this power is also fond of using the instrument of *propaganda*, that is, nonobjective suggestion for the purpose of "forming the will" *(Willensbildung)*. The very phrase "forming the will" is characteristic. For it indicates that propaganda does address itself to man as the bearer of a will, but nevertheless influences this will in such a secret and insinuating way that it is almost unconsciously changed and then accepts and carries out secretly imposed and suggested decisions as if they were its own.

Once more then, the demonic is not an opponent who becomes objectively tangible like flesh and blood—Paul says we are *not* contending with flesh and blood!—but rather works through us nonobjectively and retreats into invisibility behind us. To use Paul's terminology, this constitutes his principality, his power, and his invisible, atmospheric character (Eph. 6:12).

An unusually profound expression of this thought is presented in the New Testament image of the "dominion of darkness" (Col. 1:13). This, so to speak, translates the atmospheric imperceptibility into optical invisibility: he is the master of darkness or, as we said above, of "obscuration." But in the darkness everything looks distorted and nothing can be identified. We unheedingly and unsuspectingly skirt great perils and at the same time are terrified by the rustling of a leaf. I shall indicate only a few forms of such indiscrimination and confusion.

First, in the darkness created by the demonic power we fail to distinguish between what is "great" and what is "small." We consider some things important which in the face of eternity dwindle to nothing or should be counted as refuse (Phil. 3:8), for example, everything that has to do with Mammon or our reputa-

tion before men. On the other hand, the "one thing needful"
(Luke 10:42) we consider merely marginal, a certain religious ad-
dendum to life which may exert an uplifting and strengthening
influence but does not represent any central necessity of existence.
Thus our standards are confused. And therefore it is not merely
accidental that Jesus again and again proclaimed that in the kingdom of God all values are reversed and all existing standards are
overthrown—for example, when he said that the last would be
first and the first last. It is out of this situation of confusion and
perversion of all things and all values that one of the church's
hymns prays:

> O life eternal, cast thy beam
> Into our daily life in time,
> That small things ever small may seem
> And great things shine in light sublime.[15]

Precisely in this darkness it becomes very clear how the *diabolos*
performs his diabolizing: the demonic power throws our values
into confusion.

The same confusion and diabolizing manifests itself in the confusion of dream and reality. In the secular mind God is thought
of as something that "belongs in the Beyond," making him not
only something marginal but also unreal, a mere projection of
our religious feeling upon heaven. Since for this kind of mind
"religion" has only the character of an ideological superstructure
that has its basis in the economic or even the biological conditions
of life, God, too, takes on the character of unreality. Actual reali-
ties consist only in the forces that rule in this world, in economic,
biological, military, and similar processes. The well-known saying
that God is always on the side of the biggest cannon expresses well
this functional dependence of God, which is only an ironical way
of saying that he is quite unreal. Here again the devil diabolizes
in the darkness!

Finally, a very characteristic form of this diabolizing confusion
is to be found in the fact that it leads us to confuse the creator and
the creature, in other words, to deify the created powers instead

---

[15] From a hymn by Marie Schmalenbach (1882), *"Brich herein, süsser
Schein."* (Trans.)

of worshiping the Creator himself. We have seen the confusion that arises when individual parts of God's creation are raised to the divine. The fact is that they are incapable of controlling the whole of life and thus leave broad areas of life without restraints and exposed to chaos. The absolutizing of the intellect, for example, as in the world view called idealism, leaves untouched the area of vital, organic life and thus encourages the rebellion of the gods of "blood and soil." And these in turn leave the mind to its own unbridled impulses and produce a fresh revolt of intellectualism. This process of rebellion can be seen in many—no, *all* areas of life. Here we are interested only in showing that here again the "confuser" is at work.

His workings can be traced down to the very structure of the world of nations; for the deification of created powers, which expressed itself in the time of National Socialism especially in the deification and mythical glorification of nationalistic virtues, leads only to increasing misunderstanding between the nations. What is lacking is the common acceptance of the authority of God, which is binding upon all. If "Aryans" and "Non-Aryans" alike were to operate only on the basis of "national authority" and say "good is what is good for my people," there could never again be any sanctity of treaties or any supernational, absolutely authoritative obligations.[16]

When this universally binding power is renounced, then inevitably fear and distrust ensue, because the other person can never be tied down and therefore he becomes unpredictable, undependable. The result is the drive for "security" and then on the other side a corresponding drive for countersecurity. And then it is only too clear that these pathologically strained relations will inevitably lead again and again to violent explosions. The tre-

---

[16] We are, of course, not so unworldly as to think that even among Christians there may not be crises over treaties and contracts and conflicts between political necessities and the validity of God's commandments. It is a sign of the fallen world that it can never be without conflict of values. But it is one thing to confess that this structure of the world is an inevitable necessity that burdens the conscience and can be borne only because there is forgiveness, and quite another thing to make a virtue of this necessity and declare that no international treaties are binding by saying, "Good is what is good for my people," or "My country, right or wrong."

mendous harshness of modern military encounters undoubtedly lies not only in the technological development of instruments of war but also in this basic philosophical attitude. The *diabolos* has, quite literally, a "diabolical" interest in producing a nationalistic polytheism. This polytheism is one of the very best means of conjuring up chaos. And when the Revelation of John speaks of an increasing of evil and confusion at the end of our aeon it is doubtless referring to this diabolical function of the Adversary.

4

The demonic is therefore an actual, active *power*. He is the *prince* of this world. We have already discussed various characteristics of this power, such as its anonymity, its function as tempter, accuser, and disintegrative ferment. There are still two outstanding characteristics which we must describe: (*a*) The demonic power rules the *spirit*. It by no means has its seat, as all forms of Idealism would have it, only in the "flesh," in "sensuality," the so-called "inferior" levels of man. (*b*) The demonic power seeks to bring its victim into the state of *subjection*.

a. Paul speaks in Ephesians 2:2 of their former way of life "in which you once walked . . . following the prince of the power of the air." (We now know what is implied by this atmospheric symbolism.) But Paul also applies this statement concerning the Ephesians to *himself*. We were all under this subjugation in that we "lived in the passions of our flesh," performing the "resolves" (*thelemata*) and the "thoughts" (*dianoiai*) of the flesh.

What this says is that our "flesh" and our "thoughts" have a *will* and not merely an *urge!* The reference to the will, or better, "resolves," "things willed," however, can only mean that here purposeful power is in control, holding us in thrall, a power which is not simply the instinctual urge of flesh and blood. For, after all, as intelligent beings equipped with reason and will we could to some extent control and curb these merely instinctual desires. But here we are given to understand that the will is confronted not simply with a sensual urge but with *another* will. This is a personal power—"personal" simply because it has a *will*—a personal power with a claim, a demand, a *nomos,* which does not simply "overpower" us (as we may be overwhelmed by the violent passion and sensuality) but rather "convinces" us, that is, persuades us that submission to its norms is really a service of God.

It is relatively simple to make this clear; for when Paul and the Ephesians before their conversion obeyed their "resolves" and "thoughts" they by no means thought that they were only compulsive sinners responding to instinctive urges. On the contrary, they were in all earnestness convinced that they were offering a service to God (cf. John 16:2). For these "resolves" of the flesh had wormed their way into the mind and reason by way of the devious path of sensual self-assertion and there determined their rational arguments accordingly. We are all aware of the extent to which "the wish is father to the thought." But since wishes and desires form our thoughts, these wishes are not merely the sensual part of the self which is antagonistic to our thoughts— as the fateful oversimplification of idealism would have it—but are rather inextricably and invisibly mingled with these thoughts.

Usually our thoughts are wont to change covertly from enemies of desire to advocates of desire—again a form of demonic anonymity! And at the same time an indication of how the demonic never reveals itself in the light of our own thoughts—how could anything so dark ever cast any light!—but only in the light of God himself. This is made clear also in Romans 1:18 ff., where Paul speaks of how the thoughts of the natural man concerning God are darkened and finally end (as it were in the twilight between God and Satan) in the worship of the images of birds, animals, reptiles, and even of mortal man himself. In other words, they worship the symbols of their own creatureliness and thus themselves. In this blasphemous form of worship they assert themselves over against God, so that in reality their service of worship is not a serving of God at all but rather an arrogant and autocratic elevation of themselves above God. But since the sensual self-assertion of man has thus captured his thinking, since man is not *overpowered* "from below" but rather *convinced* "from below," he will never admit that he is against God, but when he is taxed with rejecting God he disputes this by adducing religious and rational arguments.

This is why the gesture of Prometheus, passionately shaking

his fist at God, never happens in reality at all. Through its diabolical obfuscating maneuvers the demonic power will always see
to it that a person never feels that he is an *enemy of God* (for he
would know only too well that this would be evil and damnable,
and would therefore recoil in horror), but rather that he thinks
he is acting in the *name of God*. This is exactly like the technique
of the devil's temptation, in which he likewise conceals the fact
that he is approaching me in the name of evil, and appears to be
demonstrating *ad oculos* that he wants only to show me something
beautiful, grand, and pleasurable. So the people referred to in
Romans 1 by no means thought that they were worshiping the
creature instead of the Creator. But what does human thinking
and subjective honesty amount to once it has become clear that
the level of man's thinking is the playground of another, alien
power, and how far he is from being the independent subject that
idealism makes him out to be; how far from being "intelligent"
and "autonomous," and how very much he is the object of this
secret, atmospheric, and insidious power!

Once more, then, we see the force of the saying in Ephesians
6:12 that we are not contending with flesh and blood. Sensuality
is not the exclusive medium of the demonic; rather it has established itself deep in the mind and spirit. In the last analysis it is
not a matter of idealism's antagonism between flesh and spirit, but
of a far deeper antagonism between spirit and spirit, between
God's Spirit and man's spirit. This is where the deepest mystery
of evil appears.

b. With respect to the second characteristic of the demonic
power, its constant effort to bring us under *subjection,* we have
already said a good deal concerning the nature and form of this
subjection. Here we may sum up in a few sentences what has been
said.

The words of Goethe's magician's apprentice, "Those spirits I
conjured up—now I can't get rid of them," surely represent a confession which could only have arisen in the Christian West; for
they bring out two features of the biblical concept of the demonic
power. First, we can summon the demonic powers, and up to the
moment they are summoned we still retain a position of freedom
with regard to them, but, second, after they have been summoned
we can no longer dispel them; then *we* are under their spell.

This process becomes palpably clear in the biblical story of the Fall. At one moment, when she looked at the tempting fruit, Eva had freedom of choice. But in the next moment, when she used her freedom to take it, she lost this very freedom. For then this act undertaken in freedom immediately dictated all succeeding events, totally usurping the initiative. The history that followed from this act, from Cain to the Tower of Babel to this present day, became a history of rebellion in which with a dreadful consistency the face of this *one* act keeps peering out of a thousand masks.

More strictly speaking, however, we should have to say that it is not the once-performed act that dictates the law of succeeding action; it is rather the "spirit" to whom one has sold oneself by this act who dictates this law. The important thing to realize is that what happens when a man sins is far more than committing an act. By this act he is submitting himself to an *exousia,* a power, an authority. The doctrine of original sin is a monumental expression of this truth. In order to understand this one must, of course, strip oneself completely of all idealistic presuppositions. For these presuppositions always regard man as an individual acting subject. Hence from this point of view we can never understand how it is that this subject can suddenly become an object, how the hammer can become an anvil and be shifted from free spontaneous activity into compulsive slavery. This becomes intelligible only on the basis of the biblical presupposition that man always finds himself vis-à-vis another person, whether this be God or the demonic power. Therefore it is always a question of *either* the dominion of darkness *or* the kingdom "of his beloved Son" (Col. 1:13). In both instances we are subject to an *exousia.* It is profoundly symbolical that Faust binds himself over to Mephistopheles by signing the compact with *blood.*[17] All life is either giving oneself or selling oneself.

Naturally, at this point in our course of thought the important question of responsibility arises. If my actions are performed under compulsion, to what extent is this *my* act and to what extent can I be held responsible for it?

There are two things that must be said in reply to this question. First, every action performed under compulsion always

[17] Goethe, *Faust,* Part I, Scene IV. (Trans.)

points back to the moment when I sold myself to this compulsion, the moment when, still acting as a subject, I walked up to it and offered it my hand. When Hitler, who believed in all seriousness that it is men who make history and that he himself was such a man, declared in a New Year's proclamation in 1941 that providence often puts one in places and sends one into situations which one would not want to enter oneself, but the entering of which is the consequence of our initial acts,[18] he was giving very clear expression to this consciousness of an inevitable, compulsory necessity which is nevertheless provoked by an initial step on the part of the man.

Second, we should have to make the following observation. In his discussion of the question of responsibility Luther expressed the thought in his book *De servo arbitrio* ("The Bondage of the Will") that the compulsion referred to here does not have the character of a *coactio* (i.e., a compulsion which overwhelms us from the outside without our being able to do anything about it) but rather the character of a *necessitas* (i.e., an inner necessity, analogous to Goethe's idea of the "minted form which develops as it lives"). This means that I can never disassociate myself from this compulsion as being something supposedly alien to myself, but must rather admit that as a subject I am involved in it. To use a very drastic example, even in the case of an inherited alcoholism (if there is such a thing), I can never argue that "I am compelled to drink" or "The 'it' in me"—and thus not I—"drank to excess." I must always say, "I allowed myself to indulge" and thus admit the indissoluble interaction of my being at once both subject and object. This confrontation between "myself" and the *exousia* cannot be eliminated even in thought.[19]

We described this indissolubility earlier when we said that the demonic power exercises its power with the aid of self-love (*amor sui*). Precisely when I seem to be completely myself, alone by myself, as I am in self-love, I am actually bound to myself. And how-

[18] Cited from memory.

[19] If I think of this entity that stands over against me as *God*, this indissolubility of "subjecthood" and "objecthood" becomes very clear in the relationship of predestination and free will. I cannot disassociate these things theoretically and apportion my life between these two components. Both represent only two perspectives from which I must see my identical act.

ever much self-love may appear at first sight to be a supreme act of
"subjecthood," at second sight it turns out to be a state in which I
am passively carried away and seduced. In any case, I must admit
that I am subject to compulsion and accept personal responsibility. This is the answer to the question of responsibility.

5

Now, though it is true, as we have said above, that it is man's own
"self" which acts here, we must nevertheless admit that in Jesus'
encounter with the demonic powers still another estimate and
judgment of demon-bound man plays a part, an estimate which
absolutely must be taken into account as a corrective of what has
been said thus far. And this brings us to a number of concluding
thoughts concerning Jesus' encounter with the demonic power.

The accounts of demons in the New Testament show that
Jesus never *identified* even the most demon-bound of men with
the demonic power itself. On the contrary, he always sees that an
alien spirit is speaking out of him and dragging him down. And
this alien spirit is always to be strictly distinguished from the
person who harbors him. This, after all, is the only reason why
he can be driven out. His driving out of demons is therefore actually the abolition of the demonic incarnation and the restora-
tion of the person "to himself."

This distinction between the person on the one hand and the
power that holds him in possession becomes clear when we think
of the commandment to love one's enemies.

When we consider that when Jesus spoke of enemies he actually meant the opponents of the church we see that he was trying
in this commandment of love to show the disciples that they must
distinguish two things in their persecutors and tormentors: First,
the people *as such,* as they came from the hands of God; and second, the enslaving demonic power, which is now holding these
people captive and so distorting the original image of God in
them that it is almost unrecognizable, and also constantly goad-
ing them on against the church and its Christ. It is actually the
"ancient foe" who has taken hold of these opponents and blinded
them, so that they rage against the church despite the promise
that the gates of hell shall not prevail against it. When Jesus

says, "Love your enemies," he is not saying, "Love the mire in which the pearl lies, but rather, love the pearl that lies in the mire." These words of Ralf Luther express precisely the sense in which the man "as such" must be distinguished from the power that holds him in thrall. Here we encounter the central and decisive point of Christian anthropology.

Not only do the eyes of Jesus penetrate the deceiving veil of good works and see the evil thoughts of the heart (cf. the Sermon on the Mount), but the hearing of his ears also perceives, behind the alien noises of the demons, the voice of the child of God who has gone astray and fallen victim to alien tyrants. His healings of the demon-possessed therefore consist in his snatching the "children" out of the hands of the "power" that possesses them.

Thus Jesus' mission can be described as being twofold: first, it is a battle *against* the demons, and second, it is a battle *for* men. Here we see the profound antithesis between New Testament thought and idealism. As we have seen, in idealism there is a dialectical relation between good and evil. Evil has the significance of a necessary transition to the good; in the last analysis it is a creative entity, such as Goethe personified in the figure of Mephistopheles. In any case, in this view of things good and evil are two principles that define each other: the good would be impossible without the antithesis of evil. In the New Testament, however, there is no such thing as two constituting principles; here two powers, two *exousiai* clash. Here the issue is joined and involved are the blood and tears of God, the agony of Gethsemane and Golgotha.

Characteristic of this breakthrough of Christ into the kingdom of demons is the feature that constantly recurs in the accounts of his casting out of demons, namely, that they *recognize* him; they sense that they are in extreme peril. It may be that the remembrance of the fallen angel enters in and gives them a subtle sense of the presence of the divine. Goethe says that one can understand only what ones loves, and we may add, "or what one hates." Even though the demons are so base that they can only be sent into a herd of swine, even though intellectually, ethically, culturally they are less than trash, they nevertheless have this mysterious scent for things divine (cf. Mark 5:1-21).

But the demons react not only in *recognizing* Christ; they also resist and rebel. We mentioned earlier that the demonic forces are potentiated in the face of the coming Christ. According to the vision of the Revelation of John, this will become apparent at the end of days; the nearer the returning Christ comes to this aeon the more the opposing forces mass their strength and the more energetically the Adversary mobilizes his last reserves, until the demonic excesses reach their climax and Christ returns and the new aeon of God begins. Even apart from this eschatological view of things one may say that wherever the living church exists, conscious of the nearness of its Lord, there the demons rebel and persecution ensues. So rebellion and persecution are not at all a sign that Christ has departed and left the battlefield of the world to the opposing forces. On the contrary, all this is a sign that he is coming, indeed, that he is very near. It may very well be that a church which has the public with it and is surrounded by the world's applause is in a hidden way far more dreadfully exposed than the church which is threatened and surrounded by howling demons.

How, then, does liberation from demonic subjugation take place, how are the demons driven out? Properly at this point we should deploy the whole doctrine of justification. For "justification" means nothing less than our being liberated from the demonic *exousia* and transferred through Christ into the paternal realm of the divine *exousia* ("the kingdom of his beloved Son"). We shall confine ourselves, however, to two decisive features of this liberation.

Jesus Christ is the light of the world over against the power of darkness, and he is that light in two senses.

First, he confronts this man, who in his darkness wants to "be like God" and because of the darkness even thinks he *can* be like God, with the light of Christmas. In this Christmas light that shines upon the darkness of the earth and the peoples, man discovers that there is no way to God that he can ascend, that there is no way that he can become God. He perceives that the way between God and man runs in just the *opposite* direction, that God comes down to men in the birth of the Christ-child, "suddenly" appearing in the darkness of the earth and the peoples as the Son of God made flesh.

Because Jesus Christ comes as the light of the world, he shows us the right *precedence* of all values. He shows us that there is only *one* thing needful and that man gains nothing if he gains the whole world and forfeits his soul, his very life. He shows that man is living his life in dreadful confusion, mistaking dream for reality, and he wakes him from sleep and dreams and gives him a knowledge of the ultimate reality.

Second, the Adversary is cast out; he is already judged (cf. also the "slavery" in which we were before, and the freedom to which Christ frees us, Romans 6). In this sense it is of absolutely vital importance that Christ takes away our subjugation to sin. It is true, of course—if we may give to this thought the special note that Luther gave to it—that we remain *de facto* sinners (*peccatores in re*). The evil thoughts of the heart go on lurking within us and even the Christian cannot disassociate himself from the catalogues of vices that are set forth in the New Testament, especially in the Pauline epistles. But the thing that is decisively *new* is that now all those sins against the *second* table of the commandments of God can no longer exclude us from being the *children of God*, and that God does not take all these trespasses as occasion to sever our fellowship with him. The real nature of satanic temptation lies not so much in his tempting us to commit individual concrete sins, in other words, to commit offenses against the second table of the Law, but above all in separating us from God *by means of* these offenses or *also by means of correct observance of the commandments*. Luther clarified these multiple possibilities of being separated from God by using the words "security," "pride," and "despair" (*securitas, superbia,* and *desperatio*).

Security consists in our lulling ourselves into the illusion that we are capable of fulfilling the commandments of God. This leads us into security from *God*. We no longer think of him as the threatening Judge and we no longer find him disturbing. We feel that we can cope with him and we think we can settle the accounts ourselves. This form of *moralistic* separation from God is illustrated in the so-called Pharisaic attitude.

The second possibility is that we may cherish our pride and remain defiantly disobedient to the commandments of God, insisting that we have the right to prescribe our own laws of conduct. This is separation from God by way of *defiant disobedience*.

The third possibility of breaking away from fellowship with God becomes a reality when, even though I recognize the greatness and validity of God's commandments, I nevertheless conclude in despair that that I can never fulfil them. Then God becomes an opponent and an enemy with whom I know I cannot cope, a persecutor and tormentor whom I must inevitably *hate*.

These three possible ways in which the demonic power can snatch me out of the hands of God are taken away from it the moment I enter into the allegiance of Christ. True, sin remains, but it is only a larva, only a poisonous snake whose poison-fang has been drawn.

In other words, something in it has been decisively changed; no longer can it be a "foothold" for the demonic power that would separate me from God. No longer can it drive a wedge between me and God. On the contrary—to continue the metaphor —it has become a foothold for the mercy of God: "Where sin increased, grace abounded all the more" (Rom. 5:20), and our "sins are like scarlet, they shall be as white as snow" (Isa. 1:18); and the more the lost son goes astray the more mightily does God's mercy work upon him and the more will he glorify his Father.

Behind the unchanging façade of sin—for outwardly a pardoned sinner can hardly be distinguished from an unpardoned ethically upright sinner—a total change of sovereignty has taken place: whereas before we were obliged to say that it was precisely our sin that gives the demonic power a claim upon us, now the intervention has changed this completely. Now it is precisely my sin that gives the Christ a claim upon me, since he takes it upon himself and tears up the bond of indebtedness. *O felix culpa* (O happy fault), said Augustine. Now the concrete individual sins *(peccatum in re)* are really like a serpent's skin from which the satanic serpent has crept away. Outwardly it may look the same, and yet it is only an empty skin. What is a joke without a point? And what is sin if it has been stripped of its point? And now we see that the real point and purpose of sin in the hands of the Adversary is to separate me from God. But I am in the mighty fortress where the terror of hell cannot daunt me. Even my fear, my vulnerability to temptation, my trembling subjectivity, only cause me to praise God more confidently. Inevitably one thinks of that great hymn of Johann Franck, "Jesus, my Joy" *("Jesu, meine Freude")*:

> Though sin and hell affright me
> Jesus will defend me.
> . . . .
> Despite the ancient Evil,
> Despite the jaws of darkness,
> Despite the fear of death,
> Rage, O world, snarl and spring;
> Calm and confident,
> Here I stand and sing.

If anywhere, here surely is a strong expression of the faith which knows that all the threatening sins that swarm about me are only empty serpent skins. Here the Christian faces hell and death, the ancient serpent himself. And we who live in praise of God are not beyond the reach of all this; we are only beyond the reach of the "ancient Evil." No longer dare he accuse and tempt me; for God no longer listens to the "prosecutor"; he listens only to my "Advocate."

"Who shall bring any charge against God's elect? It is God who justifies; who is to condemn?" Who shall accuse, who shall come between God and me? Christ is here! Even if my own conscience accuses me, it no longer counts, for this, too, has all been changed. Luther said: first God confronts me as my accuser, and my conscience confronts me as my defender; but when I am in fellowship with Christ this is reversed. Then my conscience is my accuser, but God is my defender. *(Deus accusator, cor defensor; cor accusator, deus defensor.)* Then the devil can no longer use the scruples of my conscience, my fears, my whole shaky subjectivity to harass me. "For I am sure that neither death, nor life, nor angels, nor principalities, nor things present, nor things to come, nor powers, nor height, nor depth, nor anything else in all creation, will be able to separate us from the love of God in Christ Jesus our Lord" (Rom. 8:38-39).

IN OUR STUDY OF MAN IN GOD'S CREATION WE HAVE
discussed the problem of *history* and our conclusion was that
God's sovereign rule includes even those who oppose him in history. And this brings us to the last round of questions to which
we are led by our consideration of God's power over the world
and history. It is the problem of free will and predestination.

More precisely the question is this: If there is one great Subject, "God," who in his omnipotence rules everything that happens, if "not a hair of our head" falls without his willing it, and
consequently not a single impulse of our nerves, much less our
wills, can occur without his consent, then how can there be any
room for our own will to act? Does not this cause our own will to
dwindle to the point where it vanishes entirely? Does not our
faith leave us constantly wavering between views of man that
make him either an unrestrained Prometheus or a will-less
puppet?

The question goes even further: If, as would appear in consequence of divine omnipotence, man is more like a marionette,
then what becomes of his *responsibility?* For a will which is con-
trolled by an entity outside of itself and is therefore "under
duress" cannot be made responsible. Is an "enslaved will" a will
at all? Here we would seem to be shackled and deprived of all
activity by an utterly paralyzing thought.

In any case it is important right at the beginning to make the
following observation. The idea that our will is subject to a
power which largely or even totally determines it is also familiar
to us in non-Christian thought, indeed, in almost all systems of

philosophy. In every age mankind has wrestled with this perhaps most difficult problem of metaphysics. For this very reason one hopes to receive from the Christian faith a different answer, an answer that will free us from bondage.

For the sake of illustration I mention only a few brief examples from non-Christian thought. The biological world view, which I dealt with in a previous chapter, has developed a very pronounced concept of *fate*,[1] namely, the iron laws of heredity in which I am imprisoned in my thinking, my feeling, and naturally also in my willing, and which consequently deprive my will of pure freedom. (One of the most striking contradictions in this world view is the attempt to combine in thought this dominant note of "fate" with an appeal to the power of the will and human activism.) For good or ill I am bound to my given heredity. Mephistopheles sardonically makes the same observation on an essentially higher level, and in view of this fateful bondage tries to mock and break down Faust's every effort of will and every aspiration to get beyond himself.

> You are, when all is done—just what you are.
> Put on the most elaborate curly wig,
> Mount learned stilts, to make yourself look big,
> You still will be the creature that you are.[2]

This is as it were the reverse side of the great Goethean imperative, "Become what you are." This imperative appears at first to give us a lofty ideal for the will, namely, that it should be the goal of my life and therefore of my will to develop the innate gifts (the "minted form," the entelechy) within me, and in a higher sense to find myself. As so often, Mephistopheles shows us the ironical reverse side of these great maxims. He shows us

---

[1] Oswald Spengler has extended this biological concept of fate beyond the sphere of the individual's life and applied it to the history of whole civilizations. The life-span of civilizations passes through stages of rise and fall according to a rhythm like that of the seasons of the year, and when their hour has come no volitional resistance is of any avail. The only contribution which the people of the declining culture can make consists in the noble dignity with which they accept that involuntary fate.

[2] Goethe, *Faust*, Philip Wayne, trans. (Baltimore: Penguin Books, 1959), Part I, Faust's Study (3), p. 91. (Trans.)

that actually I have no option but to realize myself and that consequently I am only making a virtue of a necessity when I set myself the task of "becoming what I am." What appears at first to be a grand goal for the will turns out to be—from the devil's point of view, and in its way a quite true point of view—merely a tyrannical fate that actually enslaves my will and determines it by way of the unalterable givenness of my own self. For, as Goethe says, we can only end our journey "according to the law that governed our setting out." So in the framework of the biological as well as the Goethean world view we cannot even think of the word "freedom" without immediately thinking of Mephistopheles' counterargument that I have only the freedom to live out my destiny. But is that any freedom at all? How then can anybody ever say something clear and unequivocal about freedom? So there is no thinking in which the question of the freedom of the will does not arise, no thinking in which we are not aware of the dark powers of fate that limit our freedom; the great tragedies and all the philosophies tell the same story.

The first question this confronts us with is whether this problem is merely a *reflection* of the age-old question of human life when we find it appearing also in the Bible and the Christian faith? It would appear that what we have here is something very similar, except that in the place of tyrannical "fate" we find a no less tyrannical "Almighty." Are we to conclude that not even the Christian faith can rescue us from the dreadful circle in which we are enclosed?

Before we tackle the question of free will and predestination, however, let us first allow Luther to tell us when and where this question arises for us Christians, indeed, the only place it can be *allowed* to arise.

We observe that this question usually emerges on the purely *intellectual* level. You will see this at once if you stop to think of how people as a rule "discuss" this question, and the intellectual acrobatics that are employed to arrive at some kind of logically plausible answers (which to the distress of all the participants are ultimately nonexistent).

Even a young person who is also waking up mentally during the years he is developing physically often feels it to be a worrisome problem that, on the one hand, absolutely everything should be "fixed" by divine omnipotence (or other fateful determinative factors), but that on the other hand we should have room for our freedom and responsibility. After all only one of these alternatives can be true! Or is there some other answer?

Then come his first experiences with life, in which he learns that man is obviously largely determined in his development (he learns, for example, that the physiological manifestations of puberty, which profoundly determine his whole future life, simply "happen" to him), and that this means that the curve of his life is simply a given fact.

But these thoughts do not remain on the level of the intellectual or vague surmise for long. In the next moment they become tremendously *practical*. This transition to the practical may work out in two ways (not only the pastoral counselor but every living human being knows these tendencies by observing his own and other minds).

Either one says to oneself: If God ordains everything anyhow, then I can *wait*—especially with regard to my concerns about God. In fact, I *must* wait. In any case, logically—and therefore practically—I cannot take the initiative in getting things straight with him.

Or one says (or rather one feels impelled to say): God is *unjust* if on the one hand he insists upon determining everything and then on the other hand insists that I am to be held responsible. The figure of Judas Iscariot seems to be illustrative of this argument: How can God hold him responsible when he was obviously predestined to play his evil role in the history of salvation? Or how can he hold accountable the ambitious, power-hungry, demon-driven Napoleon Bonaparte, when perhaps besotted Europe badly needed him, and accordingly one may justly assume that the Almighty ordained him to do what he did for Europe? Again one is reminded of the aged harper's plaint in Goethe's *Wilhelm Meister,* "You let the poor wretch incur guilt, then leave him to his torment."

Having thus briefly considered how these thorny questions about free will and predestination begin on a harmless intellectual level and end on a threatening existential level, it is now high time that we hear what Luther tells us about the only side from which we should allow this problem to approach us.

In his preface to the epistle to the Romans Luther says:

Here, now, for once we must put a stop to those wicked and high-flying spirits who first apply their own reason to this matter. They begin at the top to search the abyss of divine predestination, and worry in vain about whether they are predestined. They are bound to plunge to their own destruction, either through despondency, or through delivering themselves to sheer chance.[3]

In other words, this road through the labyrinth of the problem of predestination dictated by *reason* leads to inner catastrophe. These two forms of disaster mentioned by Luther we today would call "despair" and "nihilism." In every case they lead to complete paralysis.

Then Luther proceeds to point out that one can learn from the order of the Epistle to the Romans the one and only way to approach the mystery of the doctrine of predestination. Well, how does Paul deal with the problem in Romans?

The first thing to note is that the doctrine of predestination does not stand at the *beginning* but rather at the *end* of the epistle. It does not begin—as one standing on the intellectual level would logically expect—by first undertaking to demarcate the areas of the divine will and the human will in order to stake out the zones in which man is either free or subject to divine determination.

No, the epistle begins with something entirely different. The question that stands at the beginning of the Epistle to the Romans and at the beginning of the Christian life is: *How can I have fellowship with God?*

Paul then proceeds to answer this question in detail by saying that I do not gain this fellowship with God through my personal action, through any principle of accomplishment whatsoever, but only as God gives himself to me in undeserved grace, by becoming my Father in Jesus Christ.

But first let us keep our eye on the question itself: How can

[3] *Luther's Works* (Philadelphia: Muhlenberg Press, 1960), 35, p. 378, altered. (Trans.)

I have fellowship with God? Because *this* is what is at stake for a man and this is what ultimately matters for him (here I am following Luther's exposition of the epistle)—he finds himself in a profound struggle with sin. Or better, he finds himself delivered over to the battle of two powers which are fighting to possess him. The one power is his own self, which in its pride and self-security and defiance is determined to ground its life upon itself and "sow to the flesh." The other power is the seeking, forgiving, renewing love of God in Jesus Christ which breaks through this locked and barred domain of our ego and brings us home to his peace.

There, because a man knows that he has been found by this strange and undeserved love, because he sees the grace of God winning the victory in that battle without any contribution on his part—"if God is for us, who is against us?"—he realizes in wonder and adoration *that the reason why he became a Christian and countless others have not does not lie in himself, but that it was all a miracle that simply fell to his lot.* The unanswerable question *Why?*—unanswerable because no human mind can answer it—is given classical expression in Spitta's hymn:

> Whence came this boon, why was it done?
> Compassion, that and nothing more.

It is very important to catch the tone in which the question *Why?* is asked in this hymn. It is not the cool, calculating tone of logical inquiry, seeking to solve the hidden meaning of the ways of God in order to be able to answer the question *Why?* with a rational conclusion. No, the tone is rather that of praise and thanksgiving, and it breaks from the lips of one who honestly confesses that he deserves only God's wrath and marvels at his grace. The word "compassion" by which he then answers the question *Why?* is in reality not an answer at all, but only the result of the direction in which he looks, namely, toward the heart of the unfathomably, incomprehensibly gracious Father. Putting it this way indicates how much depends upon the "direction" from which we approach this heart and the questions it presents to us.

The point is that here we must see just when it is that predestination, the sovereign preponderance of the divine Subject over all human volition and achievement, comes into the picture. It appears in that moment when I have struggled with the devil and my own flesh, when I have passed through the mortal conflict, engaged to the quick in the battle of God and Satan for my soul, and suddenly find myself on the side of the victorious Christ, without really knowing, and certainly not being able to explain, how I got there. Instead of questions, I have on my lips only gratitude that I have been drawn over to that side by a power which is greater than I. *This is why predestination appears at the end of the Epistle to the Romans, after our mortal encounter with God has been dealt with.*

In other words, this question does *not* emerge in the first act of the Christian life; it does not emerge as the noncommittal dalliance of the carefree intellect, but rather as praise of God in the midst of and after the mortal struggle which has been won, not by me, but by Christus Victor for me. That is what Luther meant when he said, "In the absence of suffering and the Cross and the perils of death, one cannot deal with predestination without harm and without secret anger against God" (This means that the uncommitted intellect cannot deal with it and dare not dabble in it; this doctrine dare not become acute for us until we face it in dead earnest.) "The old Adam must first die before he can tolerate this thing and drink the strong wine." Luther then concludes with this warning: "Therefore beware that you do not drink wine while you are still a suckling. Every doctrine has its order, its time, and its age."[4]

So if my speculative and inquisitive reason insists that first it must plumb the mysteries of predestination, it will surely be shipwrecked; it will only lead me into a dark labyrinth of unanswerable questions. Reason gazing at the majesty of God is blinded, consumed, and staggered.

On the other hand, if in going through "suffering and the Cross and the perils of death," that is, through the ultimate earnestness of life when the chips are down and the worst has come to the worst, I win through to the certitude that the saving fellowship of God is not something that grew up out of "my flesh and blood," but is rather an assurance given to me through a *miracle*, a miracle

[4] *Ibid.*, altered. (Trans.)

that lies completely outside the realm of my self, solely in the unfathomable, self-authenticating love of God, *then* the concept of predestination becomes the ultimate expression of praise and gratitude. Then it is the adoration of a man who is at the end of all his potentialities, who is conscious only of the disaster to which his guilt has doomed him, and now is snatched away from all this by the strange initiative of God and led by the Father's hand into the cheerful light of home.

From this point of view, the word "predestination" suddenly takes on a rather cold and flat sound; we ought rather to speak far more of this hand of the Father drawing us home. The word "predestination" denotes only the "act" of predestination; but far more important than the act is the Subject who performs it, the fact that it is the *Father* who so mysteriously forms our destiny. The *act* of predestination is perhaps a staggering mystery; the Subject of predestination, however, is so comforting and familiar to us that suddenly one can feel secure even with this staggering mystery.

For a quite similar reason we also ought not to speak of *providence*, since this term for an act says nothing anyhow, and the Mohammedans as well as fatalists also use it. Here again one should speak of the *Father* who foresees and provides. Then we shall come to rest in the face of all the oddities and labyrinthine intricacies of the act of providence, because we "rest in God." Only then will we also understand the special note in Paul's paean of praise at the end of Romans 11: "From him and through him and to him are all things." The essential note in this utterance does *not* consist in the fact that "all things" are not determined by themselves but by another entity. The essential thing is rather that this other entity is *God*, whose heart we know in Jesus Christ and to whom we therefore can calmly and peacefully entrust all things.

I may sum up what has been said as follows: *The Bible does not present us with a pat answer to the problem of predestination which simply "solves" it; it rather delivers us from the problem by setting us down in the right place.*

That is what Luther meant when he said, "Every doctrine has its order, its time, and its age."

Therefore there is no point in trying to help a young person who is wrestling with this question by furnishing him with logical arguments. There are such arguments, of course. And even if one has only a smattering of philosophy there are plenty of them available. But in the last analysis all this is humbug and I have therefore honestly tried to eliminate all such ingenious arguments from this discussion.

Rather one can only tell a person who is having difficulty with these problems to put off worrying about them for a while and for once face the struggle with death and the devil—to take his stand at this point, to take very seriously his personal destiny with God, and work out his "own salvation with fear and trembling" (Phil. 2:12-13), in order at the *end* of this procedure to gain some idea that it is *God* who works in us "both to will and to work for his good pleasure," that it is God who rules our life with his gracious and inscrutable predestination. This can be learned only in *practical* experience, only in total personal engagement and the venture of discipleship. In *no* case can all this be learned through a process of intellectual cogitation in which one remains a pure spectator.

On this basis, then, there are still several problems which should at least be mentioned.

1. The question of how "divine omnipotence" and "personal freedom" are related to each other is never solved *logically*—even for the person who asks the question existentially. We have seen that this is not at all necessary; for what really matters is not the *solution* of the question but rather the way in which we *approach* it.

The reason why it cannot be solved logically is that here we are dealing with the mystery of "personal life," which *always*—even on the human level—eludes logic.

Let me give you an example of this. When you look at a human life "from the outside" you see that it is predestined, predetermined by a great number of factors—heredity, environment, in short, by all those factors which Mephistopheles described when he said, "You still will be the creature that you are." Looked at in this way, all the decisions this person makes in supposed freedom (in matters of love, his vocation, etc.,) appear to be part and parcel of a fundamentally predestined and inevitable process.

But the moment I *myself* am that person, the moment I really have to make a decision and consequently see it not "from the outside" but rather "from the inside," all this is suddenly changed completely. Then I cannot appeal to the fact that I am bound to my heredity and therefore have to let everything take its course. To use a rather drastic example, when I pull a drunken man out of the gutter and chide him, saying, "Aren't you ashamed of yourself?" he is not likely to reply, "My father was a drunkard too," in order to indicate that he has only acted according to the inevitable law of his heredity and therefore in a realm beyond good and evil. If he is at all sober, the drunkard will know very well, despite his possible hereditary taint and despite all the abetting circumstances, that when he got drunk it was his own free, responsible act. Freedom is something that is unmediated and logically nondeducible, and it exists alongside of and within the predetermination of heredity, or we may say that it is the other side of the same person who is thus determined.

In his *Critique of Practical Reason* Kant adduced the example of a kleptomaniac to illustrate this paradoxical circumstance. When a person who is afflicted with this morbid passion for stealing sees a silver spoon unobserved, just as surely as one can predict an eclipse of the sun he will slip it into his pocket. Nevertheless, says Kant, he acts "in freedom" and therefore he can be accused on the basis of his act and held responsible. Man is never a merely passive and therefore morally neutral "object" of his inherited structures; he is always at the same time the "subject" and responsible executor of these structures and tendencies. Even the "addict" can never say: Something in me (the addiction, the sickness) did it. He has to say: *I* did it. Man cannot shake off his selfhood, no matter whether his acts are good or bad.

And this is also the reason why the biblical statement that God works in us "both to will and to work" does not result in my saying. "Therefore I can do nothing, I must let things run their inevitable course," but rather is actually coupled with the imperative statement, "Work out your own salvation with fear and trembling." It is precisely this unconditioned sovereignty of God, to which I am subject in every impulse of thought and will, that now constrains me to bring my whole life into accord with this divine sovereignty and not to spurn the beckoning hand that would draw me to the Father's house The absolute sovereignty of God therefore does not condemn me to the slavish passivity of a mere instrument, but rather liberates me for activity and responsibility.

2. Therefore, to go back to the unpleasant example of the drunkard, but this time to a version of it given by Luther, we must not think of predestination as something which coerces our will from the outside in the way that a policeman forcibly shoves a helpless, will-less drunkard ahead of him. Luther says that it is rather an "inner necessity" (*necessitas* rather than *coactio*), which lies in the logic of our nature, so that it is actually *ourselves* who *act* as those who have been thus determined.

To make this clear we go back again to the mysterious figure of Judas Iscariot. We must point out, however, that everything we say is only illustrative and that the impenetrable mystery remains. We are attempting only to deal with the mystery in such a way that it will be helpful to us, so that we can use it in facing our own predicament. This is the only form in which one can approach a mystery anyhow.

In the case of Judas Iscariot the question of freedom and responsibility is peculiarly crucial; for it is simply obvious that he has a definite function in the divine plan of salvation, that he is the one who must set in motion the events that led to Christ's passion, and that consequently his life and his actions are set within the framework of a superpersonal predestination, which necessarily forms the course of his life and, so to speak, makes of it a necessity.

But then can he be held responsible?

Despite this objection we must nevertheless declare that by no means was he simply coerced by the "function" he exercised, by no means did it force him to venality and treachery; it rather merely utilized his venal and treacherous nature and allowed it to run the full scope of its consequences.

I shall try to explain this by using a modern example which is certainly faulty at many points but nevertheless fairly accurate so far as the main thrust is concerned. The state department of

any country of necessity requires espionage in order to keep itself informed. As is well known, this is to a large extent a very
dirty business, not infrequently involving bribery, corruption, and
extortion. In this business of espionage the state department does
not operate by proceeding to force an officer of impeccable character to engage in these sordid affairs. Rather it "utilizes" persons
who are suitable for these jobs, persons whom it then gives the
necessary scope for developing their evil instincts, in order, if not
to hallow these shameful means, at least to make them productive
for positive ends. Otherwise these ends in no way correspond with
this evil person's own inclinations, for his own tendencies are bent
only upon enrichment and miserable profit.

In other words, Judas Iscariot is not coerced by his predestination (any more than the officer with an unblotted scutcheon is
forced by the state department to perform shameful tasks). Judas
Iscariot therefore cannot say, I was "forced" to do it. He can only
say that he fell victim to the consequences of his own nature. And
this is why he does not accuse the predestinating gods, "You let
the poor wretch incur guilt . . . ," but rather dies in self-judgment
and thus in self-accusation. So for Judas himself the enigma of his
life, which is always the figment of the spectator attitude, did not
exist. In his own eyes he was very definitely *not* the mere object
of dark determinative powers, but rather a responsible subject of
a condemnable act and therefore exposed to judgment.

So the dark and inscrutable relationship between higher determination and freedom can only be expressed in two paradoxical statements: (1) God "gave up" Judas Iscariot to his own
nature (Rom. 1:24); he left him to the consequences of his own
nature. (2) God took what Judas "meant for evil" and made it
good and thus caused his individual act, which was aimed at his
own selfish ends, to enter into his higher divine plans.

Once more one must emphasize that all that we have said "explains" nothing, but only "describes" the mystery at a deeper
level, seeking to find in it what may be profitable to us in terms
of judgment and grace. (At this deeper level the purely logical
questions emerge exactly as they do in our first, more naïve encounter with the problem.) The profoundest description of this
mystery, which we can only refer to here, is again the one Luther

gave us when, in an obscure and profound passage in his book *On the Bondage of the Will*, he says that God himself is actively at work carrying out his higher purposes even in these dark "Judas-regions" of human life in which a man is completely abandoned to the demonic element in his own nature; declaring that "God rides the lame horse and carves the rotten wood." That is to say, he does not *make* the horse lame, but nevertheless he *rides* it. He does not *make* the wood rotten, but nevertheless he *carves* it.

We may conclude this darkest and most mysterious chapter of our faith, of which I have been able to give you only a mere sketch, by referring once more to the ultimate meaning of the doctrine of predestination: *it constitutes the dark foil against which the light of the gospel shines.*

To put it quite simply, the child who knows that he is being called by name and taken by the hand, the lost son who knows he is being drawn to the father's heart, suddenly realizes that he has found his way back home, not because of his Faustian strivings or his accomplishments or his character, but rather because of that voice which calls him and that hand which reaches out for him in Jesus Christ. And so he sees that he has been graciously overtaken by a predestination over which he had no control, a destiny which, in a very mysterious and incomprehensible way (at least to our eyes), seems to pass by others who likewise have no control over it.

But now because he looks at the mystery of predestination from this vantage point, namely, this point where he sees the heart of the Father, it can no longer frighten him. What made his brain reel when he tried to fathom it with mere reason now becomes a blessed mystery, the mystery of the fatherly love which has called him by name and thus assured him that this predestination applies to him personally, and even more, that his plan of grace is operative in the *whole* world—including even those realms where Judas and others linger in their stubbornness and blindness. "For God has consigned all men to disobedience" (i.e., the dark predestination), "that he may have mercy upon all," (i.e., the luminous, gracious predestination).

And so there is no other way; I must close this chapter on the terror-filled and yet comforting mystery of predestination with the same words of hymnic praise that Paul uttered, words which have long since abandoned the endless circle of argument because they originate at the heart of the Father and are spoken out of the blessed security of a child of God:

O the depth of the riches and wisdom and knowledge of God! How unsearchable are his judgments and how inscrutable his ways!

> "For who has known the mind of the Lord,
> or who has been his counselor?"
> "Or who has given a gift to him
> that he might be repaid?"

For from him and through him and to him are all things. To him be glory forever. Amen.

Rom. 11:33-36

POSTSCRIPT FOR
THEOLOGICAL READERS

THE THEOLOGICAL AND PEDAGOGICAL ATTEMPT WHICH
this book sets forth is so hazardous and so unguarded in the form
of its presentation that I feel the need to address a few words to
those readers who have proved to be least tolerant and also find
it hardest to follow when one presents the old message in an unusual form and thus departs quite radically from the traditional
pattern of theological argument.

I may therefore say in the first place to my theological readers
that I should feel badly misunderstood if the theological presentation in this book were to be regarded as "popular," and that
on the other hand I should feel that my intention had been appreciated if the form in which I have expressed them were regarded as being "postscientific" or "postscholarly."

It seems to me to be very important, not only in connection
with *this* work, but also with regard to all our theological instruction in the church and congregation, to make a sharp distinction
between these terms.

I should call a piece of instruction "popular" if its author does
not regard it as necessary to get down to a full scientific investi-
gation of his problem, but rather stops at the "prescientific" stage.
If he does this—and it would seem to me that a large part of the
more popularly written literature, by no means only in the field
of theology, is so expressed—the author will presumably justify
himself with the argument that the only thing that matters in
popularization is a certain compact and summary form of presentation, and that it would actually be a pedagogical mistake—so
to say an evidence of a lack of pedagogical instinct—to face up
to the deepest levels of the problems. In reality, however, this
kind of "popular" literature thereby only renders itself untrust-

213

worthy and acquires the distasteful smack of low-brow tracts. And speaking of instinct, I should like to point out that the intellectually alert and responsible reader who is not himself a trained theologian has a very precise intuition for this lack of depth in theological argumentation. Not that he expressly demands that he be led into the area in which forbidding problems are dealt with in detail, and where the difficult and abstract distinctions in terms begin. As the theologian traverses this area because this is his calling, he performs a vicarious act for the "layman" and therefore will frequently not take him along with him. Moreover, in this area he will not be able to dispense with academic theological language and he will have to thread his way patiently through the confused mass of tradition, the stages of which govern and help to promote the process of knowledge only after long effort (and to that extent are indispensable), but are only discouraging and really confusing to the person who has not been professionally trained. But the independent lay thinker, on the other hand, will *demand* this vicarious act and will always have a very sure sense of whether it is really being performed and whether he can properly take what sounds so easy and intelligible as being the result of such a lonely and onerous pilgrimage.

What I have said already indicates what I mean by the term "postscientific." I mean by it the equality of a presentation which has actually worked through the area, even though it contains no footnotes and other scholarly apparatus to display its findings to the reader and thus furnish proof that the author has actually been there. The "postscientific" method of speaking thus adds to scientific-dogmatic labors a further chore, namely, that of translating the results into generally intelligible terms and utilizing them in the educational task.

Concisely put, it may be said therefore that the "popularizing" method cuts off the process of scholarly work at its most important and difficult stage, whereas the "postscientific" method extends the process by an additional tour of duty. It can therefore be pursued only out of a serious theological concern. And in this sense I admit that in working on these chapters I have learned some very important things, not only pedagogically but also theologically. Perhaps it may not be altogether unimportant to my fellow workers in theology if I say this to them for their stimulation, encouragement, and comfort in their own endeavors in this very important area.

However, there is still another admission I must make to my theological readers. I would have complete good conscience about this undertaking (in so far as such a thing exists at all, and if in this aeon we can expect any more than what Luther called a "comforted" conscience) only if I had before me a thoroughly worked-out dogmatics from which the present attempt to speak to lay people evidently and demonstrably differed only in its additional pedagogical concern. Instead of this I can only refer my theological readers to a number of monographs, which are preliminary studies for the real lifework I hope to complete, and in which they will be able to see how I present the same *loci* in strictly academic form. I can also assure the reader that there is no problem in these chapters which I have not repeatedly dealt with in strict dogmatic form in my academic lectures—and here professionals do not need to be told that, so far as form is concerned, academic lectures and addresses to laymen have nothing whatsoever in common (except the theological conviction that lies behind them).

Consequently, I have no desire whatever to evade responsibility for the content of these chapters by asking the theological reader to study this book merely for its pedagogical interest and thus to look at it only from the point of view of practical theology. I have no intention of waving aside the criticism of my theological reviewers by resorting to the argument that, after all, in a practical book one must make compromises and dispense with strict principle. On the contrary, I should regard my office as a teacher as meaningless and even at this date transfer to the Salvation Army (which, incidentally, has my deepest respect), if I were convinced that I should prepare my students for the kind of practical ministry which would blunt all the sharp contours of honest theological work in the name of the *usus delphini* and accommodation to one's hearers. I should not wish to expose myself to the reproach of presumptuous self-confidence, the impropriety of which I am all too keenly aware of in venturing to publish this book; but nevertheless I think I can say that I fear the judgment of the "little" experts more than that of the "great" ones, because in the case of the latter I dare to cherish the expectation that they will detect the theological contours which have been hidden for pedagogical reasons, and see the theological work that lies behind it. In a work intended for laymen there is, for example, no room for methodological discussions. And yet the theological reader may be assured—and I hope he will believe this not merely because of this perhaps emotional-sounding assertion, but will actually see it—that for myself I have at every point reflected upon these methodological considerations and have not spared myself this labor. In any case, he may be assured that in employing formulations which may often sound rather bold, since they have been sought in a kind of speech which is far from academic, I have not merely extemporized, and that however fortunate or unfortunate my experiments have been, there has been no lack of serious self-control—with regard not only to the hearers but above all to the subject itself, i.e., the Holy Scriptures.

There is another misunderstanding I should like to preclude, but in this case I am in the fortunate position of being able to refer to other publications of mine (especially my book *Fragen des Christentums an die moderne Welt*—"Questions Christianity Addresses to the Modern World"). I refer to the misapprehension that I am here concerned with *apologetics*. It is perhaps inevitable that this characterization will be used, sometimes approvingly and sometimes ironically. The many controversies with other views which this book contains present too great a temptation to apply the term to it.

There are, however, three characteristics of conventional apologetics which I have diligently, and I hope with some consistency, sought to avoid.

The first is that apologetics incorporates both the content of the Christian faith and the opposing ideologies in one common system of co-ordinates and then, on the basis of this superior system which embraces both phenomena, exercises its judgment with the tendentious purpose of condemning these anti-Christian ideologies and reducing them to absurdity. This kind of apologetics leaves no room for genuine offense because it seeks to *demonstrate* the Christian faith as well as the absurdity of the arguments against it. It therefore confuses faith with sight and sets itself, not *under* the Word, but rather above it (even though its honest intention is only to be helpful). The chapters of this book, however, seek throughout to keep open the possibility of offense, and even at points where the biblical affirmation that sin corrupts a people is expounded and illustrated, this is never presented as a proof of God, but always in such a way that the possibility of genuine rejection is kept in view and faith always proclaimed as a *miracle*. I admit, of course, that the "lay-dogmatics" style of speech makes it difficult and sometimes impossible to introduce explicitly the methodological safeguards which are particularly important here. In the present book this applies especially to the treatment of those areas that lie between theology and physics. It is precisely here that I feel a strong dissatisfaction with regard not only to method but also content. Though I hope that in my own studies on these questions I have since made some appreciable progress, I have had no practical opportunity to incorporate the desired reconstructions and additions into the book for this translation. Moreover, it would seem to me to be better first to bring out a scientific (scholarly) work which would provide this kind of foundation.

The second characteristic of apologetics is that it proposes to give Christian answers to human questions. In the above-mentioned book, however, I have tried to show *in extenso* that Christ is actually the one who prompts the real questions, and that by no means does he accept as binding upon him the questions men put to him and then proceed to answer them. I hope that the readers of these chapters will sense something of the fact that the faith of Christianity is not simply the solution of human questions about life and its meaning, but that rather, on the contrary, it attacks the world with *its* questions and forces it to face them. In any case, this book is meant to be emphatically antiapologetic. To be sure, it may well be—and perhaps this may even be the particular goal that hovers before the author and his work—that it must take over the task of previous apologetics in a new way and perhaps contribute in a small way to transplanting the task of Christian discussion to a different and theologically genuine level.

The third characteristic of apologetics is that it speaks from a position of certainty and from its secure position addresses others who have gone astray. The apologist is sure that he possesses the truth and is confident that error is abroad somewhere fairly far from his gates. Contrary to this point of view, however, real conversation can take place only in genuine solidarity with those who are "outside," and this is so not merely because it is a pastoral "method" which, after all, requires that communication be established in order to become effective, but above all because of the theological fact itself, namely *justification*. For all the apostasy and paganism I meet with on the outside is actually what can happen to me; what is more, it is actually what I am, a condition from which I have been removed only by an act of grace over which I have no control. Looking at this objective reflection of myself I can only say: *Tat tvam asi,* this is I—and yet no longer I, "but Christ who lives in me."

Consequently the dialogue with those outside can be carried on only if it has first taken place within myself as a monologue, that is to say, as a dialogue of the spiritual man within me with the natural man within me. And to that extent this dialogue is carried on, not in certainty and security, but in *Anfechtung*, in faith assailed and tempted by doubt and despair.

All theology which pursues the genuine goal of an ungenuine apologetics has the character of a "theology of *Anfechtung*."

But in the last analysis is not *all* theology marked by this *Anfechtung?* In the first place it lives under the "Law," and to that extent it must always call itself in question and thus again it exists in constant *Anfechtung*. (After all, we do not theologize as the angels do; we have a *theologia viatorum*.) And in the second place it lives under the gospel, and to that extent it is a "comforted" theology, a theology which is aware that the act of thinking—even in the realm of *theologia sacra*—is a human work and therefore in need of forgiveness. Theology without *Anfechtung* is either (in so far as it carries on a conversation with those outside) apologetics, or (in so far as it cultivates dogmatics in the narrower sense) it is confessional morphology; i.e., as an intellectual endeavor it is an esthetic construction and as foundation for ecclesiastical practice it is repristination. In both cases it loses its relevance—notwithstanding the intellectual and scholarly accomplishments it may achieve and pride itself upon.

The present book is a modest attempt to gain this proper relevance and—without seeking to make any theological display—to represent a theological concern.

INDEX

INDEX

221

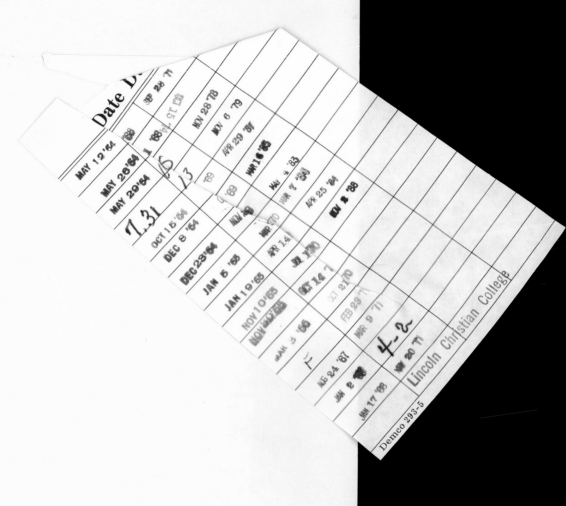